The Theatre of the Dream

The New Library of Psychoanalysis is published in association with the Institute of Psycho-Analysis. The New Library has been launched to facilitate a greater and more widespread appreciation of what psychoanalysis is really about and to provide a forum for increasing mutual understanding between psychoanalysts and those working in other disciplines such as history, linguistics, literature, medicine, philosophy, psychology, and the social sciences. It is planned to publish a limited number of books each year in an accessible form and to select those contributions which deepen and develop psychoanalytic thinking and technique, contribute to psychoanalysis from outside, or contribute to other disciplines from a psychoanalytical perspective.

The Institute, together with the British Psycho-Analytical Society, runs a low-fee psychoanalytic clinic, organizes lectures and scientific events concerned with psychoanalysis, publishes the *International Journal of Psycho-Analysis* and the *International Review of Psycho-Analysis*, and runs the only training course in the UK in psychoanalysis leading to membership of the International Psychoanalytical Association – the body which preserves internationally agreed standards of training, of professional entry, and of professional ethics and practice for psychoanalysis as initiated and developed by Sigmund Freud. Distinguished members of the Institute have included Wilfrid Bion, Anna Freud, Ernest Jones, Melanie Klein, John Rickman, and Donald Winnicott.

NEW LIBRARY OF PSYCHOANALYSIS

6

General editor: David Tuckett

The Theatre of the Dream

SALOMON RESNIK

Translated by
ALAN SHERIDAN

TAVISTOCK PUBLICATIONS
LONDON AND NEW YORK

First published in 1987 by
Tavistock Publications Ltd
11 New Fetter Lane, London EC4P 4EE

Published in the USA by
Tavistock Publications
in association with Methuen, Inc.
29 West 35th Street, New York NY 10001

Set by Hope Services, Abingdon
Printed in Great Britain by
Richard Clay (The Chaucer Press) Ltd.,
Bungay, Suffolk

British Library Cataloguing in Publication Data
Resnik, Salomon
The theatre of the dream. – (New library
of psychoanalysis; 6).
1. Dreams
I. Title   II.Series
III. La mise en scène du rêve. *English*
154.6'34   BF1091
ISBN 0–422–61040–2
ISBN 0–422–61830–6 Pbk

Library of Congress Cataloging in Publication Data
Resnik, Salomon.
The theatre of the dream.
(New library of psychoanalysis; 6)
Translation of: La mise en scène du rêve,
which is a revised translation of: Il teatro del sogno.
Includes index.
1. Dreams. I. Title. II. Series.
BF1078.R4613 1987 154.6'3 87-6538
ISBN 0–422–61040–2
ISBN 0–422–61830–6 (pbk.)

Contents

To

Aldo Pellegrini, doctor, poet, critic, and friend, who
has helped me to discover the metaphors of night . . .

Wilfred Ronald Bion, psychoanalyst, master, and
friend, who conveyed through his teaching profound
sensibility and humanity. He guided me in the
understanding of the dream metaphors of day: day-
dreaming . . .

Introduction

This book has as its background Venice: the scene is set in Venice, a dream city in which dream and reality, the two modes of the real, cohabit. On these same spaces and on these same stages, in the Venice of the sixteenth century, Giulio Camillo Delminio conceived his dream of constructing the theatre of memory and bringing together the traces of the 'drama' of man and the universe: 'The wisest and most ancient authors were always wont to reveal in their works the secrets of God, but these were hidden by very dark veils.'[1] The visions of the prophets and mystics, myths, dream (a personal myth, according to Freud) constitute, for some cultures, messages of a divine origin that reveal the secrets of being behind dark veils.

For Freud, dreams are traces, a phylogenetic and ontogenetic memory, an experience of life, a way of thinking and personifying unconscious fantasy, largely veiled from consciousness. The actors of the dream move within a 'theatrical' space-time: from a physical point of view, the dream landscape fulfils the same function as that of the chorus in Greek tragedy.

The dream stage is three-dimensional in form, but the content of what is acted out on it is multidimensional. The dream stage is like a signifier undergoing constant transformation. It may be flattened, enlarged, blown up out of all proportion until it loses its outlines. In the chapters in which I speak of the dream and of madness, I stress this absence of outlines and boundaries. The dream territory penetrates this space of the world in the form of a language that is different from that of the waking state. The space-time of the dream does not necessarily coincide with existing 'scientific' notions and raises the problems of mental space and of the 'locus' of thought. My

1

work on psychosis, psychotic thought, and the dream have led me to conceive of a multiple, complex topology that is 'metadimensional' (Bion) or 'adimensional' (Matte Blanco).[2] Utopia, the nowhere of Campanella's *City of the Sun*, corresponds to a conception of ideal space-time that is not that of either natural man or cultural man. Utopia possesses a place in the 'nowhere' and it may be conceived as a different dimensional register. However, what is sometimes met with in both dream thought and in insane thought may not correspond to the usual idea of place, of dimension and time, but be constituted as another, atopical and achronic reality.

This book is an attempt at critical reflection, through clinical experience, on the difficulty of interpreting the dream phenomenon. In the narration of this experience, stress has been laid on the restrictive, phenomenological process and on the aesthetic experience. The aesthetic experience, *qua* discourse and style of the dream, is representative of a structuring, creative process on the part of the unconscious. The interpretation of dreams is a maieutics, a dialogue, an art. The oneiromancers of antiquity were skilled in the 'divinatory' art that made it possible to unveil hidden 'truths'.

In a way, Freud takes up the idea of the vocation of oneiromancer who enlightens the consciousness concerning what is hidden in the darkness of the unconscious. This book is offered as an open study, without denying possible contradictions, and its various chapters follow an order that does not always correspond to that of linear logic, for it belongs to a real, imaginary, labyrinthine adventure, experienced in the course of an encounter-seminar. In fact, this book is born out of that encounter; it is the result of it and its structure and spirit conform to the seminar.

The Latin word *seminarium* is made up of the word *semen* (seed) and the suffix *-arium* (the place where the seed is laid). Cultivating knowledge means growing and fructifying, producing fruit. Learning together becomes a co-birth, which means to be present at the gestation and discovery of the metaphor that heralds and illuminates, throws light on the unknown. Our search takes the form of a fruitful adventure, a state of waiting, an undertaking that does not exclude fear.

The world of dreams is a living forest in which fantasy dwells in a state of riddle; since antiquity the interpreter of dreams has embodied curiosity for the obscure, invisible forms of nature and being.

The members of this seminar were actors in a living, durable scenic experience that actively nourished the common *logos*, of which I have become the spokesman. I would like to thank:

2

Edith Aromando
Anna d'Amico
Giuseppe Maffei
Bianca Napolitani
Adele Pavia
Fulvia Pes
Cori Ranchetti
Tonci Zumaglini
Laura Tremelloni

and in particular

Ana Taquini-Resnik, who has closely followed my work, helping me with her suggestions and patience.

Notes

1 *L'idea del theatro*, Tutte le opere, Venice, 1552.
2 Ignacio Matte Blanco (*The Unconscious as Infinite Sets*, London, 1975) speaks of the dreamer who sees 'a multiple-dimensional world with eyes which are made to see only a three-dimensional world' (p. 418). According to Matte Blanco, the notion of multiple dimension was suggested by Freud himself in *The Interpretation of Dreams*, when he speaks of trains of thought starting out from more than one sentence, though having points of contact.

   Matte Blanco's book is a contribution of fundamental importance in the understanding of dream spatiality. The observer may assume different roles at the same time (Freud): for Matte Blanco this is a way of escaping the limitations imposed by three-dimensional space. 'We may establish a correspondence between contradiction and interpenetrability. Finally we arrive at a very interesting aspect of the dream, i.e. that frequently the images appear nebulous and not well delimited' (p. 421).

1

The stage and the dream

'We are such stuff
As dreams are made on, and our little life
Is rounded with a sleep.'
(Shakespeare, *The Tempest*)[1]

Man is made up of dreams and the dream is a latent, profound reality. The dream is a mask that, in enveloping wakefulness, denotes its uncertain but real presence; it is the path that drives man to rediscover his own essence; it is the primordial 'stuff' that turns 'the unconscious' into discourse; it is manifested to the consciousness and to 'the reality of the body' as an ambiguous presence, both internal and external. The man who dreams, surrounded by a kind of fog, makes the boundaries between life and death uncertain, but true. It is not only man, says Prospero, that lives in dreams:

'The cloud-capp'd towers, the gorgeous palaces,
The solemn temples, the great globe itself,
Yea, all which it inherit, shall dissolve.'[2]

The man who dreams, the places where his dreams take place, the great palaces, the solemn temples, his experiences, inherited and acquired, form part of the same fog that is constantly forming and dispersing.

Existence is a dream-life, a path, an interpretation of that permanent stuff that is the dream, a stuff woven in the unconscious, the centre and starting-point of any psychoanalytical semantics of dreams: for Sigmund Freud the interpretation of dreams was the highway that brings man to a knowledge of the fundamental riddles that inhabit his mysterious reality.

In *The Interpretation of Dreams* Freud studies the unconscious aspect

4

of the dream world and tries to develop a cryptological methodology and an 'epistemology' of the unconscious.

If the conscious is a mediation between the unconscious and relational life (Freud situates the 'origin' of speech between the unconscious and the preconscious), *qua* language it articulates the structures of the unconscious and those of the preconscious with the conventional rules of 'rational' language.[3]

The language of the dream is primitive and universal; to become manifest, it uses specific principles, rules, and laws that give rise to a specific system of values and a specific spatio-temporal perspective: the dream world.

Freud seems to deny the temporal and spatial dimension of dream experience. As a result the structures of the unconscious unveiled in the dream sometimes seem detached from the 'corporal reality' in which they live. The theatre of the dream, the title of this book, implies not only an idea of organization, but also the idea of adventure; this dream adventure is played out in a 'formal' way in a three-dimensional space (like the body and like the stage of a theatre) and in an informal way within bi-logical dimensions (Matte Blanco), which are difficult to specify. To speak of the 'theatre of the dream', of its theatrical 'representation', already suggests an idea of spatio-temporal organization different from that of *objective reality*. The vicissitudes of the dream unfold, like life, according to a rhythm and to grammatico-oneiric rules that are difficult to decipher. The interpretation of dreams is an art, a technique. To decipher the secret of the dream, to make it apparent, is a challenge, a risk, a 'transgression'; to penetrate the stuff of dreams is a vocation, a desire, a curiosity for the hidden truth.

For Freud the 'reading' of dreams emerged from a profound personal experience bound up with his self-analysis, while working on his own dreams in order to try to recreate and to understand his relationship with his dead father.

The pain caused by his father's death, the ambivalent nature of the loss of the loved object, Freud's difficulty in working through the process of mourning, find expression in his work as an essential ontological problematic of his own existence.

In a letter to his friend Fliess, Freud writes of his father, who had just died:

'By one of those dark pathways behind the official consciousness the old man's death has affected me deeply. I valued him highly, understood him very well, and with that peculiar mixture of deep wisdom and fantastic light-heartedness he had a significant effect

5

on my life. By the time he died, his life had long been over, but in [my] inner self the whole past has been reawakened by this event. I now feel quite uprooted . . . I must tell you about a nice dream I had the night after the funeral. I was in a place where I read the sign: "You are requested to close the eyes."⁴ I immediately recognized the location of the barbershop I visit every day. On the day of the funeral I was kept waiting and therefore arrived a little late at the house of mourning. At that time my family was displeased with me because I had arranged for the funeral to be quiet and simple, which they later agreed was quite justified. They were also somewhat offended by my lateness. The sentence on the sign has a double meaning: one should do one's duty to the dead (an apology as though I had not done it and were in need of leniency), and the actual duty itself. The dream thus stems from the inclination to self-reproach that regularly sets in among the survivors.'⁵

Such a situation of ambiguity in pain is expressed through a resistance to facing reality, to opening his eyes, to acknowledging absence. The refusal to see is a way of opposing the idea of death and the 'duty' to assume mourning. The familiar super-ego criticizes Freud and makes him feel guilty for shutting his eyes to the reality of his father's loss.

In *The Interpretation of Dreams* Freud describes the same dream, but in a different way:

'During the night before my father's funeral I had a dream of a printed notice, placard or poster – rather like the notices forbidding one to smoke in railway waiting-rooms – on which appeared either

"You are requested to close the eyes"
"You are requested to close an eye"

or,

I usually write this in the form of

"You are requested to close $\frac{the}{an}$ eye(s)".'

Each of these two possibilities has its own meaning, which leads the interpretation of the dream in different directions:

'I had chosen the simplest possible ritual for the funeral, for I knew my father's own views on such ceremonies. But some other members of the family were not sympathetic to such puritanical simplicity and thought we should be disgraced in the eyes of those who attended the funeral.'   (S.E. pp. 318–19)

6

For Freud, guilt with regard to public opinion and the opinion of his family takes the form, on the one hand, of 'shutting his eyes' to a painful reality, despatching things as simply and quickly as possible, and, on the other, 'closing one eye', entering into complicity with an indulgent side of himself – monocular vision is two-dimensional, while binocular vision is stereoscopic and three-dimensional. The classic theory of the dream in Freud uses the notion of the dream screen. In this book, on the other hand, I speak of 'stage' and of 'theatre': the same dream is a film or theatre stage depending on whether one dreams with one eye or with both eyes. The person recounting the dream becomes the theatrical director who, on waking, will re-create the new version of the dream: it is another stage, another space-time (the 'transference' in analytical experience). The narrative of the dream is a dramatization, a different interpretation: thus the scene that appears in the letter to Fliess is not the same as that described in the 'book of dreams'.

For Freud the 'dream work' does not manage to become integrated; it remains ambiguous, ambivalent, and bi-valent: two different approaches to the same phenomenon.

In *The Interpretation of Dreams* Freud dates the dream cited above from the night preceding his father's funeral, whereas, in the letter to Fliess, the dream takes place afterwards. The transformation of the dream in the version intended for Fliess seems to be influenced by Freud's unconscious need not to assume responsibility for mourning ('closing his eyes'). In *The Interpretation of Dreams* there is an alternative: one may either deny mourning or sustain a manipulative alliance with oneself in order to avoid a confrontation. In the first few pages of *The Interpretation of Dreams*, Freud speaks of hypermnesic dreams:

'I may mention a dream of my own, in which what had to be traced is not an impression, but a connection. I had a dream of someone who I knew in my dream was the doctor in my native town. His face was indistinct, but was confused with a picture of one of the masters at my secondary school, whom I still meet occasionally. When I woke up I could not discover what connection there was between these two men. I made some enquiries from my mother, however, about this doctor who dated back to the earliest years of my childhood, and learnt that he had only one eye. The schoolmaster, whose figure had covered that of the doctor in the dream, was also one-eyed. It was thirty-eight years since I had seen the doctor, and so far as I know I had never thought of him in my waking life.'

(p. 76)

7

It is difficult not to take into consideration these two 'monocular' characters without linking them to the dream of *The Interpretation of Dreams*: 'to close one eye' means to identify oneself with the physician-father and the teacher-father who represent the monocular or 'flat' position of the dream. From the phenomenological point of view, the three-dimensional version is affectively more vivid; it even attains colour and sound in the dream. (In a conversation, Borges also talked to me about the sound dreams of the blind.) On the other hand, in cases of depression or excessive emotional blockage (psychosis), both dreams and the emotional world are flattened; there is a correspondence here with certain individuals' 'monotonous', detached tone of voice.

The significance of the eye, the act of looking, of visualizing the father's absence are expressed for Freud in two different states of mind. In the letter to Fliess, which precedes *The Interpretation of Dreams* by three years, the text is highly personal: Freud confesses to his friend how affected he was by his father's death, how difficult it was for him to assume the pain of that loss, and how a whole past history had been reopened for him.

Freud was so attached to his father that he did not want to leave Vienna at the time of his death, even to the extent of giving up the pleasure of meeting his friend Fliess. In the version to be found in *The Interpretation of Dreams*, he accuses himself of wishing to 'close one eye', criticizes his negligent, self-indulgent side, and tries to justify his position with regard to the reality personified by the family.

The excessive simplicity Freud wanted to give the funeral and which his family did not accept apparently accorded with the father's wishes; and he used every possible reason to simplify the ritual of mourning. From a rational point of view, he is concerned with his behaviour and confronts here the problem of self-criticism and self-reproach. Freud was to speak later of the problems of 'self-reproach' at the psychopathological level, in 'Further Remarks on the Neuro-Psychoses of Defence'. In 'A Case of Paranoia Running Counter to the Psycho-Analytic Theory of the Disease', he studies the relationship between self-accusation and projection.

In the case of paranoia, projection would seem to derive from the attempt to redirect self-accusation out into the world; thus one gets rid of self-reproach but, while the reproach disappears, the external world becomes inhabited by allo-accusations or hetero-accusations. The price to be paid for avoiding self-criticism is to create by projection an allo-critical situation: the externalization of the 'critical sense' is placed here at the service of the negation of one's own 'guilt' and one's own pain. *The Interpretation of Dreams*, written in 1899, seems on the face of it to be dedicated to Freud's father and to be an act of reparation for the father's death: to interpret one's own dreams is for Freud a way of re-creating a paternal image, a 'guide' who points the way in order to understand and to give meaning to his relations with all those who belong to his 'private' life.

In the letter to Fliess (no. 48), which precedes his father's death by some months, Freud confesses to his friend that he is not entirely convinced by the theory of repression and that he is waiting impatiently to discuss the matter with his friend, for he is sure that in this way he will be able to find a secure foundation, not only in psychology, but also in physiology, for his theories.

Freud's attachment to Fliess, which for him represents the fraternal aspect of the medico-scientific world, which he admires and respects, seems to have the character of dependence and reparation.

Furthermore, because of the medical world's criticism of his scientific discoveries and theories, he 're-creates' the conflictual vicissitudes with the father, as well as his own ambivalence with regard to his relations with his father. *The Interpretation of Dreams* is surely his most important contribution to the theory of unconscious thought. In the first chapter of his book Freud recapitulates the pre-scientific and scientific literature concerning the interpretation of dreams.

For Freud the most original and most representative author is Artemidorus of Daldis: 'To interpret dreams', Daldis writes, 'is merely to gather together similar things.' And Freud, who knew Artemidorus only through the writings of T. Gomperz, warns: 'An insuperable source of arbitrariness and uncertainty arises from the fact that the dream-element may recall various things to the interpreter's mind and may recall something different to different interpreters.'

Later Freud was to add: 'The technique which I describe . . . differs in one essential respect from the ancient method: it imposes the task of interpretation upon the dreamer himself.'[6]

The interpretation of dreams is a search by two persons into the past-present of the individual and of the culture; it has something of the character of an anthropo-archaeological research. Freud was very fond of archaeology, the 'logos of the arche' (ἀρχή); he liked to discourse on what was old and hidden in our culture and in each of us. In a definition that became famous, he stressed the interrelationship between the personal dream and culture: 'The dream is personal myth and myth is the dream of a culture.'

Thus to interpret a dream would have a cultural implication. The

9

reading of a dream has the value of an anthropological, archaeological, and yet at the same time phenomenological experience.

In his hypothesis on the dream, Freud stresses the hallucinatory satisfaction of unconscious wishes – the basic notion of the genesis of dreams.

But this way of interpreting the reading becomes too 'reductive'; it neglects the fundamental heritage of the classic view, which conceives of 'the dream as a message', a complex, vital message. The technique of the ancient oneiromancers, including Artemidorus, consisted of translating into conventional, comprehensible language the hidden, 'mysterious' meaning of the dream discourse.[7]

The dream is a complex, profound, iconological whole. It is an articulated polysemic iconography. If the discourse is too extended, there is a danger that the interpreter will lose his bearings; on the other hand, he must also avoid another danger, that of reducing the meaning overmuch in order not to get bogged down and thus to make the message univocal and rigid when it should not be so.

The hallucinatory satisfaction of unconscious wishes in dreams is a complex truth whose discourse remains open: it is a question of knowing who desires and what is desired. Who desires? The ego, the super-ego, the 'internalized' object, the instinct, or the drive?

A psychoanalytic reading of the dream phenomenon *qua* expression includes various possible points of view. Each interpretation is a point of view, a way of placing oneself, a choice from among a multiplicity of phenomena. The interpreter of dreams, like the ancient oneiromancer, often becomes involved in the dream himself and thus runs the risk of no longer being a true witness (which often happens in the analysis of psychotic patients). How does the 'oneiromancer-analyst' participate? Between the narrative of the dream and the dream itself, there is a gap of time between awaking and the analyst's experience of the narrative, a gap in which a whole series of perceptible transformations has taken place. In his *Matter and Memory* Bergson suggests that the images of the past are constantly mixed in the narrative with new perceptions deriving from the present, which may even go so far as to replace the preceding ones. This means that, if one recounts 'the experience of the night before', between yesterday and now, a whole experience of symbolic transformation appears and becomes established. The narrative of a dream is also a dramatization, a psycho-oneirodrama in which several objects belonging to the 'scenography' of the locus of the analysis play a part in the new representation of the dream.

For certain oneiromancers the interpretation of dreams was a true linguistic analysis of the narrative: the way in which the message was received and judged conditions the meaning of the interpretation (in ethnology, in field-work, the way of gathering the material together has a similarly interpretative character). Any interpretation is part of a 'technique' ('techne' means 'art' in Greek), but it is also part of an epistemology; to collect and classify the material of the narrative is an 'art', which tends to uncover the mystery of the dream, its 'laws', and its own syntax.

The language of the dream is symbolic. Any mental symbol is a representation. Freud draws a distinction between *Repräsentanz*, *Vorstellung*, and *Darstellung*. (*Stellung* means that which is placed, which stands up and confronts us.) Presentation is what is offered to us, whereas representation is a 'new presentation'; the notion of representative image implies a 'new presentation' in thought of what is presented before us (*Vorstellung*). Representation is an intentional impression: it leaves its personal trace. For Spinoza representation is a sensory apprehension different from the conceptual. For Leibniz it is different from perception and, in Locke and Hume, from the notion of ideas. For Kant representation is an intuitive, conceptual, or ideal apprehension. It is the reproduction of an object presented as present, past 'in the depths of the present', or as 'to come' when a project experienced in the present.

Representation is a mediation: it represents a person, a thing, an idea, a memory, a hope, an ideal. Taine gives the notion of representation a particular sense:

'It seems that nature has taken it upon herself to set up within us "representatives" of those events. . . . External facts, present, past or future, particular or general, simple or complex, have their internal "representatives", and this mental representative is always the same internal event, composed, repeated, and disguised to a greater or lesser degree.'[8]

For Melanie Klein the internal world appears as peopled by internal representatives that she calls 'internal objects'.

In waking or in dream, the internal object is an actor that 'represents' mentally or 'somatically' (a hysterical conversion, hypochondria, and somatic phenomena in general) a role, a situation, or an idea on the inner stage. In the transition from presentation to representation, a certain space-time is crossed. This crossing implies changes, 'transformations', which make the difference between the object perceived and its 'presentification' in thought: the thing perceived is an object that exists as an image (an internalized object).[9]

Freud may well have been influenced by the Herbartian notion of a 'mechanics of representations' (*Vorstellungsmechanik*), which he

11

integrates into his notion of 'unconscious representations'. For Freud *representation* is what is inscribed of the object in memory (the mnesic system). For him, memory is not a mere receptacle of images: in 'A Note upon the "Mystic Writing-Pad"' (1924), he suggests that the psychical apparatus may give new life to and elucidate through affective evocation what was imprinted and repressed in the unconscious as a mnesic trace. Freud speaks of the representation of words (*Wortvorstellung*) and of the representation of things (*Sachvorstellung* or *Dingvorstellung*). In his article 'Repression' (1915), Freud speaks of *Vorstellungsrepräsentanz*, the representative of the representation, when speaking of the content of the unconscious, but also of its constitutive aspects. Freud accepts the existence of a primary repression and a psychical representation of the drive, as well as of an inscription or 'fixation' of the representative perception in the psychical apparatus. This involves several layers of inscriptions for signs (*Niederschriften*). In *The Interpretation of Dreams* (1900) there is the hypothesis of a change of inscription that may be manifested for certain representations, going from one system to another. The notion of *Vorstellungsrepräsentanz* is also present in the texts in which Freud provides the definition of the relationship between the somatic and the psychical, especially in his metapsychological works of 1915 ('Repression' and 'The Unconscious'). For Freud the drive is somatic; he speaks of a psychical representation of the drive, which also seems to be somatic, and of the representation of the affect, stressing their different roles. Laplanche and Pontalis, following Freud, speak of a *representative of the drive* (*Triebrepräsentanz*), which suggests the way in which the drive finds its psychical expression.[10] Sometimes this word is synonymous with *Vorstellungsrepräsentanz*; at others, it has a much wider sense, taking in the affect, the affect 'quantum' (*Affektbetrag*). This interpretation by Freud stresses the affect.

Psychoanalytic experience is an experience of life, and therefore a relational one. If there is no affective charge, if there is no relationship, if space and time are experienced as trapped, blocked, denied, then the psychoanalytic discourse also comes to a stop. This is the problem with certain obsessional neuroses and certain psychoses.

Freud considers that we always think with words at the level of the consciousness and that non-verbal conscious thought – as in dream or day-dreaming – is an 'experienced intuition' of the unconscious. In schizophrenics we often notice the absence of affect in the representation of words, which are perceived by the patient as 'things'.

Melanie Klein's notion of the internal object poses the problem of the three-dimensional representation of that object and of its way of experiencing internal space, the 'internal world'. In this book I use the notion of internal object, *Darsteller* (actor), which has an imaginary body and an imaginary space, which loves, hates, moves in psychical and 'somatic' space, lives in day-dreaming, dreams, or the waking state, and becomes assimilated with the world of objects and with the inner stage, whether real or oneiric. In psychopathology the immobilized and often unassimilated (Paula Heimann) internal object is 'isolated, dissociated from the rest'.

The internal world lives in representation, in *Vorstellung*: *Vorstellung*, then, is a theatrical representation; the stage is that part of the theatre where the actors (*Darsteller*) act and where the sets that create the atmosphere of the production are placed. The dream stage may be vast, tiny, superficial, or deep . . . The characters of the dream, the actors, come on to the stage and present themselves to public view. The dreamer is also the public that sees, listens, and perhaps even recounts, if he remembers it, the representation of his dream. The actors of the dream make their exits and their entrances, appear and disappear as on the stage of a theatre. The sets are the landscape of the dream, and its shape and colours form part of the *Bildsprache*. A dream may be divided into several scenes, which may all take place at the same time, as in Leonora Carrington's play *The Flannel Shirt*, in which diachrony is synchronic.

'The theatrical production begins with life,' writes Gémier: 'One is not only performing before a visitor, a friend, a relation, one is also performing before oneself.'[11] The dream is a performance in which all the actors are part of the world of the dreamer, who, in the multiplicity of his roles, becomes at the same time the producer and the public. The dream is a performance before oneself . . . The preparations for the production, as in the theatre, consist of whole series of perceptual and imaginative experiences in a waking state: several real or imaginary places will appear on the dream stage, but the director will add his own 'ideas', transforming them and adapting them to the argument of the dream.

The production of the dream belongs to the art of the 'animator': gesture, silence, words, the way the protagonists walk about the stage and make their exits are part of a general and specific rhythm.

Linguistic research on the dream implies a revision of the notion of perception and imagination. Perception is not a mechanical apprehension of things; *percipere* means to grasp with the senses, to take with the senses, it is a way of com-prehending; *capere* means to grasp, to capture with the head. Comprehending is an instinctual-reflexive apprehension of the thing perceived: to take with . . . , 'to dialogue with the object'.

In his studies on symbolic forms and mythical thought, Ernst Cassirer attributes prime importance to the transforming, creative function of the 'intelligence'.[12]

W. R. Bion suggests that any description or transmission, whether on the part of the patient or on the part of the analyst, operates in a 'mutative' way according to the 'private' and cultural ideology of the individual. The world of ideas is made up and developed according to sets or 'transformation groups'.[13]

The object perceived, the sense-perceptible, extra-corporeal, or intra-corporeal thing is transformed into a representative image, as the result of a spatial movement through experienced time. Each movement in space has a duration. The Bergsonian notion of space and experienced time and Minkowski's remarks on psychopathology are of fundamental importance.[14]

Freud deepened the concept of the symbol and studied the particularities of the dream symbol, which he defined as an 'oneiric distortion'. In dreams, too, there is a critical psychical function, always exercised by the super-ego, which 'awakes' in dreams to censure and impose its cultural rules.

In order to avoid criticism, the ego works out a strategy to mask the individual's unconscious wishes and needs. For Freud the disguise of wishes played an important role in the theory of symbolism and in the relationship that it has with the super-ego: in order to avoid the censorship of the super-ego, the figure on whom the individual's wishes are directed is masked. The 'vocation' of desire cannot be expressed directly: the symbol is an indirect expression, a manipulatory 'solution' in order to avoid the criticism of 'society', which is always present, 'suffering from insomnia' and disguised as the super-ego (the super-ego is also, for Melanie Klein, an internalized object). What the super-ego censors in the super-ego-dominated mentality of Freud and his time is above all sexuality: the Victorian society of Freud's day demanded that 'desire' be hidden. The symbol is the privileged mediation – and mask – of desire. In *The Interpretation of Dreams* Freud considers the dream symbol and its mediating function as the product of a distortion characteristic of the modalities of the dream world. Disguise and transformations of both the form and content of the dream symbol are based on the need to communicate while avoiding the demands and opposition of the super-ego.

In the dreams related by Freud concerning his father's death (which inspired his theory of dreams), the super-ego appears in a

14

critical way, apparently hidden, but often in complicity with Freud's defensive ego: pain and guilt close his eyes.

On the other hand, the super-ego cathected by Freud's guilt-laden intentionality forms an alliance with him by suggesting to him that he should not open his eyes. The reality of the father's loss is too painful to assume and the super-ego assumes a defensive role in the service of negation, as if he were saying: 'My son, you must not look beyond what is necessary, what is permitted'. This 'limit' imposed by the super-ego is to be found in several myths: beyond certain limits, Narcissus must not look at himself in the pool and Oedipus must not look too closely into the abyss of his origins.

In Ovid's version Narcissus is the product of a violent copulation between a river, Cephisus, and the stream Lyriope. Narcissus, then, is the son of water, beloved of the nymphs (aquatic creatures), and he wants to look at and return to his origins. He wants to transgress the law, *dike*, but he is punished for wanting to see the moment at which he was conceived – the primal scene.

In *The Birth of Tragedy* Nietzsche speaks of Oedipus as a hero who wanted to look into the depths of the abyss and who had to pay a price, his eyes, for doing so.

In Sophocles' *Oedipus Rex* Jocasta expresses herself in two ways on this matter. First, she expresses relief at the announcement of the death of Polybius, king of Corinth and Oedipus' presumed father: 'Great eye open is the paternal tomb'. The Greek expression 'tafos', meaning tomb, might be translated as funeral, which allows us to use Sophocles' text again for a reading of Freud's dream concerning his father's death.[15] Second, Jocasta says to Oedipus, who wants to know at all costs the truth about his past: 'By all the gods, do not seek further, if you love life, my pain must be enough for you'. Like Narcissus, Oedipus wants to discover the mystery of his origins, his identity, and for that reason he dies: mythical morality says that any search into origins is a need to know, an explanation, which becomes a transgression. Narcissus looking at himself in the water and Oedipus looking at himself in his genealogy form part of a risky ontological adventure: looking into the mirror of the past also means contemplating one's own history.

The bivalence between seeing, exploring, and knowing the forbidden appears in pre-Socratic philosophy, especially in creation and other myths.

Any cosmogony is a cosmography, a spatio-temporal structure invested with curiosity and fear. The unknown is attractive, one is afraid of transgressing the law, *dike*, but there is also unbridled desire, *hubris*, which is opposed to the law.[16] For Hesiod the ethics of

15

being, doing, and knowing appear as a structure of thought, a mythical, religious, and sacred space, an order that must not be transgressed. Law, the measure of things, the idea of order and measure, is personified in the image of the father. In various myths, stories, and initiation rites, one of the fundamental conditions is not to look back. In the myth of the 'labyrinth', 'not looking back' is a *conditio sine qua non* of the return (*nostos*). Orpheus goes down into the underworld to free Eurydice from the world of the shades, and he knows that in order to succeed he must bring her back without looking at her. But Orpheus does not resist his curiosity, he turns round, and loses Eurydice for ever.

Looking back, in space or time, opens up the way of nostalgia: Ulysses wants to return to his past, the locus of desire to which he has always remained attached. Narcissus looking at himself in the water, or Oedipus looking into the abyss, is a way of looking back. Between the water and Narcissus' look, there is a play of mirrors; similarly Echo, the female version of his 'androgynous being', an acoustic mirror, sends him back his own voice.

According to Pausanias' version, the image that Narcissus sees reflected in the water is that of his dead twin sister: a specular double of his femininity that he wishes to rejoin, inspired by nostalgia, in order to complete himself in the form of a divine androgyn.

Listening to oneself in an attentive, prolonged way robs discourse of its fluidity and petrifies one's own image: Echo is turned into stone. Narcissus remains a prisoner of his 'narcissism'. In his ever circular space, love finds neither solution nor outlet, and in the end it is consumed or becomes a flower. To look, to look beyond certain limits, poses the problem of the riddle of death, of the world of the shades, and of all that which has remained in the shadow of the past or in the shadow of the future.

A way of defending oneself against the fear of death is not to look at the unknown directly – or not to look at oneself. In this way one seeks a mediation: the shamans, for example, had a mediating function between the natural and the supernatural; the psychoanalyst is a mediator between the natural or conscious life and the unconscious, which remains in shadow.

Thus a child under analysis, who had never known his father, remarked: 'I'd like to see everything, know everything, but it frightens me; I'm afraid of dying . . . I'd like to know how a star falls or how the astronauts went up there and why they disappeared.' And he added, 'Where are they?' Like the shaman, the psychoanalyst is a bridge between the known and the unknown. The shaman used the technique of ecstasy, which consisted in projecting oneself beyond the limits of nature in order to make contact with the planetary world. The shaman also had ritual instruments, his mask, his stick, and several objects that helped him in his 'journey'. The fear of death, which is bound up with research into the unknown, is often personified by comic characters, such 'diabolical' figures as the Harlequin in the *commedia dell'arte*, or the fools in kings' courts or churches,[17] who always appear as bearers of some essential, masked truth.

In the theory of dreams Freud uses the dream symbol as a mediator: the dream symbol is a masked character, the spokesman of a truth. In the classic interpretation of dreams, 'to interpret' meant to translate the riddles of the dream, that which is hidden, obscure, and masked: the manifest content of a dream is a hidden 'truth', a latent reality as yet unveiled.[18]

When Freud speaks of the manifest content and the latent content, I understand him to mean (every reading is a personal interpretation) that the manifest aspect is an appearance, a mask that carries a message, and this message must not be revealed overtly. For Freud the dream is not directly understandable. It is expressed indirectly: the dream symbol is a mask, a 'model of absence', which is present in a certain way. For Freud, there is a cleavage, a 'strict' separation between the manifest and latent registers – the unconscious cannot be known directly, its mediator is consciousness. The problem of 'appearance' poses the problem of 'being': the manifest content is a mask that hides, expresses, and 'betrays' the latent content. The interpretation of dreams is a phenomenology of the mask: the dream mask, whose features psychoanalysts must learn to read and to describe.

Beyond the dissociation of manifest content and latent content, one must see the dream as a physiognomic unity. Just as there was a science of 'physiognomony' (Lavater), or art of knowing the language of physical features, one must conceive of the façade of dreams as a series of dream features to be unveiled. Through a reading of appearance, the manifest content, one finds in the manifestation of the message its latent content.

As in the theatre, the dream is acted out and the author's discourse is unveiled through the dramatization of his characters. In the Greek theatre there were masks to express every mood: the actor had to 'bear' the traces of his feelings: sadness, joy, or irony . . . What is shown is the implicit expression of what is present beyond appearance. There is a mediation between the actor and the public: the author's mask. I am using the theatre as a 'true' metaphor in order to speak of the interpretation of the theatre of dreams; the place

17

where the actors dramatize the dream is the *dream stage*. The notion of stage and dramatization brings the three-dimensional perspective of the dream at the spatial level, or four-dimensional perspective if one includes the rhythm of the play as an idea of time. The theatrical conception of the dream diverges from the two-dimensional conception of the dream screen. The notion of the dream 'screen' was introduced by B. Lewin to suggest the projection of the dream on to a white screen, which symbolizes the mother's breast.[19]

In some dreams, called blank dreams, the screen appears alone, without actors, classically representative of primary narcissism. Lewin interprets the dream screen as a symbol of sleep and considers that the dream experience is connected to the child's earliest experience of his first object, the mother's breast.

O. Isakower has studied the hypnagogic phenomena that correspond to the gap between waking and sleep, analysing the meaning and difference between 'day-dreaming', coenesthesis, and dream hallucination.[20]

F. M. Cornford, in a note on Plato's *Republic* concerning the 'Cave', speaks of the three-dimensionality of the stage and the two-dimensionality of the screen – a wall on which the shadows of the world are projected.[21] The external world is projected in a two-dimensional way on to the wall of the cave, with the shadows of noises and sounds that are 'reflected' on to the screen as an echo – an 'anticipation' of the 'talkies'.

In the dream the actors on the stage represent a theatrical or cinematographic language, depending on the observer's point of view: one eye or both eyes. The notion of stage introduces into the dream a three-dimensional space and the idea of theatrical rhythm as a fourth dimension. This theatre of dreams is made up of acts, or parts of acts, not always clearly articulated. In some cases, as in the myth of the Cave, the surrealistic plays of L. Carrington or the Living Theater, several acts appear simultaneously. W. R. D. Fairbairn – like Melanie Klein – speaks of the dream as a 'short' acted by different parts of the 'self', the ego, the internalized objects.[22]

Following the schema of the two registers of the 'real', one masking the other, Freud distinguishes between different types of 'dream distortion', that is to say, different mechanisms of *Vorstellung*: 'condensation' or *Verdichtung* (the fusion of different containers and contents) and 'displacement' or *Verschiebung*, the movement of one original content to another that will represent it symbolically, the representative form of an original 'signification' displaced and transformed. Displacement is a defence that consists in distancing the original meaning and the distancing is equivalent to avoiding the reading of the super-ego, and to 'taking one's time'. Distancing is a mobilization and transformation in space and time. Freud studies Silberer on dramatization: *Vorstellung* also means a theatrical performance.[23] In the theatre everything that takes place on the stage concerning the actor or the setting helps to build up a total image of the play. In the act of recounting a dream, one also 'plays' with space and the objects that form part of the analytic stage. All the formal elements, the actors, the text, and the setting form an inseparable *Gestalt*: the stage is an overall experience with unpredictable vicissitudes; one performance is never the same as another. One cannot understand an author's narrative and his 'messages' if one does not understand where the action is being played out, thought, spoken, or felt, with what rhythm and in what time. When I interpret a dream, I always ask where the stage was set, what were the objects and characters on the stage and what the setting was: it is a way of situating the history and topography of the narrative.

Each story is part of a geography and each geography has its own story to tell. This chapter is also a geography and *The Theatre of the Dream* has a history, which takes the form of a seminar. The intervention by one of the 'actors' in the seminar (a psychoanalyst), who recounts the dream of a patient, enters the stage of my narrative in this way:

> 'The patient is a 40-year-old woman from Milan who suffers from psychotic anxieties: she tells how she dreamt that she had mislaid her mackintosh; in fact it had been stolen. In the dream, she receives a telephone call from Bari. She is told that her mackintosh has been found in a train and that it will be sent to her. The mackintosh appears in the dream, but it is in poor condition and she isn't sure that she'll be able to wear it again.'

After recounting the dream, the patient remarks that 'Bari' is a town that she doesn't know and which, therefore, she has imagined, though she has often telephoned to it in her work: indeed, in her job, she often has to contact Sicily or Africa and always does so through Bari. The patient realizes that Bari is a *mediation* represented by her analyst, who is the bridge between her and several geographical places in her personal history.

The patient's personal, private world, her history, is spatialized in the dream in order to deny a painful time element: the pain of loss and nostalgia for the lost object are dissolved in space, being transformed into new spaces. The patient's 'impermeable' (*impermeabile* is the Italian for 'mackintosh') attitude during certain sessions appears

19

as the expression of the sign *impermeabile*, and the lack of the *impermeabile* links her to the fear of 'opening up' and therefore losing her protective impenetrability. On the other hand, making herself more open to the transference triggers off both her fear of communicating and the need to return to her closedness: her *impermeabile* was losing its effectiveness – it had got into a poor state.

To recount a dream means to unveil oneself to discover oneself, to open oneself to others. Communicating, establishing contact with the world, is a 'normal threat'; Heidegger speaks of exchange, of commerce (*Umgang*) with others. When exchange becomes difficult and the intentionality of commerce increasingly threatening, one can always stop. The autistic defence is a way of stopping exchange with the world and of retreating to one's own body. Making oneself distant in this way and even impermeable to any external stimulus characterizes the autistic position (Tustin); the autistic person cannot assume experienced time.[24] In the schizophrenic, where the autistic phenomenon was described for the first time by E. Bleuler, there is a transformation of too painful experienced duration into a sense of surface: morbid geometricism (E. Minkowski).[25] One finds again the 'spatial thought' characteristic of psychosis in the dream mentioned, even though the patient was not psychotic. Spatial thought is a 'way out', a pathological solution to autism: a colonialist expansion to control the world. Withdrawal, impermeability, and expansion are the three stages of an extreme movement of being 'in danger'.

The dream is a dramatization and the patient's account of it to the analyst 'a new dream adventure', a reactivation of yesterday's dream. The theatrical representation of the dream in the session is also a ritualization of the 'dream myth'; the dream is a 'journey' and the account given today in the session is an encounter with new variants that transform the meaning of the message. To interpret a dream means, on the part of the analyst, to assume 'an adventure', to introduce a new variant: the interpretation acts upon the narrative, just as the narrative acts upon the interlocutor. In so far as the Milanese patient is more confident in communicating to the analyst, the analyst becomes a privileged part of her personal geography, which she calls Bari. The analyst is the mediator who will enable her to make contact with the various 'geographical places' of her history.

In Indian cosmography and cosmology, the world of the cosmos is made up of the parts of a super-human body. In the hymns of the *Rig Veda* there is a description of a social geography of the world; starting from the idea of a superior body (*Purusha*), the world is a body dismembered in accordance with the laws of sacrifice, a dismemberment that constitutes a categorization of castes.[26] From the body of Brahma the priests take his mouth, the warriors his arms, the workers his hips, and the servile class his feet.[27] For the Milanese patient 'Italy' is also the expression of her surface body, with a particular cathection of each of its geographical points. At a given moment the patient recounts to her analyst that, one day, as she was walking in the street (Italy is a leg), she saw a labourer working in a man-hole; she imagined that he might be trapped there and suffocate. According to her analyst, she identified with 'being shut up in his impermeable world', like being a prisoner in a hole.

To dream, to sleep, to close one's eyes to everyday life is also an experience of death, a journey to an unknown world from which one is never sure that one will return (insomnia is an expression of this fear). The dream is an 'enigmatic' discourse; what is called the interpretation of the dream is a way of translating certain of these enigmas, which is never exhaustive. The language of the dream is personal and specific; as Freud indicated, it is a privileged discourse; dream symbolism has peculiarities that differentiate it from all other forms of symbolism.

At times it is difficult to distinguish between the interpretation of the dream and the interpretation of the transference. But it may be said that the dream narrative unfolds in the transference and it is through the transference that one may understand the dramatization and reactivation of the dream.

It has long been said that psychotics cannot distinguish between the world of dream and the world experienced during waking (Bion). I would add to this hypothesis that the dream has its own space; and when the dreamer and his characters go beyond those bounds, they occupy the stage of the world, while being unaware of the frontier between dream and reality. The psychotic, even if he says that he does not dream, dreams all the time with his eyes open: he dreams reality. The world is a dream, the characters in Calderón de la Barca's *Life is a Dream* would say:

> 'Though I see that I am awake,
> Maybe I am dreaming.
> No, I am not dreaming; I touch and believe
> What I have been and what I am . . .

> The world is so strange
> That to live in it is to dream.
> And experience teaches me
> That man dreams what he is
> Until he emerges from sleep . . .

What is life? Madness.
What is life? An illusion.
A shadow, a fiction;
The greatest happiness is little enough,
For all life is a dream
And dreams are worth what dreams are worth.'

The difference between normal life and psychosis is a matter of degree. Day-dreaming, the intermediary state between dreaming and waking, occupies a privileged place for the poet. The Chilean poet Vincente Huidobro speaks of 'a poets' madness', which is not necessarily delusion.

The psychotic dreams all the time without being able to wake up. In 'normal' life we are unaware that we are dreaming until we wake up. When we dream, life is a dream, but we don't know that it's a dream. If we don't wake up, the space of the dream remains a reality with its own time and history, in which the characters are 'awake'.

The oneiric conception of the world and the oneiroid possession of reality pose the problem of the relationship between dream, delusion,[28] and reality. But delusion that is not a dream tries to make the world go mad, to go off the rails . . .

Freud always linked dream, myth, and delusion, as also did Otto Rank[29] and Geza Roheim:[30] the dream is a myth, a conception of the world, a way of living in another register. Delusion tries to transform the world and to restructure the chaos that it has projected into it.

In Freud's 'The Schreber Case',[31] delusion is a way of occupying and invading the waking world, of colonizing reality by the real of delusion, by the real of one's 'waking' dreams.

Beyond delusion, the poet and artist in general experience a dimension of the world that is not strictly oneiric, situated between dream and waking. They are thus able to assume an ambiguous space and time that allow them to think and create simultaneously in different horizons. The world of creativity is a mediation between dream and waking: that is why the surrealists always tried to bring together the world of dream and the world of waking, and to experience both through fantasy.[32]

Notes

1 Shakespeare, *The Tempest*, IV. i. 156–58.
2 Shakespeare, *The Tempest*, IV. i. 152–54.

3 Cf. S. Resnik, 'Inconscio', *Enciclopedia Einaudi*, Torino, 1979, VII.

4 In *The Interpretation of Dreams* Freud relates two other dreams of his in which the element of the eye, the gaze, seeing/not seeing reappears, always in relationship with his father. Thus his childhood doctor (as we shall see later) is confused in the dream with his secondary-school teacher (paternal images) through the common elements that they share: both had an eye missing. In another dream Freud is in the company of an old gentleman who pretends to be blind, or at least to have only one eye. Freud associates this image with the glaucoma that afflicted his father ('Material and sources of dreams'). The eye and the problem of the father, in relation to the Oedipus complex, appear therefore 'inscribed' in Freud's biography.

5 Sigmund Freud, *Complete Letters of Sigmund Freud to Wilhelm Fliess, 1887–1904*, trans. Jeffrey Moussaieff Masson, Cambridge, Mass., 1985, p. 202.

6 *The Interpretation of Dreams*, Standard Edition, IV, p. 98.

7 Aelius Aristides was another oneiromancer of the Roman period. He was a native of Asia Minor and had had the same teachers as Marcus Aurelius. Aristides developed mystical and therapeutic conceptions of the dream inspired by ancient traditions; Aesculapius (Asklepios) appeared to Aristides in his dreams in order to guide him. According to Elemire Zolla ('Conoscensa religiosa', *Le Nuova Italia*, no. 1, 1976, p. 54), Aristides speaks, like the shamans, of the dismembering and reassembling of the body at the moment of dream ecstasy. He thus introduces the notion of time and history (as 'remembrance') into the dream space. The intuition of a connection between the biological body, the dream, and memory is essential.

8 H. Taine, *De l'intelligence*, Paris, 1870, I, p. 236.

9 For Eugen Fink, a pupil and collaborator of Husserl (*Studien zur Phänomenologie*, 1930–39, The Hague, 1966), 'representation' *qua Vergegenwaertigung* cannot be conceptualized without the notion of 'image' (*Bild*) [von Schubert speaks, on the subject of the dream, of *Bildersprache*] and of *fantasizing* (*Phantasieren*). The elucidation (*Aufklärung*) of the problem of representation becomes, for Fink, the subject of a phenomenological analysis. Fink speaks of the representation of images or *Bildvorstellung*: imagination is a modification of experience as apprehension. There exists a multiplicity of horizons in space and in time that partly 'determine' the modalities of apprehension. But any horizon is the projective expression of an intentionality. The future of the imagined object will depend, therefore, on the modalities of *retention*, *protention*, and *appresentation*, living horizons of an experienced presence. The phenomenological complexity of the representative process (in space and in time) is not for Fink a mere making present or only modes of

representation (in time), but the expression of what he calls de-presentation (*Entgegenwaertigungen*).

10 In *The Language of Psycho-Analysis*, trans. Donald Nicolson-Smith, London, 1973, p. 223.

11 F. Gémier, 'La Mise en scène au théâtre', lecture of 15 June, 1919, quoted by P. Paraf in *Les Métiers du théâtre*, Paris, 1923. Together with Copeau, Gémier was one of the masters of theatrical production at the time.

12 Ernst Cassirer, *The Philosophy of Symbolic Forms*, New Haven, Conn., 1955, and *Language and Myths*, New York, 1946.

13 Wilfred Bion, *Transformations*, London, 1955.

14 Eugène Minkowski, *Le Temps vécu*, Paris, 1933.

15 *Tafos*: for Hesiod 'grave' and for Homer 'funeral' or 'funerary festival'.

16 In Greek *dike* means 'measure' and *hubris* means incommensurate 'violence', excess, arrogance.

17 In the Middle Ages a distinction was drawn between 'domestic' mad-men, 'seigneurial' madmen, 'ecclesiastical' madmen, and 'wandering' madmen.

18 Riddle or enigma – in Greek *ainigma* – means 'the darkness speaks'.

19 B. Lewin, 'Sleep, the Mouth and the Dream Screen', *Psychoanalytic Quarterly*, XV, 1946; Interferences from the Dream Screen', *International Journal of Psycho-Analysis*, XXIX, 1948; *Dreams and the Uses of Regression*, New York, 1958.

20 O. Isakower, 'A Contribution to the Patho-psychology of Phenomena associated with Falling Asleep', *International Journal of Psycho-Analysis*, XIX, 1938.

21 F. M. Cornford, *From Religion to Philosophy*, New York, 1957.

22 W. R. D. Fairbairn, *Psychoanalytic Studies of the Personality*, London, 1952.

23 H. Silberer, 'Symbolik des Erwachens und Schwellen-Symbolik Über-haupt', *Jn. psychoan.-pyschopath., Forsch*, 3, 1912, p. 621; *Probleme der Mystik und ihrer Symbolik*, Leipzig and Vienna, 1914.

24 Frances Tustin, *Childhood Psychosis and Autism*, 1967.

25 Eugène Minkowski, *La Schizophrénie*, Paris, 1927.

26 In the hymns of the *Rig Veda*, the body of Brahma was described as the giant Purusha, the cosmic man whose dismembered body formed the universe.

27 Quoted by Ernst Cassirer, *The Philosophy of Symbolic Forms*, New Haven, Conn., 1955, vol. II, p. 90.

28 From the Latin verb *delirare*, meaning 'to leave the furrow', and therefore 'to lose one's reason', 'to go off the rails'. The idea that delusion is related to the dream and that to be in the grip of a delusion means 'to dream' without waking up, and without end, was already

formulated by nineteenth–century French psychiatrists: cf. P. Tissié, *Le Rêve. Physiologie et pathologie*, Paris, 1898; Régis, *Les Rêves*, Bordeaux, 1890, and 'Le Délire du rêve chez le vieillard', *Journal de médecine de Bordeaux*, 1895.

29 Otto Rank, *The Myth of the Birth of the Hero*, New York, 1932.

30 Geza Roheim, *Magic and Schizophrenia*, New York, 1955.

31 Psycho–Analytic Notes in an Autobiographical Account of a Case of Paranoia (Dementia Paranoides), Standard Edition, 1911, pp. 1–82.

32 In particular André Breton's *L'amour fou* and *Nadja* pose the problem of the representation of the day–dream and the marvellous in the everyday. Also in the literary domain one might mention Joyce's *Ulysses*, in which the discourse unfolds in an ambiguous space-time, between conscious and unconscious, between waking and sleep.

2

The birth and itinerary of the dream discourse

Dream reality confronts everyday reality: thus in his normal development, the child must confront the world of dreams with the waking world and gradually discern the differences.

I would like to illustrate this process through a dream dreamt by Clive, a 2-year-old boy, who was in analysis with me in London and who was recounting his first dream.[1]

Clive did not know exactly what recounting a dream was. At one point during a session, Clive looked at my hand and started talking to it:

'I saw you yesterday.'
'Are you sure you saw me yesterday?'
'Yes', Clive replied.

He took my hand and led me off to a corner of the room. He put my hand into the wash-basin there and turned on the tap. He picked up various objects and threw them into the wash-basin, saying, 'Take out everything you find there'.

Clive was using my hand as a tool to gather up objects from the bottom of the water: small bits of wood, tiny dolls, and bits of card, which he had thrown into the wash-basin. The game consisted of putting my hand into the water and sometimes his own hand, to fish out immersed objects.

'What's happening?' I asked.
'They're little children', Clive replied.
'Where and when did all this take place?'
'In my room, at night', Clive replied.

26

What happened under the water, below his consciousness, and in his room at night? As he looked at the objects under the water, Clive spoke of the little children; he made a movement with his body and a noise with his mouth rather like an explosion: 'Bang'.

The various bits and pieces thrown into the water probably represented pieces of children's bodies linked, in his inner world, with an explosion: it was a reactivation of an 'explosive time' during which his mother was pregnant. And it was precisely on that occasion that the parents felt the need to take Clive to a child analyst. During his mother's pregnancy and even after the birth of his younger sister, Clive was very anxious and sad: he couldn't sleep, he suffered from insomnia.

In that period of time that I call 'Clive's dream', the child tried to personify and dramatize his destructive fantasies. His words 'I saw you yesterday', spoken as he looked at my hand, corresponded to a daytime memory: the analyst's hands of the previous session. It was this 'daytime' hand that he incorporated in his night life, which acted as a mediator and therefore as an 'analyst' in the account of the previous night's dream.

Between the daytime memory and the reality, an element of the night before, part of the analyst's body became part of Clive's dream. The reverse is also possible, the affect of yesterday's dream may inhabit today's world; the child uses nocturnal memories in dramatizing today's dream: the narrative of a dream is a new dream.

The nocturnal memory is thus linked with the *déjà vu* (and *déjà connu*) phenomenon. The daytime memory and nocturnal memory are integrated with the reality of the night before, a possibility of mediation between two aspects of the real: daytime reality and dream reality. During the dramatization the wash-basin played the role of 'dream belly', the 'maternal' belly, while the analyst-fisher-of-immersed-and-hidden-objects personified the guide and mediator: a super-egoic function.

For Freud the dreams of young children are relatively simple. In children's first dreams the distance between the latent content and the manifest content is seen to be minimal; the 'dream work' is reduced, for, in the infant, wishes and their direct fulfilment predominate.

For me the development of the dream is already the expression of a primitive capacity for dream symbolism, the sign of an adaptive dissociation between two cognitive activities: 'waking' thought and 'dream' thought.

The fact of recognizing the dream as such, of perceiving it as a different, specific reality, is, for the infant, the sign of an ego becoming integrated and acquiring a sense of the 'real'. In the case of psychotics, oneiroid or persecutory thought has the opposite significication: loss of reality sense.

The child may project himself on to the analyst – the maternal 'container' – in order to collect misunderstood 'signifiers': in Clive's case, the 'wash-basin/belly' was the place where the analyst's hand was to help him to repair his 'fragmented world'. Archaic fantasies, dramatized in play, correspond to a reality invested with great anxiety: the wish to rediscover the mother's body – the first 'habitat' – and the wish to attack the pregnant mother are rediscovered and merge. Melanie Klein devoted herself to a study of the infant's world and of his precocious relational anxieties.[2]

The notion of reality appears as a fundamental problem for the development of the unconscious stages of the child's imaginary (fantasies). A few aspects of Clive's dream, in particular the nocturnal memory, show that my hand played the role of intermediary between two realities: daytime reality and night-time reality. The words 'I saw you yesterday' may mean that Clive had perceived my hand in the dream, a dream reality that was merging with the daytime reality of the session. At this precise point, we should examine the problem of the distinction between dream space and time, daytime space and time, and between the daytime and night-time *forms* of thought.

'I saw you yesterday' probably meant that Clive wanted to know where and when, to what space and time, the hand that he had seen belonged. Clive had incorporated me into a dream world (proof of the existence of the transference), and the dream element that represented me appeared to him in the form of my 'being-hand'. For him I was the analyst-tool, the actor-tool, the actor in the drama that was taking place on the dream stage and on the analytic stage: two spaces and two times. The unconscious was represented by that immersed world: that presence under the water and the objects-toys constituted the characters, the inhabitants of that unconscious world. The role of the analyst was that of translator-mediator, which brought out of the water what was hidden there. The fishing out of those objects did not happen of its own accord, it was work that had to be done with the child: gathering facts is already a way of organizing the reading. Like the oneiromancer of old, the analyst is he who listens, reads, and interprets *what the dream says*: the dream speaks. The dream becomes a subject when confronted with the dreamer and the interpreter, the element that forms the triad of the dream message. The variants of this dynamic triad form a complex, multidimensional reality. The theory of wish-fulfilment is a ideological, one-dimensional interpretation.

28

In the psychotic crisis the third party, the dream, leaves the dream stage and invades the space of waking life; the frontier between dream and the waking state disappears and dream space becomes day-time reality. This confusional experience (con-fusion of boundaries) is a delusional discourse that may suddenly be experienced as cata-strophic: the crisis is an 'event' that changes the order of the world. 'Delusional' change is an overthrow of the meaning of the real, a distortion of the everyday, sometimes accompanied by a sense of disaster.

At the moment of chaos and disorder, the private becomes public. The acute crisis is not only a loss of the sense of the real, but also a *moment of truth*, an instant of psychotic lucidity. This is why the psychoanalytic approach is of crucial importance in acute crises. Bion distinguishes a pre-catastrophic phase, a catastrophic phase, and a post-catastrophic phase: the first phase is characterized by an increase in aggressiveness, which turns into violence in the next phase, when bound up with a 'new view of the world' (the delusional view), and regresses in the post-catastrophic phase.[3] During the crisis the link with reality seems to be lost: the tool-hand, the third party (the father-phallus that links the disorder) is attacked and destroyed. In the psychotic crisis delusion is an attempt to recompose 'fragments', the debris of a catastrophe: the crisis is also a regrouping, an 'odd', personal way of regrouping the fragments of shattered time. Cata-strophe and chaos are borderline situations, life and death at the same time. In several cultures death represents a new initiation, a way of opening up to the unknown, to the mystery of non-existence. There is an ambiguous meaning in the term 'birth-death', which is bound up with a universal ontological anxiety consisting of wanting to know what is beyond the known. The unknown is situated in origins (what pre-cedes life), or at the end (de-cease), or in life itself, in that space between origin and end: the space of life, the adventure of exis-tence. The mechanistic, causalist, or finalist 'scientific' approaches are so many ways of mentally organizing chaos from a starting-point called origin and in relation to a horizon, something called end. This mental organization, this reductive, simplifying view appears simpler and more 'tranquillizing' than the threatening multiplicity of a world in crisis. To know, to capture the mystery, is a challenge, an act of arrogance, a transgression.[4] Tiresias says: 'Do not wish to know beyond certain limits'. The most painful figure in Greek drama, the unfortunate Oedipus, had excessive curiosity; he wanted to decipher the riddle of his past: Dionysiac wisdom, says Nietzsche in *The Birth of Tragedy*, is an unnatural monster.

The analysis of the psychotic is also a challenge, a confrontation, at once 'dangerous' and fascinating, with the mysteries and riddles of the beyond: any fascinating experience arouses fear. The psychotic is not concerned with the everyday; he is preoccupied by fundamental ontological problems that appear in the form of 'mythical' thought, the thought that lies at the origin of all language (Cassirer).

In our culture there is a manifest relation between the mythical world, the world of the 'dead', and the world of dreams.

In the myth of Orpheus and Eurydice the narrative is made up of two themes: curiosity about death, about the unknown, and the ambivalence between 'knowing' and 'not knowing'. Curiosity for the world of dreams and for the knowledge of the secrets of existence belongs to borderline states in which prohibition and punishment are manifested.

The interpretation of dreams is bound up with the unknown world, with darkness, with the world of the dead . . . In the first chapter of his *Traumdeutung*, Freud summarizes the pre-scientific literature on the interpretation of dreams and speaks of the obscurity of dreams and of interpretation as a journey into night.

Hesiod discovered the secret of Greek mythology through the night that hides the light that is to be born.

In ancient Babylon dreams played a very important role in cultural and religious life. In dreams the gods appeared as the expression of the will of Heaven, predicting the future. He who wanted to be helped by his dreams prayed in the temple and invoked Mathir, god and goddess of dreams.

At Nineveh, in the library of King Assurbanipal (5,000 BC), a rich collection of books on oneiromancy (or the interpretation of dreams) was used by Artemidorus. In the oneiromantic science of the time, there was already a technique, an interpretative reading of the dream context: to fly was interpreted as a way of escaping from a dangerous situation; to dream of flying was therefore the sign of that dangerous situation. It is possible to deduce the moral principles of certain interpretations of that time, already implied in the dream narrative: to dream of drinking wine meant to have a short life, while to dream of drinking water was the sign of a long life. Such a principle denotes the presence in the dreams of a 'social', critical character, corresponding to what, since Freud, we call the 'super-ego'. The system of values of the time belonged to the grammar of the dream discourse, just as did a certain socio-political and religious interpretation. In Egyptian and Mesopotamian society dreams played an important role. In Egypt divination through dreams was officially recognized. The Egyptian 'Book of the Dead' takes account of the 'world of dreams' and its interpretation. There is even mention of miraculous cures through dreams in which certain gods intervened. The Egyptian god of dreams was Serapis. A temple, the 'Serapeum', was dedicated to him. At Memphis too (in 3,000 BC), in one of the most important temples of the city, there was an oracle for the interpretation of dreams.

In Greece people invoked Aesculapius (Asklepios), who was also to be venerated as the god of medicine. The interpretation of dreams was also used as a means of cure and in order to arrive at an understanding of some primordial message. The Greeks linked the world of dreams with the world of theology (demonological and divine). At the time, substances or 'medicines' were used that had hypnagogical and hallucinatory functions, by means of which the god Aesculapius appeared. He appeared in dreams in order to give advice and to 'interpret' and explain to the 'believer-patient' certain aspects of his life and health. The oracle, a mediator between the 'patient' and the god of medicine, made it possible through a sort of personal, medical *transference* to introduce the interpreter of the dream – the god – into the dream.

Hippocrates, the father of medicine, who was himself worshipped as a god, was also concerned with the interpretation of dreams. According to an astrological concept, he linked the 'personal body' to the 'universal body'. Certain pains in the head or the intestines were due, according to him, to a change in the position of the stars.[5]

According to Hippocrates, dreams were a representation of one's personal situation in relation to the universe and vice versa: a dialectic between the microcosm and the macrocosm.

The classic notion of the dream as a message from the beyond is bound up with the idea of a universal mystery.

Aristotle denied the idea that dreams were of a divine nature and were thus of supernatural origin: he declares that they belong to the rules and laws of being and mind. He also suggests that the slightest external stimulation – bodily sensations, for instance – may condition certain dreams to a considerable degree. The heat of certain parts of the body, Aristotle said, may cause a dream in which one is walking on fire.

Freud takes up these same associations when he links dreams of fire with enuresis: it would appear that there is a link between the sensation of heat and a burning sensation caused by urine.

The most important interpreter of dreams in antiquity was Artemidorus of Daldis, who lived in the second century BC and was a native of Lydia. Even in his own time, he was regarded as a philosopher expert in the interpretation of dreams; in his treatise on oneirocriticism or *On the Interpretation of Dreams*, he divides dreams into two categories: the first comprises 'insomnia', or relatively clear dreams, connected to the present, and 'fantasies', or exaggerated amplifications of fear, fantastic tensions, ideas that may also find expression in nightmares. The second category comprises dreams connected to the future and therefore to the oracle: these dreams refer to the world of divination, to the notion of 'vision'; 'symbolic' dreams or 'somnia' (from the Latin *somnium*, 'dream') are connected with the notion of interpretation.

For Artemidorus the dream is a living thing, a movement of the mind that, when it refers to the future, may have a positive or negative premonitory meaning.

The dream is a movement or 'fission' of the mind, a mode of thought. In fact the dream includes various elements and its interpretation seems to be a way of making evident various phenomena of a symbolic or allegorical kind that are not directly understandable.

Artemidorus distinguishes between the 'non-personal' dream and the 'personal' dream. In the first there is a 'character' in the dream who 'becomes embodied': for example the dead father, whom the dreamer identifies with the bearer of the dead object, implies his death. Setting out from that point, one may imagine that a dream character (a dream 'object') may be the 'true dreamer', the 'director' and the ego of the formal dreamer, an actor: in this case, the dreamer's ego is at the mercy of one of his characters.[6] The personal dream is linked to things that concern only the dreamer, such as speaking, singing, dancing, diving, dying: it is a sort of dream 'soliloquy' or theatrical monologue. In this case one must seek the 'other characters' in the dream setting: Freud suggests that all the characters of the dream are part of the dreamer's world; but the setting and the stage also create characters. Artemidorus draws attention to the connection between the dream and its fulfilment (Freud speaks of wish-fulfilment).[7] He also speaks of generic dreams and specific dreams, dreams asked of the gods and dreams that are sent without request. He classifies dreams according to themes: birth, the body and parts of the body, art, craft, occupation, sexuality.

Artemidorus' interpretative hypothesis has linguistic implications: to dream that one has a big head, in the case of someone who practises usury or banking, foretells large sums of money; indeed, the Greeks called money *kephale* ('head'). Another example, concerning an episode in the life of Alexander the Great during the siege of Tyr, and which is cited by Freud, was already regarded by Artemidorus as the most precise interpretation of the dream: Alexander was very impatient and preoccupied because the city continued to resist, which lost him valuable time. One night Alexander dreamt of a satyr dancing on a shield. He questioned Aristarchus, his oneiromancer, who made the following 'linguistic' interpretation: 'Satyr signifies *saturos*, that is to say, "Tyr is yours", and the dance on the shield signifies triumph'. Thus reassured and encouraged, Alexander attacked and took the city. Artemidorus also speaks of theorematic and allegorical dreams. The first are those in which the fulfilment follows as the dream depicted. For example a sailor dreamt that he was shipwrecked and this happened to him. For, scarcely had he woken up, than his ship went under, and he himself was rescued only with great difficulty. Or again, someone dreamt that he was wounded by an individual with whom he had agreed to go on a hunting expedition the following day. During the hunt, the other man wounded him in the shoulder, exactly where he had been wounded in his dream. Or, again, someone dreamt that he received money from a friend and next day he received from him 10 minae. There are many other examples of the same kind.

Allegorical dreams, on the other hand, are those that signify certain things by means of other things: in such dreams it is the soul that, according to certain natural laws, hints in some obscure way about an event.

'The dream is a movement or polymorphous modelling of the soul that signifies good or bad events to come', Artemidorus writes. The event is a privileged fact, not yet born, but latent, and therefore present in dream. All this poses the problem of dream time and waking time. In the theorematic dream of the sailor, the dream 'speaks' and signals to the sailor that he is perceiving a sensation of danger. Allegorical dreams pose the problem of indirect knowledge which, through attentive listening, tries to understand what the soul is communicating 'obscurely'. It is in obscurity that mystery dwells. The understanding of the dream message is a cryptography of mystery. Artemidorus operates a strict semiological approach to the meaning of dreams. The dream occupies a space and, like the body, it has different meanings according to its various constituent parts. There is a topography of the dream as there is a geography of the body. Artemidorus studies the meaning of the various parts of the body in dreams, the body of cultural man also to be found in folklore and in the popular thought of the time: the interpretation of dreams is not dissociated from the social.[8]

There is a correlation between the dream world and culture, and the interpretation of dreams is also, for Artemidorus, a moral science that demands rigour and prudence, that is to say, respect, on the part of the interpreter. In a series of dreams it is important to note the relationship and articulation between them: to see whether the series of dreams forms part of a wider discourse, with revealing ontological and social implications. Artemidorus takes up this ethnological and 'culturalist' approach, trying to discover what facts or events influence the dream. He also believes that it is necessary to know the identity of the dreamer, his occupation, and his life.

The dream is often experienced as a journey into the unknown . . . A journey towards death.[9]

> A patient recounted how after a long coma following a serious accident, in which her mother and sister died, she awoke with a sensation of perceiving a blinding light coming from a long, dark tunnel, like a living form that ought to have woken her from the world of the dead or taken her to it.

The dream is bound up with life and culture; it is a discourse, a message, and not merely the fulfilment of wishes (the causalist or finalist, but always linear concept of Freud).

Freud, Jung, and Binswanger note that the interpretation of dreams can in no way be separated from life and that the dream must be related to the analytic transference. The transference is the alpha and omega of psychoanalysis, but the interpretation of the transference cannot take the place of either the specific feelings or the meanings of the dream world. Each must be integrated with the other.

Certain authors consider that the interpretation of dreams is inseparable from the 'work of the transference' and from free associations. However, a phenomenological distinction should be made here: the dream is 'expressed' in a language bound up with daytime memories, but the language of dream 'in itself' is a specific kind of experience. The world of the dream is both archaic and belonging to the present, and the structure of the dream with its 'symbolism' represents a 'grammatical' system with its own particular linguistic rules which, according to Freud, are constitutive of the laws of the unconscious. The dream is a mode of thought that may be expressed equally well in sleep or in waking. Bion speaks of 'dream thoughts'.[10] He also speaks of 'sense impressions' that are connected to what he calls the 'alpha' function, which itself produces 'alpha' elements that are useful and necessary in accumulating reserves for the gestation of the 'dream thoughts'. The transformation of each emotional experience into 'alpha' elements must be regarded as a process of abstraction, an aspect of the 'alpha' function.

'Sense impressions' transformed into 'alpha' elements are used in dream thought and in unconscious thought that belongs to waking life. The degrading of the cognitive and unconscious aspect of the 'alpha' function (or when a child is not prepared to use 'sense data' and to transform them into 'alpha' elements) becomes an intolerable fact, empty of emotion and significant content, which begins to be experienced as persecution. The 'alpha' element that loses its capacity to contain a sensitive and emotional experience becomes an 'empty object' or 'beta' element. The empty object becomes an object 'full' of persecutions whose fate is to be evacuated.

A child whom Piaget had asked what, for him, dreams were replied: 'A dream is something that appears in my bedroom when I shut my eyes and go to sleep.' When young Clive, looking at my hand, said to it, 'I saw you yesterday', it was as if he had said to me, 'I saw you with me in my bedroom when I shut my eyes to go to sleep'. To shut one's eyes means to turn one's gaze to the internal opacity. The darkness is a mediation between the epistemophilic point of view (curiosity for knowledge) and what is hidden in the darkness of the night: the unconscious lives in the opacity of being. The insomniac is afraid of the night and develops a sense of danger with regard to his own opacity.

For Clive, putting my hand in the water with various objects constituted the context of the dramatization of the dream: the bits of wood were children and fragments of children. During his mother's pregnancy Clive had developed deep depressive and paranoid anxieties, which I interpreted during the session as a need on his part to penetrate into my body or into the piece of furniture where the children's toys were locked up (in accordance with Kleinian technique, each child has his own box of toys, his personal code, which he has the right to lock up). Clive wanted to go back to his mother's womb in order to occupy his place and to attack and smash the other children. This phenomenon corresponds to the mechanism of pathological projective identification, by which one projects oneself inside the object of need and desire, the mother, in order to resume occupation of one's original habitat and to expel 'strangers'. In his omnipotent view of the world Clive considered that the maternal–analytic space belonged to him, was his property and his body: there was no room for other children and he therefore had the right to invade the space, to wage war on intruders, to smash all those occupying the space that he had invaded.

How do we know that we are dreaming? The psychotic dreams, but he can never wake up. In order to know that we have dreamt, we have to be able to wake up, otherwise we may live in a world of dreams, like Calderón's dream world, which has a poetic, nostalgic

35

meaning bound up with day-dreaming and magic in everyday life. The psychotic does not always have access to day-dreaming and metaphor, 'dream thoughts' emerge from their original space and invade daytime space: this is the phenomenological basis of delusion. An Argentine poet, Macedonio Fernandez, writes on the subject of poetry and metaphor: 'If a dove or a bird comes in through the window, is it a real fact or a dream? The difference is difficult to grasp because we would have to know whether the bird came in when our eyes were open or when they were shut.'[11]

Silberer, whose work on the phenomenological and formal aspects of the dream interested Freud greatly, defines the concept of 'functional symbolism'. Among the constitutive elements of functional symbolism, the most important is the somatic element: it is connected to the bodily sensations and to the material data that belong to the dream stage, the actors, and the setting. One is reminded here of the production of the dream as a theatrical performance, *Vorstellung*.

There is also an element of functional symbolism that is related to movement: the dream is movement, in the sense understood by Artemidorus. The third constitutive element is time: Freud suggests that time does not exist in the dream.[12] However, the notion of dream time is very important: it is revealed as a rhythm that may be slow or quick, more or less harmonious within a space-time. The spatial elements of the dream setting have various meanings: to be on a mountain does not have the same meaning as being in a valley. Minkowski[13] and Binswanger[14] have spoken of the sense of exaltation associated with finding oneself on the crest of a mountain, 'on high', and of the sense of depression produced by the fact of being 'below', in the valley. This is also valid for the notion of time: there are sickly, maniacal dreams, with a great deal of movement, and depressive or catatonic dreams in which there is a slowing down and immobilization of time.

The dynamic or functional aspect of the characters and constitutive elements of the dream *qua* spectacle is fundamental; there is no dream or delusion without spectators.

W. R. D. Fairbairn conceives the dream as a film in which each character represents an aspect of the dreamer himself, who is both the director and the actor in a one-man show.[15] Like the dreamer referred to by Freud, this dreamer is selfish, since each element of his dream is dependent, with no life of its own. Two examples of dreams dreamt by one of my patients are useful in showing the analyst's *commitment* in his double role as witness and audience.

In London, I had an analysand, a 40-year-old woman, who manifested a state of psychotic anxiety with many schizoid mechanisms:[16]

Sitting on a chair, she stared at the couch and began to speak: 'This is a bed couch, which I saw yesterday in a dream.' And she went on: 'I was in Camden Town. In that district, which is not far from Regent's Park, is the institute in which I work.' (It should be said that my psychoanalytic office is also in that district.) My patient went on: 'I was asleep, but not at home. I was at the institute, in a bed that was at the same time the psychoanalytical couch. In my dream I was suddenly awoken by the telephone: "Hello, hello", said a voice and I didn't answer. It was Susan, one of my colleagues, who was expecting a baby at the time and who is a very educated woman, but whom I don't care for very much – it irritates me that she knows so many things.' As she was saying the last few words, my patient's gaze settled on my bookshelves. 'What a lot of books!' she exclaimed. She said no more and I had the impression that her mind had wandered, that she was miles away. In fact, I spoke to her and she said nothing, until I said, 'Hello! Hello!', and she suddenly woke up, saying, 'Yes, yes . . . I dropped off.' 'In Camden Town, in your institute', I said. 'That's right', she answered.

I pointed out to her how the couch of her dream yesterday had been transformed today into a 'bed couch': the reactivation of the dream message became today experience and drama, between us and between two spaces, the analytic space and the space of her place of work. By saying 'Hello, hello', I had personified Susan, that Susan for whom my patient was pregnant with so many books and so many ideas, whom she envied and admired at the same time. When I, her analyst, spoke to her, the patient, she preferred to transport herself to Camden Town, where she became more important: here she lost her image of a patient and found once again her character as a teacher. The recall to order given by the analyst-Susan had woken her from that megalomaniac ideality in which she had placed me in a subordinate position so that she could deny her condition as a patient and a child who could not bear that her mother should be pregnant with so much knowledge.

To my explanations, my patient replied with a few childhood memories: 'When I was small', she said, 'I was very fond of playing the schoolmistress with my dolls. I had decided that certain of my dolls were bad dolls: they wouldn't keep still and were disobedient, while there were other dolls whom I called good dolls, who kept still and obeyed me.' At that precise moment, I started to move and the patient exclaimed: 'Why are you moving?'

My movement had not been premeditated and I answered: 'Because I'm a bad doll.' The patient smiled and I explained to her how she experienced analytic dependence as a 'class' difference: I belonged quite definitely to the 'analyst-master' class, whereas she belonged to the 'doll-child' class. But, in an informal way, she had projected on to me, up to a certain point, the image of the doll who is dependent on a maternal, authoritarian super-ego, which was immobilizing me and categorizing me as a bad doll. The patient's infantile, omnipotent ego may personify the tyrannical aspects of the super-ego, which, in order to live, cannot allow others to live.

I had thus allowed her to recover the projected, dispersed, or fragmented elements in these various characters and to become aware of her function as 'director' of her dream.

My patient reacted to the analytic interpretation of her narcissistic wound with a violent stomach-ache; she had absorbed my message, but found it very difficult to digest: for her to become aware that she was fond of me, that she wanted to come to see me – in my office, where she was a child and I the master – was a painful experience. On the other hand, all this meant for her that she was losing her infantile omnipotence. The analyst who had 'fed' her and whom she had internalized allowed her to understand herself and helped her to understand and digest the painful reality of her dream.

According to Freud the dream is a narcissistic regression, a fundamental, archaic state in which the 'primary process' predominates. If the regression is deep, as in psychosis or in an excessively pathological narcissism, the other, the analyst, may be so inhabited by the patient's omnipotent projection that the relationship of otherness disappears: narcissism does not tolerate diversity and tries to abolish the identity of the interlocutor. It accepts only its own image or the image of the similar. When the projections are too intense, the interpersonal meaning of the dialogue is weakened, for the 'Ego-Centre' of the dreamer who aspires to 'absolute power' no longer recognizes the other's status as a subject. (This type of projective identification seems to characterize the model of the narcissistic object relation.) Otherness poses the problem of the principle of identity. All equality, like all otherness, requires at least two terms. The identical (sameness, for Voltaire) is translated by the Greek *to auto*, by the German *das Selbe*, by the English 'self', and by the Italian *sè*. A thing may be the same thing, but not quite. There is time: in so far as things exist in time, the state of the thing is not the same. Any movement in space implies time and any shift in time implies a transformation. The sense of duration is part of our conscious-unconscious system and of our perception. Any perception is a 'participation', a shift, and a 'transformation' of experience. To accept the difference between things and between beings means to recognize the locus of an identity and of each otherness. Identity is a quality that characterizes the subject *qua* person. Martin Heidegger, in *Identity and Difference*, makes a phenomenological study of the relation between identity and difference, of the 'co-belonging' of thought (simultaneity and succession in thought as identity of the act of thought), and of coexistence in relationships.[17]

In relationships, human beings are one in relation to the other in such a way that they address one another even without speaking. All coexistence is a confrontation in the space of the world: for Heidegger space is not in the subject, even if the body is extended (Descartes). 'We do not have a space within us', says Heidegger, 'that we project outside ourselves.' The world is not *in* space, because there is no space in the world. Beyond all subjectivism and all objectivism, it is the being-there (the *Dasein*) that is spatializing.

Dasein is made up of two words *da* and *sein*. Usually *da* is translated by 'there' and *Dasein* by 'being there'. But this translation does not take into account the Heideggerian sense of the word.[18] The English *there* (or French *là*) translates the *Da* as an adverb of place. For Heidegger the *Da* does not designate a certain place, but the opening of the *Dasein*: an opening that half-opens space (*Einbruch*).

To exist is to clear a path, to open up the space of the world, to find one's place as one moves forward. Moving forward is a determination, an opening towards the identity of the other, an acceptance of otherness. Exaggerated or pathological narcissism does not tolerate otherness and tries to abolish the space of the other. The dreamer's 'Ego–Centre' distributes its characters with the idea of a certain otherness, fundamentally those characters form part of a single identity. The narcissistic ego is also identified in dream with the theatrical space that is part of its representation, a way of arranging the world. The characters of the dream's dramatization wear the mask of others, but in fact they represent various parts of the dreamer's world: by a mechanism of projective identification within the dream, desire, the subject's system of values and way of life invest ideologically the dream objects.

When the ideology of the dreaming subject is in crisis, conflict appears in the dreams. Sometimes there are different points of view within the same ideology or 'ideological differences' between the internal objects: the paternal super-ego or maternal super-ego, which always belong to the subject's world, may be in disagreement with one another or with the subject's ego. In the theatre there are actors, a director, and the author; the actors play the parts assigned them and each one interprets them 'in his own way'. The dream is a theatrical re-creation of certain unconscious experiences, which are both subjective and objective at the same time: there is always a daytime and night-time 'commerce' between dreaming and waking. The dreamer introjects 'models of the world' and adapts them to his own way of life: the dream is a narcissistic representation. It expresses not only desire, but also a complex, problematic situation that is not quite resolved in waking: the dream is a new elaboration of everyday experience. There are several ways of reading a dream and each author has his own style, his personal way of elaborating the reality of the dream. The dream is the message, a 'character' who speaks: the dream says . . . This was how Artemidorus of Daldis and other oneiromancers listened to what the dream said. Freud was more concerned with the *raison d'être* and cause of dreams. This linear ideology in Freud was conditioned by the medical and scientific thought of his time. The notion of aetiology was essential in anatomoclinical medicine. The causality principle, which is the basis of the idea of aetiology, makes it possible to introduce the notion of order into time and the notion of succession into space.[19] This order allows a linear reflection of the symptom, but sometimes it also implies a loss of the phenomenological view of wholeness.

The dreamer is that which dreams and the dream that which speaks, the prophet for the ancient oneiromancers: the dream tells and fore-tells. The interpretation of dreams is never univocal and requires an attentive, rigorous reading. The interpreter of the dream is always a reader who has his own way of perceiving and interpreting what the 'dream messenger' is saying. To interpret means to negotiate with the messenger, to dialogue with dreams: interpretation is an *inter-prestation*. The dream is also a traveller in each individual's present-past, an archaeologist of the present.

For Jung the dream is an encounter with cultural archetypes, with the primordial models of a society.[20]

From a phenomenological point of view, which is not necessarily evolutionist, it may be said that the dream travels into a past that is always present in the body: the body carries its history with it, bodily space is 'animated' by its history. History is the flow of time. The dream is present-past that is part of a becoming that is always projected as future. One must find out to what extent desire *qua* messenger is not an unconscious project.

Without adopting the magical view of the oracle, it may be said that the dream is part of a thinking structure that is projected towards the future: the dream is a fundamental experience that tells, that foretells, that communicates its experience in order to be used in life.

A dream may 'anticipate' and 'advise'. In his role as mediator, the analyst may help the patient to understand what he has partly 'decided' in his subconscious or what his unconscious has been unable to decide: that is to say, show his contradictory desires, the opinion of the super-ego, which supports or censures the 'project'. The interpretation of dreams may reveal the contradictions existing between desire or wishes and the patient's attitude to reality. Showing the oppositions and helping the patient to confront them stimulates internal dialogue and enables the patient to assume the 'situation' with a 'healthy', useful ambiguity. Ambiguity that is not ambivalence is already an attempt to grasp the whole.

The dream is a theatrical representation and the space of analytical interpretation, the space of the transference, is a new representation. The analyst's attitude in the interpretation acts on this new representation. Not everybody is able to play and the 'principle of spontaneity', the coherence of the role with the character (whether analyst or patient) is essential.

Anyone who has had a psychotic crisis and who is still blocked in the transference has a strong tendency to rationalize coldly and to avoid play. Reawakening the playful transference, a sense of humour (even 'crazy' humour) is a step forward in the process of the rehumanization of a reified person. A 'mechanical' (pseudo-Kleinian) interpretation is dangerous: what the patient introjects is the mechanical aspect. To speak of good and bad objects and what one sends out or in may become an artificial, dissociative language if one has no sense of play.

Psychoanalysis is an experience of *life*. It is always a 'double transference', an encounter between childhood and adult experience, normal and 'pathological' experience, which come from both sides: the side of the analyst is called the 'counter-transference'.

The analysis of dreams will depend, therefore, on what the dream awakes in the other. In each adult, patient or analyst, there lives a child, isolated or more or less integrated into adult life.

The creative capacity in analysis is bound up with the possibility of re-creating fundamental links. There is always a 'dialogue' between play/dramatization/theatrical representation/communication and dream language. The interpretation of the dream, in the case of my English patient, was also operational in so far as I spontaneously played the role that she projected on to me. In the case of psychotics and obsessional neurotics, who have a strong tendency to

41

rationalization, a cold, abstract interpretation increases the pathological rationalism and dissociates still further the infantile ego from the adult.

To psychoanalyse is not a question of using analytic jargon, but of living through an experience and discovering the language of the transference, which is spontaneous, alive, and specific. When I met Melanie Klein in 1955, and later when I attended her seminars, I always found in her a great freshness and sense of play, which are not to be found in her writings. If my only contact with her had been through her works, if I had not had personal contact with her, my knowledge of her discoveries would have been incomplete: there would have been an absent, unexperienced stage.

In the 'theatrical' sequence from the dream stage to the transference stage of today, a whole series of living transformations has occurred. The dream of my English patient shows two acts that became confused: the stage at the institute where she taught and the living stage represented by the space of the session.

To a question asked during the seminar from which this book sprang, concerning the episode of the dolls ('Why did the patient ask the analyst not to move and why did he move?'), I replied that I moved because I was identifying with the doll, who wanted to become de-reified and live; I identified with that doll, which was opposed to the rigid, omnipotent teacher who did not allow the child to move and breathe. I reacted in an unconscious way, as I have already said: spontaneity is the rule of the game, as Moreno puts it so well on the subject of the psychodrama: 'Life is a psychodrama and a theatre and all we do is to act out roles or represent characters.'[21] I may behave like my mother, like my father, or like myself, like that friend, or like anybody. My body dramatizes the role of a particular internal object: that is the reality of the mask. The object is not hidden behind a presence, whether it is abstract or material, but it is expressed through its own body.

Any human being is a combination of roles. As in Greek tragedy, different moods correspond to different masks, while remaining one and the same person. The notion of person always refers to the notion of individual and wholeness. The body is a mask and, depending on the degree of the person's emotional coherence, it expresses his degree of harmony or disharmony. What is more personal, what has a style of its own, is recognized as an original character.

To dream normally means to wake up, to carry a message, to leave a closed dream space and to emerge into daylight . . .

To dream is a mode of expression and communication with

oneself and with others: one must be *with* oneself in order to be really with others; identity and otherness are two aspects of the same reality, 'sameness' and relations with others.[22] The communicative function of dreams is often expressed in the need to recount it, to externalize it, to find some interlocutor, whether a friend or a professional. The analyst's function is to mediate between what the dream is saying and its 'public' impact. The analyst is also an 'actor' in the dramatization of the dream, a translator, a receiver of the message.

A dream is recounted in order to understand it, but also to get rid of it (evacuative dreams, according to Bion).[23]

To penetrate the dream world, as Freud did, means to enter the forbidden, the world of demonology. For the Greeks daemons were the souls of the dead, tutelary or fearsome genii. A genie was attached to each man and acted as a secret adviser, like Asklepios at Delphi. In Christian demonology daemons (devils) are angels who have betrayed their nature.

The analysis of dreams is probably Freud's most important contribution to the understanding of the unconscious. The interpretation of dreams is an essential but difficult path to follow. Research into dreams, and into language, also makes it possible to approach the problem of delusion and hallucination. The dream is a normal hallucinatory phenomenon and, if one does not wake up, one goes on hallucinating.[24]

Notes

1 See the article 'La Psychanalyse kleinienne', *Etudes psychothérapiques*, 3 September, 1977.
2 Freud's own German term, *Angst*, has the root *ang*, meaning 'to tighten', which is related to the Latin *angor*, meaning 'pain'. In Melanie Klein 'precocious anxiety' means 'irrational fear', 'worry', which may also find expression at the bodily level as 'death anxiety'. Cf. Melanie Klein, *The Psychoanalysis of Children*, London, 1954.
3 Wilfred Bion, *Transformations*, London, 1965, p. 8.
4 For the Greeks, the concept of *hubris* represents a fundamental challenge to *méconnaissance* (misconstruction, failure-to-recognize): *hubris* is an insolent act of someone who wants to know the causal chain of things and the ultimate cause. The word 'hubris', which means pride, arrogance, is also the name of a night bird, the screech-owl or eagle owl, a rapacious creature that sees and captures its prey at night.
5 The position of the stars in the cosmos sets up the idea of structure and

rhythm; with chronobiology and the different biological times of each organ or bodily system, it may be said that there is a planetary system in one's body (to use a metaphor). Each part 'turns' according to its own rhythm, which is not associated with the rest, bound up with the idea of a 'universal harmony' – eurythmy.

6 Karl, one of my schizophrenic patients, some of whose dreams will be described in this book, often spoke of a character whom he feared in his dreams: 'the old man', who is the enemy of all change and who stimulates his delusional ego. Sometimes, in place of the old man, there appeared a young girl wearing a mackintosh (*imperméable*) – Karl's big sister, whom he sees again as a child – who is strictly 'impermeable' to any different opinion, a 'leader' who wants to control the reader's destiny and represents an apparently impersonal element, but really one that is representative of a dissociated side of himself.

7 *Apobasis* in Artemidorus who, in Book IV, stresses the dream as a source of knowledge, as experience for life.

8 The interpretation of the body, in both dreams and waking, is always a reading of the mind (*anima*). For Aristotle the body is a sign of the existence of not only the *anima*, but also its mask. 'To be' means to inhabit the body, to see and to be seen, and therefore to seem, to have a visible mask. The body is the habitat of the soul. 'Habitat' and 'to inhabit' imply a place to be occupied, mean 'to possess' and ultimately 'to have' (*habere*). It is in the body, in its habitat and its habitus, that the living and dreaming being lives. The habitus is the way of being, the appearance, the body's physiognomy, clothing, dress. The interpretation of dreams also involves a study of the 'habitus' or of the way in which the dream and its characters are dressed.

9 In the myth of Er, recounted by Plato in *The Republic*, the story of Er returning from Hades (Book X, 613e) has all the semiological characteristics of a dream.

10 Wilfred Bion, *Second Thoughts*, New York, 1967.

11 Macedonio Fernandez: 'No toda es vigilia la de los ojos abiertos' (all is not waking when one's eyes are open), Buenos Aires, 1967.

12 Ella Freeman Sharpe, in *Dream Analysis* (London, 1937), speaks of the absence of time in dreams as a characteristic of the unconscious, a reality without space or time.

13 Eugène Minkowski, *La Schizophrénie*, Paris, 1927; *Le Temps vécu*, Paris, 1933.

14 Ludwig Binswanger, *Wandlungen in der Auffassung und Deutung der Traumes von den Griechen bis zur Gegenwart*, vol. I, Berlin, 1928.

15 W. R. D. Fairbairn, *Psychoanalytic Studies of the Personality*, London, 1952: relating the dream to film implies considerations of two-dimensional perception in the dream stage.

16 I am referring to the distinction made by Brissaud (1890) between *anxiété*, a psychical worry, and *angoisse*, a somatic anxiety [a purely French distinction, not usually reproduced in either German or English – translator].

17 Martin Heidegger, *Identity and Difference*, New York, 1969.

18 Walter Biemel, *Le Concept de monde chez Heidegger*, Paris–Louvain, 1950.

19 *Causa* in Latin. The original meaning is not determinable by such Latin compounds as *causidicus*, he who expounds the case (*causa*), the advocate, he who introduces the principle of reason and truth. There is no case (*causa*) without a trial (legal language). For some authors *causa* is related to *cavere*, to be on one's guard, to beware, to call into question, to challenge. There isn't just the legal meaning; there is also the scientific aspect, characteristic of positivist thinking. There is also a theological implication in the meaning of cause – God as first cause.

In his *L'Esprit de la philosophie médiévale* (Paris, 1969) Etienne Gilson develops the concept of cause and finality in medieval philosophy. St Jerome said that God is his own origin and cause of his own substance. Such an autocentric 'accession' to God also represents an idealized image of man, who tries to identify him with his own ideal (the ideal ego accedes to the ego ideal).

20 Carl Jung, *Die Psychologie des Unbewussten*, Zürich; *The Archetypes and the Collective Unconscious*, London, 1955, vol. 9, pt I.

21 J. L. Moreno, *Psychodrama*, New York, 1946.

22 At a particular point during the seminar, someone remarked: 'The patient's dream message during the analysis is intended for the analyst. This destination may form part of a "strategy", dreaming in a certain way. Dream messages are myths, more or less dogmatic ideological systems. Kant said that "in order to arrive at the critique of pure reason", one has to awaken from the "dogmatic sleep" of classical metaphysics.'

23 In certain regions of Italy when someone has a bad dream, he is advised to recount it seven times to seven different people. Is this a way of freeing oneself from one's demons? The number 7 is a magical number in the Caballa and in several religions.

24 Geza Roheim speaks of 'dream hallucinations': *Magic and Schizophrenia*, New York, 1955.

3

Scenes and schemata of bodily space in dreams

On the dream stage and on the stage of the narrative of the dream, that is to say during the transference, a special relationship is established between dream language, expression through play, and theatricality.

As in the ancient theatre of Dionysus at the time of Aristophanes, the two stages are made up of the *skene* (stage) and the *theatron* (the auditorium). At this time the auditorium had its centre in the orchestra and was divided into *parodoi* or corridors; the actors entered the orchestra, which is the place of dancing, with their masks.[1]

It is the same in analysis: the 'analytical stage' is made up of several 'corridors' or mental *parodoi*, where the analyst–spectator, sitting in the auditorium, tries to find his 'point of view': the phenomenological reality in which the dream stage is recreated is polysemic and poly-morphic. The form and meaning of what is recited there reveal a complex network, some lines of which become privileged *parodoi*. The analyst–observer must sometimes risk entering certain of these passages in order to be able to interpret the stage from several points of view. During the analytic scene he must accept being a spectator who, placed at the centre of the theatre, looks around him. From his side, the patient presents his dream by situating himself at the centre of the dream stage : the dreamer, Freud stresses, is always the centre, the nuclear ego of the drama.

Play, childish language, recreation, reactivation, and ritualization form a complex language that integrates and condenses a whole cultural 'history'. The relationship between play, imagination, day-dream, dream, myth, theatre, and ritual is constantly present in men's lives, as in the various cultures and civilizations.

Referring to the experience of 'primitive man' – as he calls him – Lucien Lévy-Bruhl defines the 'participation principle': it is impossible to grasp any difference between a dream, an imaginary game, a hallucinatory or illusory experience, and an actual experience.[2] The participation principle is connected to the history of the development of the sense of the real. It might be said that the primitive ego, before establishing the differences between the imaginary and reality, merges in reality with reality itself.

Before the defined object relation, there must exist a state of non-differentiation and of syncretism that probably corresponds to the 'primitive confusional' state. 'Participation' is strictly bound up with the animism that invests the reality of the world with anthropomorphic intentionality. In his *Carnets* (1949) Lucien Lévy-Bruhl speaks of being and existing as modes of participation. From primitive man, who dwells in each individual just as a child dwells in every adult, there emerges a tendency to action, to playful language, and to a magical view of nature. The affective categories of the supernatural and causality are materialized in myth and ritual, which would explain in a 'natural' way what is 'supernatural': it is a way of assuaging the anxiety that derives from unknown, uncontrollable forces.

Between the waking state and the state of sleep, there is a 'normal' stage of participation that corresponds to hypnopompic and hypnagogic hallucinations.

We have already seen, in my English patient, an example of participation that takes the form of a confusion between different spaces and times. The narrative of the dream revealed the transposition that occurs between the moment one is dreaming and the moment when one re-creates the dream, on the analytical stage. This transposition implies a transformation of the original dream experience that continues to the moment of its 'presentation': the narrative.

Another dream recounted by the English patient will help us to illustrate some of these concepts. It is a strange dream, which made me participate on the dream stage to such a degree that, during the counter-transference, I myself felt suspended between dream and reality.

'I dreamt I had gone to the theatre with my husband and our two daughters, but the stage was transformed almost at once. My family had disappeared and I was looking for them. I was moving through a forest – I had the impression I was a little girl. I couldn't find anybody.'

There was a long, pregnant pause. I, too, the analyst, had got lost, like my patient, in the forest, in the space of the narrative. I then asked:

'Would you repeat to me the transition from the first part of the dream to the second?'

My patient looked at me anxiously and exclaimed:

'You got lost!'

'True', I said, 'I got lost in the forest of your story.'

In that place of dramatic re-creation, the analysis had become the theatre where the patient and I were both actors and spectators of what was being represented: the *skene* was confronting the *theatron* often to the point of becoming confused with it. The reality of the analytical session, today's dream, became ambiguous, the actors were also spectators, and the objectivity of this common viewpoint – experiencing together the dream-narrative – had become confused with the reality of yesterday's dream. The objectivity and subjectivity of the analysis have their meeting point within the ego of the observer who, at every moment, runs the risk of being submerged by the spectacle and unable to surface again.

The Freudian observing ego reveals the possibility of discovering an inner distance, an inner perspective, between a certain part of oneself and another capable of being distanced without losing emotional contact; this is an indispensable condition in order to be oneself a subject before the object.

When my patient was anxious because I had got lost in the course of the counter-transference, I felt as if I had been taken prisoner in the space of the dream, had become its prey; I could find no way out, no 'corridor' to get back to my seat in the auditorium.

While my patient was projecting her infantile ego on to me, I was identifying with a character in the dream. Looking for her parents meant rediscovering her ego, which had got lost and been projected among the various members of her family. The disintegrated ego was trying to become reintegrated. My patient accused me of inattention because her ego was confused – by projection – with that of the analyst (and therefore with mine). The atmosphere of the session had indeed made me available to assume the role of bearing her wandering, lost ego.

The analysis of the dream and of the situation that was created during the session was like 'fieldwork'. The aim of that exploration was the interpretation of the so-called 'dream' phenomenon and the restoration of the identity of the author of the dream by means of a search carried out among the actors and characters of her dream. The characters of the dream and those of the analytic session needed a director to articulate and differentiate the forms and meanings of the drama. As in Pirandello, the characters were in search of an author. The analyst, using an understanding attitude, must assume this role.

The patient's wish to rediscover her own character appeared clearly in her words. 'Sometimes I feel lost and I'm afraid I will not be able to find myself again', she said. She thus asked the analyst to assume the function of guide and director.

After re-introjecting her subsidiary ego projected on to me, the patient changed attitudes. She became extremely sad and regretful when she realized that she was no longer her own guide and had to admit her infantile dependence on the analyst, her need of someone else.

In projecting her infantile omnipotence on to the analyst, the patient tried in turn to bind the analyst to her and to make him do as she wished (maternal transference). The analyst is supposed to contain this situation and to encourage it, acceding to the wishes of the patient's infantile ego. If he does not obey, the patient's power is undermined. Indeed my patient told me: 'I am feeling flat.'

To be disappointed in our own omnipotence is the only way of assuming the role of the patient and child who needs help and is willing to be helped.

This example illustrates fairly well the phenomenon of dissociation that often takes place between the reading of the dream, the 'stage' of the transference, and the encounter situation.

J. W. Dunne, in *An Experiment with Time*, analyses the problem of dream time.[3] Future events are experienced in dreams as 'pre-presentation', he believes. There are therefore two times: the time of the dream and that of waking, which do not coincide, though they refer to the same 'truth'.

In Greek culture the interpretation of dreams sometimes appeared as an 'anticipatory' reading.

Aristotle wrote a great deal about dreams. In *On Divination* he poses the problem of the existence of a premonitory meaning in dreams, which can be neither denied nor affirmed, although it is sometimes difficult to deny the anticipatory character of certain dreams. Aristotle attempts a scientific analysis of the problem, separating out the possible divinatory aspect of dreams. From a medical point of view, Aristotle remarks, the reading of dreams may be very useful, in detecting, for example, the beginning of some disease, which may be expressed in dreams before appearing in the waking stage. Certain representations of dreams turn out to be signs or causes of diseases, even if this is mere coincidence. Aristotle stresses the difference between cause and coincidence:

'I used the word "cause" in the sense in which the moon is [the cause] of an eclipse of the sun, or in which fatigue is [a cause] of fever; "token" [in the sense in which] the entrance of a star [into the shadow] is a token of the eclipse, or [in which] roughness of the tongue [is a token] of fever; while by "coincidence" I mean, for example, the occurrence of the eclipse of the sun while someone is taking a walk; for the walking is neither a token nor a cause of the eclipse, nor the eclipse [a cause or token] of the walking. . . . Are we then to say that some dreams are causes, others tokens, e.g. of events taking place in the bodily organism? At all events, even scientific physicians tell us that one should pay diligent attention to dreams. . . . For the movements which occur in the daytime [within the body] are, unless very great and violent, lost sight of in contrast with the waking movements, which are more impressive. In sleep the opposite takes place, for then even trifling movements seem considerable. . . . But since the beginnings of all events are small, so, it is clear, are those also of the diseases of other affections about to occur to our bodies. In conclusion, it is manifest that these beginnings must be more evident in sleeping than in waking moments. . . . But conversely, it must happen that the movements set up first in sleep should also prove to be starting-points of actions to be performed in the daytime since the recurrence by day of the thought of the actions also has had its way paved for it in the images before the mind at night. Thus then it is quite conceivable that some dreams may be tokens and causes [of future events] . . . . The most skilful interpreter of dreams is he who has the faculty of observing resemblances. . . . But, speaking of "resemblances", I mean that dream presentations are analogous to the forms reflected in water. . . . If the motion in the water be great, the reflexion has no resemblance to its original, nor do the forms resemble the real objects. Skilful, indeed, would he be in interpreting such reflexions who could rapidly discern, and at a glance comprehend the scattered and distorted fragments of such forms, so as to perceive that one of them represents a man, or a horse, or any thing whatever.'[4]

Indeed it sometimes happens that a disease may appear in its initial stage in the dream message. The case of one of my patients, who is of North African origin and a biologist, is very interesting in this respect.

He had been my patient for some time when he developed a strange, complex somatic symptomatology, the first signs of which appeared in a dream. 'I saw myself', he told me, 'in a mountainous landscape, in which two armies were fighting.'[5] He stopped, touched his foot, and said: 'My foot hurts!' He went on recounting his dream, saying that the war between the two armies might have been that in Palestine, referring in this way to the fact that between him and me, a Jew, a state of tension may have crept into the transference.[6] The joint in the foot, which he indicated as being the most painful spot, may have dramatized, according to him, the vicissitudes of the transference, the way in which our relationship was being articulated. He also told me that, for some time already, he had not felt very well and that a sharp pain, beginning in his foot, rose up his leg, sometimes reaching as far as his back.

The disturbances persisted; my patient finally decided to go and see a specialist, who subjected him to a lot of tests. The tests revealed a multitude of data, which were difficult to integrate: the radiographies bore traces of a structural alteration in the bony tissue (geodes), while other examinations revealed a serious reduction in phosphates and disturbances to the exchange of the glucidic metabolism.

In his dream the patient had associated the dream landscape with that of his native country and had described it as "one of the richest countries in the world in phosphates" . . .

So my patient had dreamt what, in Aristotle's words, might be called an anticipatory dream.

However, the disturbances got worse and the clinical symptomatology became increasingly confused. The patient consulted other specialists, who came up with nothing but hypotheses: disturbances of the parathyroid, the beginning of Paget's disease. . . . My patient's own fears were of a progressive spondylarthrosis. The only disease that could be diagnosed was diabetes.

It was about this time that my patient recounted another dream, which might be called 'anticipatory'.

He saw himself sitting at a table, with other members of his family, in a house that reminded him of my consulting-room. A cousin, for whom he had high regard, suddenly stood up and began to gesticulate in a strange way, as if he had gone mad and was breaking down.

The first dream seemed to announce the beginning of a somatic process bound up with difficulties in the transference, whereas the second showed the disturbance in all its gravity and revealed the level of anatomo-physiological dissociation, which the dreamer defined, within the dream, as a 'madness of the body' or 'schizophrenia of the body'.

51

New symptoms and serious asthenia appeared; the patient found it increasingly difficult to walk; in the end, he took my advice and went into hospital. However, he was allowed to leave the hospital for his sessions with me. He still walked with great difficulty and was always afraid of falling. He experienced this situation as a profound narcissistic wound; indeed he had always practised sports and had an athlete's physique. This sense of inferiority took the form of a compensatory reaction in a dream: a strong athlete was climbing the façade of a church with great agility; once he reached the top, he launched a challenge to the whole world, threw himself off into the air and landed once more safe and sound on his feet. Before becoming a biologist, this patient had been a career soldier and he regarded himself as one of the best parachutists in his country; this conviction had largely contributed to inflating the image that he had of himself.

Enormous generosity was the other feature characteristic of the young biologist. It reminded me of the 'potlatch', the ritual celebrated by Indian tribes of north-west America, the whole aim of which was the display of wealth, the expression of a megalomaniac, omnipotent generosity: a tribal chief who wanted to show that he was the richest and most powerful of all organized a festival during which he distributed all his wealth, even his wife and children, to his guests and even went so far as to burn down his house.[7]

On the basis of these dreams and other elements, I explained to my patient that he had so closely associated his country with his body, that they had become for him one and the same thing. He had perceived the danger on the 'frontier': between his body and my body. At the conscious level, he was still fond of me, he still needed his analyst to explain to him the 'discourse' of his organism (he had come to me after reading my book on the language of the body).[8] He wanted to prove – his country is the richest in the world in phosphates – that he could get rid of all the phosphates and remain full of holes, which corresponded to a 'disarticulation' and to an overthrow of his body's physiological *language*. This was a way of showing his bravura, as if he was still a soldier on the battlefield.

This language went beyond my understanding. What was clear was the close relationship between his country, his body, and the potlatch (which he knew about, having read Marcel Mauss). He himself confirmed this hypothesis. 'It's true', he replied, 'I act in just the same way with my money! It isn't generosity on my part, I simply want to demonstrate my power. What I am doing is throwing down a challenge, like a gambler who stakes everything he has.'[9]

Of course my interpretation did not help him to overcome what I had been unable to understand myself, but he was able to become aware that it was not 'divination', but the 'reading' of a dream, which indeed had enabled him to uncover the latent and quite suicidal war that had broken out with the analysis. The schizo-phrenic cousin seemed to represent his own body, which was indeed acting in a schizophrenic way. 'In fact', he told me, 'if I don't get better soon, the skeletal architecture of my body will begin to break down.'

He then agreed to something that he had always tried to avoid, being convinced of his own omnipotence. Being himself a medical biologist, he entertained the fantasy of curing himself.

He now began to get better, though nobody was yet able to tell him what was wrong with him and what relationship there was between such heterogeneous symptoms coexisting with and suggesting the most varied diseases.

This patient's dreams suggest to me the idea of a language that could serve as a mediation between the 'biological stage' (which is expressed in the language of the body), the 'psychical stage' of the body, and the dream stage.

With time, my patient finally recognized his position as a patient suffering from psychical disturbances and displacing his illness into his body. Insisting that he go into hospital turned out to be very useful. Knowledge of the socio-pathological situation of a patient's organism is of great assistance in analytical work and allows the analyst to intervene more effectively.

Different forms of 'anticipation' are to be found in dreams. In the dream recounted by the chemist August Kekulé, the relationship between the symbolization process, dream thought, and conscious thought is clearly apparent.[10] The night before his discovery of the benzol ring (up until then only rectilinear chains were known in chemistry and no one had thought that the first and last carbon atom might be linked), Kekulé dreamt that a small serpent was biting its own tail and mockingly twisting and turning in front of him.[11] Kekulé woke up 'as if under the influence of a beam of light' and spent the rest of the night working out the consequences of his dream 'hypothesis'. He had found the solution. What one glimpses here is the very close link between the process of symbolization of dream thought and that of conscious thought. Furthermore, the two discourses, oneiric and conscious, take place on two different planes.

53

This brings us to the question of creativity and intuition. The symbol of the snake in the dream might already be a scientific intuition, represented in a symbolic, oneiric way.

It is also a way of bringing back to the level of the consciousness what had been conceived at a deeper level. All creative thinkers, including Freud, drew on their dreams for the inspiration of a process of elaboration that they could have formulated scientifically only later. This corresponds to the infantile, ludic ego, to the recreative and creative aspects of oneiric dramatization, from which repressed childhood experiences emerge.

Perhaps Einstein, in his childhood games and dreams, had an intuition of certain fundamental theoretical aspects that he was to develop only later, thanks to the acquisition of scientific thought and knowledge. Freud himself was inspired by the dream about the hairdresser, which he had at the time of his father's funeral, and it was out of that inspiration that his book on the interpretation of dreams was born.

The dream message is 'materialized' as an appearance. The appearance, the dream mask, is the manifest content or explanation of a latent discourse, both present and structured: sensations of hunger, satiety, tension, fear, various physiological phenomena, endo- and extra-perceptual phenomena of the organism . . . This notion of the unconscious as a corporalized whole is to be found in Hartmann: the unconscious is not an entity without a body, the dreamer makes his own organism speak through the dream, which perceives, judges, projects, and anticipates symptoms.[12]

As far as the dreamer or emitter, dream message, and interpreter or receptor triad is concerned, the last, the oneiromancer in classical tradition and the analyst in the psychoanalytical context, has the function of a third party: he must indicate a possible conflict between the unconscious 'deep' level of the message and the conscious, 'surface' level.

From a 'semiological' point of view, this difference of register between the 'reality' of the dream and 'reality' as it is experienced by the consciousness is very useful and leads the individual to confront his own bi-polarity.

The symbolic expression of the dream is part of a language that is both universal and personal. Freud privileged specificity: personal symbols. Jung stressed the universal aspect and cultural archetypes: universal symbols.

Steward Lincoln distinguishes between two types of primitive symbol: symbols belonging to particular cultures and symbols belonging to universal cultures.[13] In Jungian thought, primary ideas, such as birth, love, death, body, parents, are the basis of the archetypes of all symbolism; symbols are the inter-representations of ideas, whether primary or secondary, personal or universal.

I am convinced that a study of dreams in different cultures would prove the existence of universal symbolic images. I believe that it is even possible to speak of a phylogenetic memory, in the same way that Freud spoke of proto-fantasies.

There is a dream space–time proper to dream ideology: a system of ideas that expresses itself in its own way in dreams. The premonitory aspect in dreams may even be regarded as a hidden or 'unconscious' project, or even as the expression of the wish-fulfilment of an ideal . . . As the interpreter of the dream, the analyst constructs his interpretative hypothesis as the witness or actor of the narrative that is dramatized on the premises of the analytical encounter.

To speak of 'transference' and of 'counter-transference' outside the analytical situation as a whole would be a partial, reductive interpretation. Psychoanalysis is 'field-work', an anthropological experiment, but also an investigation of an anthropo–ontological nature into existence and its mysteries. Mystery and myth have a common root: the two words derive from the Greek μύω (*muo*), which means 'I shut eyes and mouth'.

To throw light on the hidden riddles of dreams is a necessary transgression.

Notes

1 In his 'Utopian' project concerning Venice during the Renaissance, Giulio Camillo Delminio conceives of the theatre according to the model of Vitruvius' theatre, which follows the astrological principle of the seven corridors, to which correspond seven doors, each representing the seven stars. The spectator is at the centre of the theatre and observes the auditorium around him. Like Pico della Mirandola, Camillo Delminio is obviously influenced by Caballistic thought.

2 Lucien Lévy-Bruhl, *Carnets*, Paris, 1949.

3 J. W. Dunne, *An Experiment with Time*, London, 1927.

4 Aristotle, *Parva Naturalia*, 'De divinatione per somnum', trans. J. I. Beare, in *The Works of Aristotle*, vol. III, Oxford, 1931, 462b–463a, 464b.

5 The landscape, an open space, and a house or room, a closed space, represent containers in dream myths: thus open space, the earth Gea, contains and expresses esoterically the idea of mother; the closed space

55

corresponds to the maternal body, to the uterus-body capable of preserving esoterically the dreamer's riddles.

6 The patient insisted, quite rightly, on the fraternal links that originally united the two peoples.

7 Marcel Mauss, 'Essais sur le don, forme archaïque de l'échange', *Année sociologique*.

8 Salomon Resnik, *Personne et psychose*, Paris, 1973.

9 This situation and behaviour might correspond to the notion of 'destructive narcissism' as defined by H. Rosenfeld.

10 Friedrich August Kekulé von Stradonitz (1829–97), a pupil of Liebig, considered to be the founder of the modern theory of organic compounds. (The dream was suggested by a member of the seminar.)

11 According to alchemical symbology, the snake that bites its own tale represents the incessant development and continuous transformation of matter and metals. The serpent Ourobouros is usually accompanied by the inscription: 'The all is one'.

12 E. von Hartmann, *Philosophy of the Unconscious*, London, 1931.

13 Steward Lincoln, *The Dreams in Primitive Culture*, London, 1935.

4

Semiology of the psycho-biological 'tissue' of the dream

'And that God gave unto man's foolishness the gift of divination a sufficient token is this: no man achieves true and inspired divination when in his rational mind, but only when the power of his intelligence is fettered in sleep or when it is distraught by disease or by reason of some divine inspiration. But it belongs to a man when in his right mind to recollect and ponder both the thing spoken in dream or waking vision by the divining and inspired nature, and all the visionary forms that were seen, and by means of reasoning to discern about them all wherein they are significant and for whom they portend evil or good, in the future, the past, or the present. But it is not the task of him who has been in a state of frenzy and still continues therein, to judge the apparitions and voices seen or uttered by himself.'

(Plato, *Timaeus*, 71 E-72 A)[1]

I have tried to introduce a phenomenological perspective into the question of time in dreams: in dreams, time is *presence*. Past experiences become a projection, from the present, towards a point of space called past; experiences 'to come', a projection, from the present, towards the space called future.

According to Husserl, the body has its roots in experience, in the material *Erlebnis*, in life itself, in the experience of 'being-in-the-world'.[2] 'Being-in-the-world' means presence and co-presence, relation between subject and object, intersubjectivity.[3]

In a phenomenological view of the dream, the present lives in the first person and is projected into the past through the phenomenon of 'retention', or *Abschattung*, and into the future through 'protention', which contains the notion of anticipation or *Vorerinnerung*.

57

In Freudian terms the past is hidden by the present just as the latent content is veiled by the manifest content. We have seen how what hides meaning is also the 'corporization' of the soul: the body as 'mask' of the soul. A thorough reading of certain aspects of the mask or of manifest content may already therefore show, or at least hint at, meanings that are not to be found 'behind' the mask, but implied and 'imprinted' in certain of its physiognomonic features. Past and future are expressed, therefore, as features of this present mask.

Another dream of the patient introduced in the previous chapter, expressive of his 'schizophrenia of the body', might throw light on this matter:

When I got back from my holidays, my patient was much better; he had taken care of himself and was walking more easily.

'Now I can walk', he said. 'On the other hand, I feel paralysed on the mental plane: I can't speak properly. It isn't that I am lost for words, just that I don't seem to be able to use them. I call this an 'ossification' of words. . . . There is a dream that I would like to tell you about. I dreamt that I was in the country with my son, who is one-and-a-half. He was very happy, because I was playing with him, admiring his prowess as a tightrope walker. Suddenly he made a jerky movement and I saw his head separate from his body and fall to the ground. I wanted to wake up. I was afraid that I would not be able to emerge from this nightmare. Then the scene changed: I found myself in a house; in the middle of the room there was a big chest, which was like a coffin, the colour of this couch [the couch is black – author's note]. I had no head. I was holding my head in my hands and looking at it admiringly, saying to myself: "I'm as handsome as my son in my previous dream." I then saw my head, going in and out of the coffin; there were people, too, who were afraid of me, which I interpreted as a sign of my power and I felt very proud. Really it was as if I had two heads: one in my hands and the other on my shoulders, but invisible, which enabled me to listen and see without being seen. . . . I was happy that I could work out everything that was happening in my body. However, I couldn't understand why first my son, then I, had lost our heads. "Losing one's head", for me, means "being mad", and I now feel the burden of all the madness of my body during the dream, as if I had really "lost my head" . . .'

What my patient somatized, 'corporized', was related to the state of tension that had come between us during the transference.[4] He had incorporated me, not into his dream-world, but into his body-world, and he was experiencing this situation in a profoundly self-destructive way. It was not, therefore, a matter of two worlds, but of a single world, a single body, split in two and on a war footing. When it reaches a particularly destructive degree, somatization becomes simply an anarchic game, which insists on opposing destruction to any attempt at construction, any re-creative aspect of true 'play': *polemos* is opposed to *dialogos*.

There is a double game in this dream: in the paternal transference, my patient becomes the analyst-father who gives back psychical equilibrium to his patient-son in order to show him, in a highly exhibitionistic way, 'how strong and brave his father is'. In fact he is himself his own son; he has incorporated the two characters into his world and into his body, personifying both his son and his analyst, in order to attempt to exclude the real analyst: a narcissistic solution.

'If you "lose your head"', I told him, 'it's because you want "to be mad" in my eyes. If you "are mad", you can neither think nor speak, and I can no longer analyse you. The double game consists in losing your head and then making it invisible. If you have no head, I can't see the expression on your face, I can't carry out a "semiology" of your body, or work with you properly.'[5]

My patient was now on the edge of tears; he had assumed the role of a child confronted by his analyst-father, someone other than himself.[6] The analyst intervened and tried to help him, and he felt better; but this ambivalent child, like a capricious 'little king', did not want to admit that his father had helped him: he refused to intellectualize, to take up once again the discourse on the disintegration of the body on the level of thought, or to confront it in a 'constructive' way. He preferred to reopen the conflict in order to make his analyst 'fail'. Destructive narcissism is a veritable challenge launched at the constructive tendencies that want to accept help.

The patient wept and declared that he was glad to weep. Our relationship is both excellent and contradictory. My patient recognizes this; he remembers how, in his first dream, the child fled and how he looked for him without being able to find him. He walked, having 'lost his head'.

'It's very difficult for me', I told him, 'to follow this child that you are, who is constantly losing his head, throughout the whole session. It makes me sick trying to follow him.'

My patient interrupted me: 'I forgot to tell you', he exclaimed, 'that my father is in hospital; although I said nothing about it before, I am very preoccupied!'

59

The war with the paternal imago is dramatized by the patient in his own body, in a dissociated and 'discordant' way: this might be called a 'discordant madness', using Chaslin's term on the subject of schizophrenic disharmony.[7]

> 'I am glad', my patient went on, 'to be able to see and look around at everything. Yet I feel as if I have something in my eyes, something that wants to come out: a sort of exophthalmia, which might be bound up with my son's admiration for me.'
>
> I explained to him that he admired me for the help that I had given him, but that his look was also greedy and envious; he could not control his wish to rob me of my knowledge.
>
> 'I feel better and I'm hungry', my patient replied. This was how his infantile ego recognized the source of his needs (paternal transference). He left my consulting-room walking quite well.

To be able to give an analytical explanation and to intellectualize does not mean understanding all the mediations that exist between the biological process (Paget's disease, diabetes, a cancerous process . . .) and the mental processes. There can be no doubt that there are links between them and one of the functions of the analyst is to be the mediator, who will help the other to establish his own relationships. When the analyst carries out his task effectively, the patient is in a position to develop his capacity to think and to re-create the links between different ideas and situations. He might thus emerge from his primordial, schizoid condition of 'compartmentalizing' totality which was intolerable to him and even inconceivable.

There is a profound dimension concerning tissular and humoral language, which is expressed on the basis of its own code, which is very far removed from verbal language. The dream speaks a language that is at the same time archaic and present: distant in time and close in space. Some authors, Jung among them, have studied the implications of the primitive language of the unconscious and its relations with the archaic models that are to be found in various cultures. The language of the body, its forms, and its systems of values – its 'linguistics' – derive from a particular culture, that of the organism seen as 'cellular society'.

Carl Jung has concentrated his research on the archaic models or 'archetypes' of our culture.

We shall now examine more closely some of the dreams analysed by Jung, and which he has interpreted as premonitory messages.[8]

These dreams were recounted to Jung by a Swiss patient in his forties, who came from a family of peasants, but who had managed to study at his own expense and to become a 'professor'. For some time the man had been suffering from disturbances – vertigo, nausea – whose cause had not been ascertained. He decided, therefore, to approach Jung, who diagnosed a 'mountain sickness': according to him, the patient had reached a 'summit' that was rather high for his abilities and, if he was ill, it was simply because he had taken it into his head to climb even higher, to 'get on further still' (in fact, the patient aspired to a chair at the University of Leipzig).

In the first dream the patient saw himself in a small Swiss village; he was wearing very formal clothes, in stark contrast with the poor milieu of the village and the relaxed air of the young lads playing nearby, who reminded him of his childhood friends.

In the second dream that he told to Jung, the Swiss patient was about to leave. He had to pack his bags, but was wasting a lot of time, because he couldn't find his things or kept leaving them all over the place. He came up against a whole series of difficulties, so that he got to the station late, just in time to see his train moving off. The train was very long; even though the front of the train was far off in the distance, the back was still very close. The patient said to himself: 'Let's hope the driver doesn't accelerate any more or the end of the train will come off the rails.' But the engine-driver went into top speed and catastrophe ensued. The patient woke up in the grip of a fear typical of a nightmare.

The patient's third dream introduces a very archaic figure in mythology. 'I'm in the country, in an ordinary peasant house, and I'm talking with a motherly looking woman. I tell her how I am planning to go soon on a long journey. I hope to walk from Switzerland to Leipzig. The woman, of course, is astonished and this gives me great pleasure. I look out of the window and see peasants hay-making in the fields. The scene changes and a huge monster, half-crab, half-lizard, appears in the background. It moves towards me, in a zig-zag movement; I find myself caught in a corner formed by its enormous claws, which look like huge scissors. I'm holding a stick, with which I touch the head of the monster, which drops stone dead. I stand for a long time observing the beast.'

Jung explains: 'After the dream about the train, the dreamer returns to the world of his early childhood; he sees himself again with a motherly farmer's wife – it is easy to recognize this as a veiled allusion to his own mother. In the first dream he wants to draw the attention of the village lads to his imposing "Herr Professor" look, complete with long, tight-fitting coat. In this second dream, he wanted to impress some inoffensive woman by showing off his importance and the scope of his ambitious project of going as far as Leipzig on foot – an allusion to his wish to get a chair. The crab-lizard does not belong to our dream experience and is obviously a creation of the unconscious.'

The crab is not simply a personal experience, but an archetype; when an analyst encounters an archetype, he may no doubt begin by explaining the relations to the patient, who is not familiar with mythology sufficiently well to be able to explain symbols of this kind. 'I may even go so far', Jung goes on, 'as to provide the necessary context when he does not have this; the patient doesn't know where the image of the crab-lizard comes from and doesn't know what it means. Since I do know, I provide him with the material he needs. So I point out to him that the theme of the hero has recurred in all his dreams and that it represents a fantastic creation of the hero, even when referring to himself, which was obviously the case in the second dream. He is certainly the hero in his role of the important man, with his long coat and big plans. And he is the hero who dies on the field of honour at Saint-Jacob.'

In analysing the first part of his dream, the patient speaks of a peasant household, which he then associates with a lazar-house, an asylum at Saint-Jacob. At Saint-Jacob, says Jung, there was a great battle, in 1844, between the Swiss and the Duke of Burgundy. During that battle 1,300 Swiss died, because they did not want to wait for reinforcements. They chose to go beyond their capacities and died as a result. Jung goes on: the theme of the hero invariably accompanies the theme of the dragon. The hero always fights the dragon: they are two images of the same myth. In this dream, the dragon takes the form of a crab-lizard. This does not explain the meaning of the crab-lizard-dragon, which is simply the reflection of a psychological situation.[9] The mental associations that follow are linked, therefore, to the monster. When the dragon–crab begins to move in a zig-zag movement, from left to right, the dreamer feels as if he is caught in a corner that might close in on him like a pair of open scissors. The result might have been fatal. My patient had obviously read Freud; he therefore interpreted this situation as an incestuous desire: the monster appeared to be his own mother; the open scissors, his mother's legs, while he himself was in the middle, as if he had just been born or was about to return to his mother's womb.

It is very curious that, in mythology, the dragon represents the mother. This mythological theme exists throughout the world and the monster is often called a 'dragon-mother'. The dragon-mother devours her son after giving him life. The 'terrible-mother' (as it is also called) awaits, in the western seas, with its mouth wide open and, when a man approaches, the huge mouth closes over him; he is lost forever. . . . She is a goddess of death. But these parallels still don't explain why the dream particularly chose the image of the crab-lizard. I believe, and I have good reasons for being convinced of this, that the representations of psychical facts in some such image as a snake, a crab, or a lizard, or some animal, of abnormal size, are an organic factor. The snake, for example, probably represents the cerebro-spinal system, the lower centres of the brain and in particular the spinal cord. The crab, which possesses only a sympathic system, represents mainly the sympathic and para-sympathic; it is therefore an abdominal image. This means that if you want to decipher the text of the dream, you ought to read: 'If you go on acting in this way, your sympathic system and your cerebro-spinal system will rebel.' This is precisely what was happening to the patient. The symptoms of the neurosis express the rebellion of his cerebro-spinal system against his conscious behaviour. 'Unlike the mythical hero', says Jung, 'he does not struggle against the dragon with a powerful weapon, but with a mere stick.' The dreamer had told him: 'In view of the effect obtained, it was as if the stick were magical.' In fact, it was thanks to an act of 'magic' that he freed himself from the monster. The stick, too, is a mythological symbol, often with sexual implications, and sexual magic is a form of protection against danger. In the dream the dreamer was convinced that he was not in danger. This often happens. One has only to think that a thing doesn't exist and it suddenly disappears. That is how all those who believe that they are made up of nothing but spirit behave. They use their intelligence to distance what disturbs them by thought, by means of reasoning. The Swiss patient acted in the same way: he distanced the monster by simple reasoning. He said to himself: 'No creature like a crab-lizard exists, there is no will opposed to mine; therefore I can save myself, all I need to do is use my intelligence. I believe that I want to commit incest with my mother; that's all right, in view of the fact that I shall never do that.' Jung replied: 'You have killed the beast, but what do you think of the fact that you stood there so long observing it?' The patient went on: 'When I think about it, I find it quite extraordinary how easily I managed to free myself of the monster!' Jung agreed – 'You were indeed magnificent!' – then told him what he thought of the whole situation: 'You have an ambitious programme and that, for you, is madness, for you are going against your own instincts. Your abilities will not allow you to realize your plans. You are now trying to remove the obstacle by the magic of thought. You want to overcome the obstacle by means of artifices provided by your intelligence, but, believe me, you run the risk of "paying for it". Your dream contains a precise warning. You are acting like the engine-driver or like the Swiss, who were so thoughtless that they attacked the enemy without waiting for reinforcements to arrive. If you act in the same way, you will go straight into catastrophe!'

'My patient considered that my point of view was too severe', Jung concludes.[6] 'He was convinced that his dreams stemmed from incompatible wishes and that he really felt an unfulfilled incestuous wish that had caused and dramatized his dream. Now that he was conscious of it, he would try to extirpate it. It seems that he then went to Leipzig. "Well", I told him, "all that is left for me to do is to wish you good luck!" The patient did not come back to see me. I know that he achieved his aims, but that, a few months later, he lost his chair and had a lot of trouble. For him, it was the end.'

What emerges from Jung's account is that any anticipatory interpretation poses the problem of power, in this case of the formal power of the analyst's status. Indeed the analyst is the spokesman of a pre-determinist view, which may have important consequences on the patient's unconscious depending on the super-ego personified by the analyst.

The example brings out the danger implied in the notion of the dream as 'prediction'. If one accepts the dream as a 'clairvoyant' message, it is possible to use it at the level of prognosis, just as in medicine prognosis is based on various investigations and clinical analyses. Besides there is the same – fundamental – difference between prognosis and prediction as between science and mysticism – and, as it happens, between Freud and Jung. Freud would have spoken of prognosis and never of prediction. Jung, on the other hand, seems to wish to ignore the Oedipal conflict that was nevertheless indicated to him by the patient himself; a conflict that was furthermore impregnated with narcissism, centred on the patient's aspiration to obtain everything that he had not had as a child, on the need to go beyond his own father – a humble peasant – especially in his profession.

The patient probably expected a word of encouragement from Jung, a possibility of mediation; on the contrary, he found himself severely condemned. 'You want to rival', Jung declared, 'with me, your father, the father in general; you want to reach something that is quite beyond your strength.'

Despite the value of a specialist like Jung, the counter-transference remains centred here on his own point of view, on his personal ideology: what evidence did he possess to be able to declare that his patient was not up to fulfilling his plans of occupying a university chair? The consequences of Jung's narcissistic identification (projective counter-identification) with his patient was catastrophic. It is clear that the personal conflict between Jung and Freud played an important role in this analysis.

To accept the dream as bearing an absolute 'truth' creates a strong dependence on the part of the subject's ego on the unconscious, which is a situation incompatible with the ethics of the analytical space.

By relating dream in images to mythological meanings that only the analyst would know, Jung assumed extraordinary power over the patient. He used the dream images as precise symbols, a sort of code to read the content of the unconscious and he forgot to take into account the patient's 'persona'.

Indeed everything seems to point to the fact that this Swiss teacher remained in analysis with Jung for only a short period of time. It may be that Jung developed a negative counter-transference, that the patient was actually antipathetic to him, and seemed to him to be someone who wanted to dispossess him of his knowledge. It is a fact that, even if one does not know the patient, in his second dream (where the train was very long and went very fast) he himself appears as a monster who wants to eat everything and go off. So much greed could make him 'mad', send him 'off the rails' of reason. He was not in a position to establish a correct object relation, or to make himself autonomous, to wean himself off; too short an analysis, a 'surgical' separation, so to speak, formed a defence against a real weaning.

In this case separation was equivalent to mutilation. The vertigo might indicate the difficulty of weaning; separation became synonymous with 'fall': to separate meant 'to fall into his mother's arms'.

What seems to me to be interesting and positive is that, thanks to the relations made by Jung in the sphere of myths and collective symbols, the patient was able to make contact with the archaic foundations of his own culture. Nevertheless the analyst should have waited for those associations to be made.

For Melanie Klein, the archaic characteristics of psychical material concern rather the child's precocious fantasies. At the fantasy level one may transgress the limits of the person, the mother, and the father, and go as far as to conceive of the couple as a hermaphrodite monster, namely 'combined parents'.

I would like to come back to the distinction between prevision and prediction. Prevision is never omnipotent; it is accompanied by a strict prognosis. Personally I am convinced that one may read the visible or hidden features inscribed in the 'physiognomy' of the phenomenon. Jung, who is usually an excellent 'reader of dreams', seems here to have forgotten that the reading of the dream must never be separated from the relationship that is established between the person who recounts his dream and the person who is listening to it. Between the two there is a 'history' of transference and counter-transference that cannot be dissociated from life. In the example cited, the patient probably stimulated the negative intentionality of the analyst, who did not thoroughly analyse the vicissitudes of this transferential relationship. In speaking in the name of 'culture', Jung lets us suppose that the analyst must – in his eyes – be substituted for the patient, like a mother who verbalizes what the child does not yet know how to formulate by himself, but at the same time rejects the patient in his illness; it is as if he had said: 'Remain a child or you'll die!'[10]

This example may not be the most suitable to illustrate the use of mythological symbols, since Jung makes the mistake here of not taking his counter-transference into account. But it seems to me to be useful from a 'historical' point of view: Freud, too, in the dream of Irma's injection, becomes aware of his mistakes and learns.

It often happens that patients ask their analyst to become a sort of omnipotent sphinx; many of us respond by fulfilling this 'fantasy': we adopt a monolithic silence or give a monolithic answer. If the sphinx-analyst spoke, he would run the risk of losing his omnipotence: God does not speak and if he speaks it is to declare an absolute, irrevocable truth. The message of the dream, on the other hand, is never a monolithic, univocal message, but it is always polysemic and ambiguous. Interpretation is an art that cannot be learnt or developed unless one is intentionally motivated and committed to the psycho-analytic experience.

The patient–analyst relationship is not a mere 'fantasy', but an experience of real suggestion and reciprocal influence.

Thus even the external image of the analyst – the tone of his voice, his gestures, his reflections, his positive or negative availability – act on the patient's super-ego. A sado-masochistic mental structure may induce a sado-masochistic relationship between patient and analyst. At a psychotic level, speech and thought may lose their symbolic status, become concrete 'acts', a 'threatening' – seductive, Messianic, violating – situation, invested with 'somatic' attributes. What matters is not the 'school' (Freudian, Jungian, Kleinian . . .), but the impact of the intersubjective discourse and the enormous responsibility that this involves in relation to the unconscious.

Some years ago, I used the notion of 'induction' to indicate that, in co-presence, the patient and analyst bear 'intentions': the intention is something that everybody *has* in relation to others or something that *induces* a certain availability or unavailability to others.

Bion has confirmed my hypothesis.[11] He believes that the patient does something to the analyst; it is not just an omnipotent fantasy. Just as the patient may drive the analyst to behave in a certain way, the analyst may also trigger off a particular (even psycho-physiological) process in his patient. The work of the analyst is a highly responsible one. An imprudent analysis may cause a great deal of harm, and even destroy a person's life . . . Analysis is not harmless. If one does not have an adequate personality, and above all if one has not rigorously analysed one's own narcissism, one may cause an abnormal, even monstrous situation.

Analysis gives great power, which the narcissistic patient himself demands, but which also stimulates the pathological aspects of professional narcissism.

I would like to give one more example of a patient with 'schizo-phrenia of the body'.

The last session was coming to an end. He began to recount in a maniacal, repetitive way that he was obsessed by a wish to possess and seduce a lot of Jewish women and that each time he felt as if he were caught in a trap, with no way out, prey to violent claustrophobic anxiety.

I explained to him that all women may be represented by the analyst as an eroticized mother image. His wish to possess-penetrate the analyst-mother was experienced as the risk of being possessed in turn, aggressed, 'bitten' deeply – to the bone. . . . He wanted to possess what stimulated him through the eroticization of thought: the act of procreating new ideas, which he wanted to seize in a cannibalistic way, making his voracity like a devouring cancer, with hungry mouths totally consuming the body.

The same dream may be conceived in a distinct way depending on the personality of the interpreter, the methodology that he uses, and his philosophical or religious view of the world.

One cannot be 'taught' to interpret dreams. Reading is a technique and a skill that requires natural capacities and an onto-cryptological vocation; only those who have such dispositions can benefit from an apprenticeship.

Furthermore (as Artemidorus emphasized), one must be very prudent, for everybody at some moment or other seeks in someone else a sort of 'witch', an 'omnipotent' image to be subjected to his own omnipotence.

The analyst's function, the reality principle, is to help the other person to 'deflate' in a creative way and to rediscover the valid, 'productive' aspects of his personality, in a less magical, more natural dimension.

Notes

1 *Plato with an English Translation*, trans. R. G. Bury, vol. VII, London, 1929, p. 187.
2 Edmund Husserl, *The Phenomonology of Internal Time-Consciousness*, trans. J. S. Churchill, Bloomington, Ind., 1966.
3 Intersubjectivity is a constitutive notion of experience and knowledge. The 'essence' of time poses the problem of its origin, which, in Husserl, corresponds to the primitive formations of the awareness of time, which are constituted in an individual, intuitive way, and are the original sources of all fundamental experience. The objective intuition of space and time, in actual experience, implies an 'a priori', which seems to suggest an anticipatory concept of consciousness itself, the 'proto-conscious' or 'unconscious'.
4 *Irresein* comprises the idea of *irren*, to wander. *Irresein* means, strictly speaking, 'to be wandering', without any precise aim, a counterpart of the known aim that has been swallowed up by tension (Henri Maldiney, letter to the author, 14 November, 1971). What is not mobilized in the transference or what escapes begins to 'wander' in the body, a transformation of the tissular and metabolic language of the organism (autoplastia).
5 'Physiognomony' (Lavater) strives to read the features of the mask that is the body.
6 Tension, like 'wandering' in the body, is restored during the transference as dramatic dis-tension – tears.
7 P. Chaslin, *Psychiatrie: traité de pathologie médicale*, edited by E. Sergent, Maloine, 1920.
8 Carl Jung, 'Le Rêve', in *Revue de psychologie analytique*, 1, March 1971, vol. 2.
9 A chronic psychotic patient, interned at the psychiatric hospital of

Sainte-Anne, in Paris, told me during a group session: 'I've a crocodile in my stomach!' Then he looked in the air and exclaimed: 'He's disappeared!' 'Does he fly?' I asked him. 'Yes', he replied, 'he's turned into a dragon!'

10 It was only after writing this chapter that I had the opportunity of reading Jung's *The Visions Seminar* (Zürich, 1976). His seminar on dreams and 'dream visions' is more convincing and led me to a better understanding and appreciation of certain developments in Jung's thought. It is not the interpretation of the dream that is important, Jung observes, but what the dream says; the dream is the subject. In *The Visions Seminar* research into archetype becomes the expression of a fundamental cultural discourse. Metaphor – the poetic form of thought (G. B. Vico) – and mythical thought (Cassirer) are integrated into the socio–cultural history of the unconscious.

11 Wilfred Bion, *Bion in New York and São Paolo*, ed. Francesca Bion, Perthshire, 1980.

The grammar of dreams

'As it is a God that moves in the whole universe, so it is in
the soul; for, in a sense, the divine element in us moves
everything. . . . They are called fortunate who succeed in
what they initiate though they lack reason. . . . The power
of prophecy of those who are wise and clever is swift, and,
one should suppose, not only what results from reasoning.
But some through experience, others through familiarity
with employing the god in inquiry . . . see well what is to
be and what is the case, and those whose reason is thus
disengaged; thus those of a melancholic temperament also
have vivid dreams. For the starting-point seems to be
stronger when reason is disengaged . . . '
(Aristotle, *Eudemian Ethics*, Bk. 8, Chap. 2)[1]

The idea of an internal world and an external world comes up against
the notion of the 'real', while the idea of the real refers us to the
notion of the 'unreal'. Eugen Fink[2] speaks of a phenomenology of
unreality, rather like Minkowski[3] and Bachelard,[4] who see 'unreality'
as the necessary element in the world of the imaginary. The ability to
fantasize, which is at the origin of the child's metaphorical thought,
is based on the principle of spontaneity. Again it is in the
'spontaneity' of nature that Paul Valéry recognizes the function of
the unreal, which allows the subject to discover the 'magical' and
'odd' in everyday life.

If the sense of the real is dormant, images and experiences felt as
'unreal' rise to the surface. Assuming such experience may sometimes
prove to be creative; but it must not be forgotten that the 'dream-
sleep' of reason, as Goya calls it, produces monsters . . .[5]

In philosophy the notion of reality is always associated with the world, with the view of the world. When he speaks of reality, Descartes refers to external space. The internal world acts on the external world and transforms it; Husserl stresses the action of 'intentionality': opening oneself up to the world is already a way of inhabiting it in a projective way and of transforming it by our intentions.[6]

The body, according to Aristotle, is the sign of the existence of the soul. One might also say that the body is a way for the soul to 'appear', its way of revealing itself; it is the mask of the soul and that is why it 'hides' and 'shows' at the same time. The phenomenology of the mask is not a simple 'surface psychology', but a way of recognizing and deciphering the most profound features of the human being.

Just as the person (*prosopon*) is defined by his mask (*prosopeion*), so the body 'unmasks' the person's intentionality.

The unconscious is not an abstract entity: it is expressed concretely in the body.

The exploration of dreams is an investigation into its way of appearing, and therefore into its mask, which is simply the manifest content. Freud declares that, in dreams, there is no notion of time, or any principle of contradiction, and that the phenomenon of 'condensation' has the function of denying and resolving contradictions.

I believe one can say that in dreams there is a very special dimension of time, proper to the dreamer's culture, to the system of values and 'institutions' that belong to one's own territory or world. Social institutions are personified by the super-ego, an entity possessing privileged functions inside the individual's psycho-physical space.

Time does not exist in the dream, in the sense in which Freud uses the classic concept of time based on linear perspective: past-present-future.

The discovery, in the domain of art, of a different perspective introduces a new dimension that makes it possible to create and dramatize the idea of distance in time and of time in space. On the dream stage, in the dream context, which is a three- and four-dimensional space, time exists, but is expressed in an unusual, unconventional way.

Aristotle's contribution is essential here: when he speaks of 'prophetic' dreams, he seems to be saying that the future is already present in the dream, as a 'project'. Similarly the past seems to be understood in the form of a 'space' in present experience and in the dream narrative.

In reaching a phenomenological concept of perspective and

71

horizon, it is important to be able to recreate the past, childhood, in analytical experience. But the way in which we perceive – in the here and now – the past as reversibility of perspective is just as important.[7] The search for what is called 'past' time is therefore a search into the way of perceiving, now and with eyes fixed on a point of space called childhood, a personal history or proto-history – a history that is dramatized once again in the present, in the form of project or wish.

Freud accepts as the hypothetical foundation of the dream the hallucinatory fulfilment of an unconscious wish, thus bringing out the notion of a wish projected into the future.

According to Ernst Cassirer, 'the specific function of thought is its capacity to transform reality'.[8] The symbolic phenomenon is not simply the result of a displacement from a primary object to its new presentation (time) or representation (space), but the product of the creative, symbolic transformation of an original experience. Thus the transition, the distance between an experience triggered off by a daytime memory and its own re-presentation, or between the latent content and the manifest content, involves for Freud a specific transformation, bound up with the function of unconscious thought. A distinction is made between various aspects of this transformation, such as the relationship between 'being' and 'appearance' or between soul and mask. The second term of each relationship – appearance and mask – is simply the dramatic 'corporization' of a subjective experience. On the subject of condensation, Freud declares that several characters or several experiences may come together and be expressed in the form of a single dream symbol, a single image.

Condensation brings with it, then, the creation of a new linguistic unit, which may be understood only through a meticulous examination of the notions and characters involved. This coming together of different elements may assume the form of a neologism.

In the case of psychosis and schizophrenia, beyond the dispersal of thought, there is sometimes an attempt at synthesis, which follows neither the rules of conventional grammar, nor the laws of syntax, and which is a personal way of bringing various elements together. The object condensed may be conceived not only as a relatively comprehensible thing, but also as a real 'invention', a neologism – a new 'logos'.

For Freud the principle of contradiction does not exist at all or is not expressed in an obvious way, whereas condensation reveals the conjunction of different, opposed experiences: an attempt to link the contradictions through the synthetic function of the ego.[9] The principle of ambiguity represents – between ambivalence and integrity – a perceptual, not a historical, synthesis of wholeness. This means to tolerate and accept different points of view or different versions of a common experience. Ambiguity, like the creative suffering of thought, condenses the bipolarity of ambivalence.

'Displacement' is another mechanism observed and described by Freud, which characterizes the phobias and obsessional mechanisms bound to the super-ego. Displacement appears as one of the solutions that allows the dream world to understand in its dramatization elements that the ego or super-ego, or the ego influenced by the super-ego, do not tolerate directly, but which they may accept through a mediation or indirect modalities.

For Freud the 'direct' presentation in the dream of certain elements, for example sexual elements, is rejected by the culture internalized by the super-ego (*qua* super-ego). It is the representation that acts as a mediation and allows the ego to arrive 'indirectly' – for they are 'hidden by veils' – at the original contents that the 'institutional system' of the personal inner world rejects. The super-ego then decides on the possibility (or impossibility) of belonging to its territory, to its culture.

It is to the vast domain of symbolism that the phenomenon of displacement may be said to belong. Psychoanalytic literature gives a great deal more importance to the mechanism of displacement than to real transformation, of which 'sublimation' is only a higher creative level.

Any displacement in space takes time and produces time. This is not simply a question of a mechanical displacement, which would imply a negation of experienced time.[10]

All primary experience relives in a secondary experience, which is representative of the first, but at a level that is more 'socialized' or more easily acceptable by the individual or social system of values.

Freud talks a great deal about the importance of sexuality in dreams and in the function of the censor, because he belonged to a society that was full of prejudices about anything concerned with sex. Freud's ideological and interpretative foundation often refers to sexual symbolism, precisely because this aspect had to remain hidden and ignored in order to be accepted by the social censor internalized by the super-ego. Freud is inclined to associate the world of dream with the world of psychosis, defining dreams as a regressive phenomenon at a very deep level, bound up with psychotic experience: 'To dream means to hallucinate.' But dream hallucination is internal to a territory and to a cultural system in which hallucination and psychosis are 'normal' phenomena: what is 'abnormal' is not to dream when all the conditions exist for doing so. The dream is a

73

dramatization in which all objects and all characters are connected with the dreamer: the dreamer is 'egotistical', whatever appears in the course of the dream relates to him, represents him. The dream world is in fact 'self-referential': whatever is found in the space and time of the dream cannot exist autonomously. There is therefore an obvious relationship between certain dream mechanisms and certain mechanisms of egocentric psychosis accompanied by delusions of grandeur, proper to a delusion of relation (*Beziehungswahn*).

For example if someone dreams that he is taking the lift instead of the staircase to get to the floor where he expects to find his analyst, this may mean a 'keen' attempt to get help. The choice of staircase or lift is indeed influenced by the patient's degree of need and haste. Haste and impatience may represent the symptomatic, corporal expression of keenness: the patient is trying to get there as fast as possible. On the other hand, if he is depressed and has no confidence in the person treating him, or if he is ambivalent, the patient will opt for the staircase or for a slow-moving lift.

The image of the lift played an obvious, very important role in the dream of one of my patients, a woman of about 40.

My patient recounted having dreamt that she was in a very high, dark temple. A coffin was suspended in the air and her mother's body was inside it. The coffin began to move up and down and her mother's body alternated with her son's body, with whom she was not getting on very well at that time. Her son was not dead, because he was moving about inside the coffin, like a clown or child performing tricks. The movement of the coffin was reminiscent of a lift going up and down. . . . Suddenly the coffin hit the ceiling and somersaulted in a grotesque movement. Inside there was her mother's body, which she watched rise upwards and go through a window, as if going 'beyond time'.

The following night my patient dreamt that she went to see her mother at her home; she was wandering through the house, which had several floors, and which appeared different from the house of her childhood, which is true, in view of the fact that the house had undergone a good many changes since then. She was looking for the place where the lift 'was born'; she went up to the terrace on the roof, inspected it, and found the lift at last. It was then that she heard a cry: the lift crashed to the ground and a small boy was inside it. Once more she recognized her son, dead (the coffin and lift had become one and the same thing).

It was a dream full of anxiety. My patient commented: 'In the first dream, the death didn't concern me, it wasn't a true death. In this second dream, on the other hand, my son is really dead. The rising movement of the first dream felt like a liberation, a mystical experience. . . . I must admit that I am always concerned to present myself to others, you included, as intelligent and clever. I've always tried to present myself in the best light, to give an "elevated" image of myself, as elevated as possible (the Freudian ideal ego). I wanted the "other", my interlocutor (in a formal way, the analyst; in an informal way, her father, her mother), to admire me.'

The patient was aware how ridiculous this feeling was and how it prevented her from communicating and feeling herself to be 'alive' in her contact with others. The grotesque or clown-like elements present in the dream express precisely this sense of the ridiculous.

The mother represents a condensation. The patient projects on to her that part of her ego that is bound up with the ideal ego, her own ideal aspect, the sense of showing off through her son. But the higher one goes, the greater is the danger of falling. My patient associates the rising movement of the dream with an idealized image of herself, which she regards as a response to the attacks of the other: the 'desire of the other'.[11] Thus the child must rise and become important because such is the wish of his parents, who tend to fulfil themselves through their child. Thus her own family expected that she, too, would be increasingly brilliant, that she would climb higher and higher in the social scale.

'My dream was like a Chagall picture', she said, 'everything in it was levitating. It reminded me of a woman who dealt in property in my home town and whom I met when I was looking for an apartment. . . . She was very tall. . . . But how exhausting it is always keeping a watch on oneself in order to give an elevated image of oneself to others!'

I explained to her that she was criticizing her infantile behaviour and was disappointed in herself, or was beginning to be, and was afraid of disppointment. The elevated image that she had of herself, of her mother or of her son, into whom she projected her 'desire of the other', contained a whole family ideology:[12] she was having to approach horizontal reality and abandon upwards, vertical movement; but to get back to earth, to return to reality, can be catastrophic and run the risk of killing the still infantile image that she had of herself.[13] Moreover, the only alternative that she could envisage to her fear of being 'deflated' on regaining contact with reality was to continue to rise to infinity, 'beyond time'. The patient perceived this situation as 'crazy'. She experienced the fall as a break in her being and rise as an idealizing, mystical expression of existence, as achievement 'upwards', towards some extra-terrestrial, extraordinary space–time. . . .

The patient was now depressed, felt 'flat', deflated. Nevertheless she felt more 'alive', though she was still afraid of that 'descent' from the ideal image of herself that she felt to be ridiculous and grotesque. To make of her own body a temple was an act of exhibitionism: the temple is a place of elevation, a place where one worships one's ideal image.

Descent also brought her closer to her own childhood and to the teenager that she was in herself; the problems that her son gave her became more accessible and understandable to her and their relations improved noticeably.

During the next session the patient told me that she had been thinking over her dream, because she was aware that it was an important one. 'I thought about it for a long time', she said, 'but it will be very difficult for me to overcome that ideal image of myself, which, really, has crushed my personality.'

According to Melanie Klein, excessive idealization beyond the ideal object is the corollary of the opposite situation, which is not always persecutory, but certainly degraded, producing a diminished self-image.

My patient went on: 'I'm losing my powers of levitation and I'm rushing back to earth without being ready for it. The image of the lift surprises me and worries me, because for me it is simply a "mechanical" object that is quite incapable of putting me in communication with the world. That makes me feel less alive, more closed in, "mechanical".'

So she was worried about the origin of her way of being. Where did it come from? From her childhood? From heaven? From God? It amounted to a cosmological, ontological, and epistemological search into the origins of the phenomenon of verticality in terms of power, and into the ideal image that the patient wanted to fulfil.

'I've a weight', she said, 'here on my chest, which oppresses me when I speak. It's as if that weight were crushing my heart. I went to consult a doctor, but he found nothing. Yet I am short of breath, sometimes I can't breathe . . .'

My patient was living through a depressive process of 'deflation' and it was quite normal that she felt she couldn't breathe freely. The self-image – formerly ascending – was now 'descending' and she felt that she was living through a catastrophe: a dead weight was crushing the very kernel of her life, her heart, which was that part of her that was still 'alive' and young.

It was a bit like the story of Icarus, whom arrogance drove to disobey his own father: Daedalus had built wings to escape with his son Icarus from prison and had advised his son not to get too close to the sun, which would melt the wax that held their wings in place. In order to fly higher than his father, Icarus came close to the sun, Helios, transgressed the super-ego censor (the sun-father), and fell into the sea. His ambitious wish to rival the sun god and the transgression of paternal authority were punished by the fall into the sea, the 'sea-mother', who welcomed him with open arms, but who could not spare him death.

'I must change', my patient said, 'but what can I do to transform that vertical world into a horizontal, socialized world? In order to stop looking down on things and people, to be simple?'

Her ego ideal was bound up with the highly idealized image that others expected of her. In order to understand the ideal image of herself, she had to understand, as we have seen, the image that others offered her, the meaning of their message.

The case of Oscar, an autistic Italian boy, may serve as an example.

During a session, Oscar said to me: 'The world goes round, it's a turn-table: it goes around me . . . around me and around you. . . . '

As he played, the child never stopped saying the word *deo*, an irregular form meaning 'god' in Italian. I thought I understood that he regarded this 'deo-god' as something like the centre of the world, the centre of the turn-table, which represented the earth and its movement.

Omnipotent as he was, Oscar could make me a god. That means that the creation of the ego ideal (Freud) – a demiurge, architect of the universe, god of some religion – is bound up with the transformation of the ideal image of oneself into God: ideal ego equals ego ideal.

In André Chouraqui's version of Genesis, one reads:

'Elohim says: "There will be light"
and there is light . . .
Elohim says to the light, "Day",
to the darkness he cries: "Night!" '[14]

The voice, the *cry* of God, creates the world, in the same way as the mortal creature, man, invokes, cries, and thus creates the name of God . . . The ideal ego cries, 'ego ideal!' And the ego ideal cries, 'ideal ego!', for it cannot live alone . . . It is a tacit, but eloquent and narcissistic 'contract' between the natural and the supernatural, between man and the supreme power, between desire and metaphor . . .

'I have need of God, but God has no need of me', Meister Eckhart writes. There is a dialogue and an exchange between the ideal ego and the ego ideal, so that we cannot conceive one without the other.

In the dream last recounted, the lift and the movement up and down dramatized the vicissitudes between idealization and dis-idealization, the inflation and deflation of the ego.

Rising and falling often recur in the history of painting. The transitional period from the Renaissance to the Baroque and Mannerism expresses the need to abandon the ascending verticality of the idealization proper to a mystical conception of the world, in order to open up to the world of horizontality and sociality, to a new dimension in the relationship between man and nature.

Gothic architecture, which is strictly bound up with a vertical vision of life, corresponds to an idealized image of the person. They shall look at God, project themselves into Him, and seek heaven more than earth.[15]

In my patient's dream, we saw that the only possible choice was to rise to infinity or to fall into the abyss. In order to avoid the fall – that is to say 'death' or dissolution, which is always experienced as a 'death' – one must accept the idea of end. To assume 'end', to confront one's own truth, means to assume the limits of a narcissistic, egocentric view of reality and to confront our ambitious, envious drives and tendencies.

The coffin that rose up contained the aspects of the patient's internal world – her history based on the inflation of the personality. The loss of the original dimension (deflation) led to her confronting the terrain of horizontality. Life outside 'natural' and human contacts is a death–life, a way of 'living inflated in a coffin'.

In her first dream the patient was self-critical. She even went so far as to make fun of herself, attack her own narcissism: the coffin containing her mother, which, after hitting the ceiling, performed a grotesque somersault, represents a critique addressed to the ego ideal, which is already inside the dream. The grotesque movement has a comic meaning that reveals the ridiculousness of all omnipotence and exhibitionism. Humour serves to attenuate the tragic sense of narcissistic oppression and deflation, which, if experienced directly, is intolerably painful.

Very narcissistic people may be highly critical of themselves and even go so far as to attempt suicide when they identify themselves with a too demanding and sadistic super-ego.

The super-ego is never a completely independent entity. Within the 'community' life of internal space, there is always a certain degree of complicity between an aspect of the super-ego and the ego, which produces a subsidiary ego that is projected into the space of the super-ego (internal and external to the individual).

After a period of *narcissistic depression*, the patient began to feel much better. The dream now represented for her a 'mental labour' that had to be carried out, suggested by the dream message concealed and partly elaborated in the course of the transference.

To become a 'living' person, to assume one's life, means to accept confronting oneself with death. That is why the patient proved resistant and was afraid of life. She seemed to be saying: 'How could I change, I who have escaped death through the window of a temple, in a mystical vision of the world? How could I rediscover contact with human beings, with nature, with the world?'

Any change in life – and psychoanalytic experience is 'attached to life' – implies the idea of death and rebirth.

When Oscar, my young autistic patient, began to speak to me again, he said: 'Ri-Ra-Ro-Ri, Ri-ra-mo . . . Mo-ri-ra: 'morirà', that is to say, 'he will die'. And again: 'Ri-ga-ga . . . Ga-ri-ra: 'guarirà', which means 'he will be cured'. To die and to be cured, the two limits, life and death, always confront one another.

Each change, then, is above all a confrontation with death. That is why, in various cultures, transformations bound up with man's physical and somatic, psychical and psychological development, as well as changes in his 'social' status, have always been the object of ritualization: they assist the individual to elaborate his 'mourning'.

Birth, puberty, marriage, death have been ritualized: for each new 'passage' that man must effect in his life, in order to be reborn in a new space-time, he must know how to assume death, he must know 'how to die', how to accept the idea of 'end'.[16]

Notes

1 Aristotle, *Eudemian Ethics*, trans. Michael Woods, Oxford, 1982.

2 Eugen Fink, *Le Jeu comme symbole du monde*, Paris, 1960.

3 E. Minkowski, *La Schizophrénie*, Paris, 1927; *Le Temps vécu*, Paris, 1933.

4 Gaston Bachelard, *L'Affirmation de l'esprit scientifique*, Paris, 1947.

5 In Spanish: 'El sueño de la razon produce monstruos': 'sueño' means both 'dream' and 'sleep'.

6 Edmund Husserl, *The Idea of Phenomenology*, trans. W. P. Alston and G. Nakhnikian, The Hague, 1968.

7 In architecture, according to the terminology used by Vasari, one speaks of 'the restoration of perspective'.

8 Ernst Cassirer, *The Philosophy of Symbolic Forms*, New Haven, Conn., 1955.

9 Karl Abel (1884), quoted by Freud in his article 'The Antithetical Meaning of Primal Words' (1910), points out that, in both myths and dreams, contradictions that, at an archaic stage of language formed an original unity, are reintegrated (Standard Edition, XI, pp. 155–61).

10 The dream work (*Traumarbeit*) means a process of dynamic, experienced, not mechanic elaboration. The translation 'dream mechanisms', as Riccardo Steiner observes, is inappropriate.

11 'The desire of the other' is a notion developed first by Jacques Lacan, then by Serge Leclaire in *On tue un enfant*.

12 This is an image that was very narcissistically idealized by the whole family, who identified the child–Messiah with the ego ideal of the group, which sought realization through 'projective identification'.

13 See S. Resnik, 'A propos de la dépression narcissique', in *Regard, accueil et présence, hommage à Daumezon*, Paris, 1980, p. 313.

14 André Chouraqui, *Genèse* (French translation from the Hebrew), Paris, 1974.

15 D. Cargnello, *Alterità e Alienità*, Milan, 1977. Setting out from Binswanger's article, 'H. Ibsen und das Problem der Selbstraidealiz-ation', he posits two fundamental meanings of 'human presence': horizontality (*Horizontalität*) and verticality (*Vertikalität*) represent two spatial schemata of existence (*Raümliche Schemata*). Connected with the idea of 'body' (*Leib*), the 'high' is what is situated above our heads, the 'low' is what is at our feet. In addition, there is everything that is not seen, and which is behind us, or even in front of us, but still invisible on the horizon, or to the left or to the right. Height is what is 'above' us, the Supreme; depth what is 'below', sometimes the abyss. In Latin the two words 'high' and 'low' were expressed in one and the same term, *altitudo* (see Freud, the article on the antinomic aspects of primitive words).

16 Arnold Van Gennep, *Les Rites de passage*, Paris, 1981.

6

Linear time, dream, and delusion

The dream is a plastic, 'living' dramatic expression of man. One may also speak of a specific, vital 'dream thought', in which acceptance of the idea of dream represents the fundamental ontological question. Ernesto De Martino speaks of a 'crisis of absence' and of a 'crisis of mourning': death is conceptualized as a loss of presence, a 'break' of or in existence (in the case of schizophrenics).[1] A break in the unity of presence signifies the abolition of the possibility of 'being' in a human history. Mourning and funeral rites are a necessary condition for an elaboration of the loss of the object. It may also be said that to sleep may be a way of assuming death in life, of closing one's eyes to the presence of others, to the metaphors of day, and of confronting the metaphors of night.

The extreme situations described by Karl Jaspers, the categories of life, death, time, space, are present in dreams in which the individual exercises his own ability to conceive and to confront reality according to its possibilities and limits: perception is already a mode of transformation and categorization.[2]

The definition of the concept 'psyche' given by Ernst Cassirer, as 'an apparatus for transforming experiences', is very useful in this regard: between perception of the object and its symbolic representation, one must consider a series of changes that correspond to successive stages in the transformation of experience from the proto-symbolic to the symbolic.[3]

The experience of life leads us to confront the problem of death. The representation of death is bound up with that of time. If one recognizes the existence of dream time, one may accept the idea that death is in some sense 'present': for Heidegger, to be born and to live already mean that one accepts and recognizes the existence of a starting-point and an end.[4]

In psychopathology we know that the patient who wants to deny death and time can paralyse and petrify time (deep melancholy and catatonia) or experience time as if it were 'infinite' (the infinity delusion described by Seglas and Cotard).[5]

The notion of time appears in dreams in the form of space: Minkowski suggests that, in psychotic experience, time is experienced as space.[6]

The dream is not, of course, a psychotic phenomenon, but it does seem to have common roots with psychotic experience.

The dream of one of my patients throws light on the spatialized expression of time in dreams:

My patient was living through the anniversaries of his brother's death with great anxiety – the brother had shot himself in the temple. He told me that he had dreamed that, on the anniversary of his brother's death, he was in a room with a low, vaulted ceiling; he had to cross the room slowly, from end to end, backwards and forwards, in a movement and rhythm like that of the pendulum, which marked the passage of time. He was holding his head in his hands, evoking the gesture that his brother had had in death. He relived the whole scene as a re-presentation of the painful drama.

Walking endlessly up and down the room, with ritual gestures, represented the space-time of the drama, the extreme situation reactivated and ritualized in the representation of a feeling that anticipated all the anniversaries to come, which it would be impossible to miss as long as he was alive: the dream itinerary of a project of 'endless' mourning.

The anniversary of a death is offered each time as the profoundly experienced recreation of a painful moment in which the space-time of the original drama appears as re-creative, experienced, and re-presented in a 'permanent' way.

Beyond any causal, deterministic, or historical prejudice, based on the formal sequence of events, the articulated and sequential structuring of a painful experience is reactivated as presence: the past is a way of being for time, which is always 'present'; diachrony is the present experienced in synchrony (the two are quite inseparable). Synchronic articulation, the 'crossing' of the room, was integrated as *experienced time* (Bergson, Minkowski).

The 'anniversary' is the meeting point between diachrony and synchrony, experienced painfully as a 'pain point', a painful evocation of the lost object. Evocation is more than a reorganization of an experienced situation. It is rather a reconstruction of the object and the object relation, thanks to the recomposition and restoration of their spatio-temporal integrity – the space of life.

The subject who 'suffers pain' sometimes lives the present as if experienced time were broken into a thousand pieces; he feels himself fragmented and forced to carry the bits and pieces of the destroyed object inside him; a persecutory death that grips, tears, destroys, takes away.

The reparation of mourning is a way of seeking and retracing the place and moment when the object was destroyed and taken away. Memory, re-membrance, restores and brings back the spatio-temporal place of the lost object, its absence and the interrupted emotional relation.

A phenomenological, structural approach to the idea of memory does not contradict the concept of chronological time, conceived from a genetic point of view, but attempts rather to integrate it in a dynamic way. Thus a reduction that would have impoverished the complexity and value of the phenomenon as a 'present' form is avoided.

To accord too great importance to genetic or linear causality, or to the final cause – in the Aristotelian sense – may make us lose sight of the message as a whole, which possesses a natural plasticity. If causality is given as an absolute, 'mechanic' hypothesis (when hypothesis becomes thesis), there will also be a tendency to read the text in such way as to give the same meanings all the time.

The richness of the dream depends precisely on the fact that it is never the same; even when it is repeated, the dream is always the new expression of a personal, mythical version of a recurring text that personifies a memory or an insistent request; a 'mannerist' way of evoking in gesture, nostalgia.

Causal theory may be conceived as the hypostasis of various points of view, in relation to the same phenomenic reality.

We must take account of the distinction between 'causality' and 'truth' if we are not constantly to invest points of view with an absolute truth and run the risk of losing sight of the phenomenon as a whole, its experience and various horizons.

Contact with the real is not always a clear, 'organizable' experience. Tolerating ambiguity experience allows a pause for thought that anticipates understanding.

The need for certainty and truth in judgement denies the tolerance and uncertainty that guarantees contact with life. Nietzsche believes that one does not do justice to life by linking concepts to a precise meaning, which merely pays homage to the idol of simplicity and univocity: 'The strength and mobility required to maintain oneself in an incomplete system, with free, open perspectives, are very different from the qualities needed by those who remain enclosed in a dogmatic world', he writes.[7]

We must distinguish between true contact with real life, the wish to organize everything too much, and the need to make the sense of 'unreality' coherent, which is also part of the real. Shaping our experience in a 'categorical' way often makes us lose that painful contact with the real, but activates the manipulatory technique that has a delusional content in opposition to a real acceptance of 'difference'.

We must also distinguish between day-dreaming, creative imagination – which has a tendency to turn surrounding reality into metaphor – and delusional thought.

An exploratory approach, of a strictly positivistic and pragmatic type, is transformed into a manipulatory technique in the apprehension of the thing perceived. Delusional thought 'transforms' and organizes the sense of the real and 'unreal' in its own way, which is different from the 'usual' way. Delusional thought is usually based on an absolute hypothesis, on delusional conviction, which imposes its rules and laws in order to affirm itself as an ideology: delusion as a system of ideas.

Delusional thought and categorical scientific thought, based on absolute convictions that often find their justification in genetic theories, find expression through a narcissistic approach that is opposed to a true acceptance of otherness.[8]

The dream phenomenon – considered in its plasticity of interpretation – is the hallucinatory expression of a 'normal' delusion that poses the problem of the dramatic, ludic dimension in the process of understanding, to which it brings all the richness of the imaginary world.

Heraclitus, called 'the obscure', said: 'Time [αἰών] is a child playing backgammon: the monarchy of a child.'[9]

This seems to mean that everything that is unknown to us in the universe is revealed only to those who have a good relationship with the ludic meaning of existence, with play, of which one scarcely knows all the rules and of which the principal protagonist is the child, even *qua* the ludic aspect of the dreaming adult.

In Chapters 3 and 4 I have examined the semiological possibility of making a premonitory reading of a bodily event (somatization).[10]

In the case of that patient, what I was witnessing was the organism's 'seizure of power' of a metabolic, physiological anarchy, which was already present in the dream 'corporal' space.

The sense of anticipation and the latent presence of a process that had not yet emerged into the light of day enabled the analyst and the patient to resort to the necessary medical measures and to understand the 'grammar' of somatization.

The transformation of the organism – going beyond any immediate understanding – was nevertheless revealed to the analyst, who had interpreted in advance a process that, having been confronted and checked in time, made possible the re-mentalization of what had already been somatized.[11] The language of physiology was reconverted into mental language thanks to the 'mutative' character of the interpretation (Strachey).[12]

The phenomenon of intellectualization appears in the case mentioned as the verbalized expression of an anarchy of a schizophrenic type, of a discordant process of the personality, which is manifested at an organic level through four or five different clinical syndromes, each having no relationship with the other: a veritable anarchy or disharmony of the organism, a 'somatopsychosis' (Bion).

What it amounts to is an exploration into somatization for what might be called the 'psycho-sociology' of the body at the level of cellular exchange between the tissues (tissular language), which is made explicit in a latent way in the dream and was in contact 'in depth' with the organism, when the psychical disturbances were not yet evident and could not be verbalized.

In one of the dreams that I related, I observed that the phenomenon of levitation is manifested as a dream law belonging to a psychotic view of the world, a view that is opposed to the force of gravity itself, in accordance with the demands of omnipotence dear to mystical anti-gravitational thought. Descent is connected to the idea of hell, it is a 'fall' into everyday life, which is opposed to the ascensional ideal (ego ideal). Nobody accepts death; the psychotic individual in particular does not tolerate the passage of time and tries to stop the descent into 'normality'. In narcissistic depression, I have been able to observe a phenomenon of deflation of the delusional ego throughout the therapeutic process of psychosis. The psychotic patient sometimes 'fulfils' his ideal ego in delusion: the ego ideal seems to represent the specular counterpart of the ideal ego *qua* super-ego. At the moment when he becomes aware of the 'reality' of the delusion, dissociated from everyday reality and systems of values, the observing ego remains disappointed and discouraged by its 'false fulfilment'. There is always a possibility of integration between delusional reality and the reality principle; but the narcissistic wound is too deep and it tends to be expressed, either in narcissistic depression, an expression of mourning on the part of the ideal ego, or as an uncontrolled increase of violence towards oneself. This may also bring with it an attack on one's own body, even to the point of self-mutilation and self-destruction.

Illusion is part of life, as is disillusion: if it is important to be able to 'have illusions', the ability to become disillusioned is even more important. One must know how to rediscover and accept the real, positive values of 'normal delusion', proper to the imaginary of the world of horizontality, of sociality. The acceptance of disappointment (the capacity for dis-illusion) arouses the creative tendencies and introduces the concept of 'creative disillusion'.

Calderón de la Barca never quite dissociated dream from waking: 'Life is a dream', he wrote.

One of my patients, who was hospitalized in a psychiatric institution, made me think a great deal about this question. Understanding delusion means above all com-prehending the dream dimension in everyday life: the dream is a part of existence. This patient, who was suffering from schizophrenia with negativity, did not speak; he had himself declared that he refused to speak because he felt that his language was 'vague' and 'mad'.

'I've always been mad, that is to say, vague', he said, making an equivalence between the two adjectives. (This was a 'phonetic equivalence', the two French words in question being *fou* and *flou*.)

He was referring to his vague language, which lacked 'substance' – it was indeed '*flou-fou*'. I remarked that his problem lay above all in a difficulty in condensing his ideas and that he felt this difficulty as madness.

'I'll tell you a story', he said. 'I was travelling by train from Lyon to Dijon. I was in a second-class compartment; someone with a South American accent came and sat down opposite me, then someone else arrived, both coming from the first-class compartment. The second individual had his head bandaged.'

As the patient was speaking, I became aware that we were ourselves the characters in the train. I interrupted him to say:

'We're both in a train.' (That was how I had dramatized the dream.)

'Yes', the patient replied.

'We are in a train and you are a patient, a second-class passenger.'

'That's right', he said.

'I'm the South American doctor, the first-class passenger. In this

86

way you interpose differences of values and culture between us. I've come to see you because you hurt your head and are in pain.'

It seemed to me to be important to get the patient to speak (in a playful way and in the terms of the waking world) about that dream view of the world, into which I had been brought and implicated, in the hierarchically imposing shape of a first-class, cultured doctor. I was the non-mad opposite the second-class, *fou-flou* patient.

The dream view of the world in delusion made me understand that what the patient had called his 'story' was in fact the dream reality within which he usually lived, so that he could not distinguish between dreaming and waking, and transported people around him into that 'world', which he believed to be real. It is a meeting of two worlds, seen from one side only, experienced from the patient's point of view. I had been included in that dream space in movement represented by the train. But I was able both to be with him 'within' the dream space as an interlocutor and also to speak to him from the outside and tell him that his way of speaking seemed to me like a dream: this was the starting-point in helping him to awaken from his 'permanent dream' and gradually to become aware of the dream modality of the transference.

This is what I call the 'dream transference': between Lyon and Dijon my patient had transported me into his own dynamic topogeography. I was taking part in that ludic communication by playing along with the 'psychodrama' of the train, thus allowing my patient to bring his space close to mine, which is simply the space of reality.

The choice of the train, in the dream, had a precise meaning: the train represented movement in space and time and a significant, articulated multiplicity (the carriages).[13] The train was simply the multiplicity of thought and the adequate articulation of the convoy corresponding to sequential, coherent grammar: the train was the symbol of an ordered, linked whole whose specific task it was always to have a destination (the notion of wandering without a destination often recurs with psychotics).

Children like to play with model trains, not only because of their articulated, ordered multiplicity (the carriages), but also because they are contained by the rails. Psychotic thought often goes off the rails. Children like to articulate and disarticulate the train; this exercise dramatizes the integrative and disintegrative vicissitudes of the ego.

In the movement of the train, through the space it crosses, there is a series of reference points – the stations. Each station represents at the same time a refuge in the wandering adventure and a stage in the wandering, in the journey without destination . . . From the train, the world means birth and re-birth, continuous change; on either side, the landscape is constantly changing.

My patient, the son of a former railway employee, could travel free of charge. Thus he saw his wandering conception of existence in the mobility of the train. For him stations were fixed points, reference points, too, throughout his endless journey through space and time. He told me how, one day, as he left a Paris railway station, he met a tramp who, after staring at him for a long time, said, 'Tell me, you wouldn't be a Martian by any chance?' The question awoke the patient from his day-dream, from his psychotic, wandering, or planetary adventure.

This patient experienced movement as isomorphic with his own absent-mindedness, his multiplicity in time, his fragmentation in space (he was a bit at Lyon, a bit at Dijon, sometimes here . . . sometimes there); it was difficult for him to re-encounter, re-discover the various bits and pieces of his person in a unifying, unified place.

To be oneself, says Descartes, one has to be aware of one's own body, of one's extension and limits: the body is matter and the unified place where one thinks.[14]

This patient, on the contrary, thought in different places; railway stations and changing landscapes were precise reference-points, but he didn't know what station he had stopped at . . . But to travel one must think in a single place, that of our body, which moves in space without losing its unity and integrity.

My patient told me a very interesting 'story', which happened to him at Marseille:

'Everything began at Marseille', he told me, 'in May 1968, when the student demonstrations broke out. I found myself between the police and the students: I had an important role, placed as I was between those two things that were about to confront one another and mustn't touch. I was both the meeting point and the point of collision, a hyphen and a separation. . . . I felt that I was invested with a shaman's power: unfortunately, I was absolutely incapable of fulfilling my role as mediator, of bringing the police and the students together.'

The origin of what some people call his 'illness' – but which he himself describes as his *fou-flou* state – appears to be linked, therefore, with a notion of challenging an ideological principle opposed to the norm. My patient, who attended a workshop in a day hospital, 'produced' curious objects, collages, which were strange, pathological condensations, masks whose function was to concentrate diversity, articulate, and bring together different worlds and materials: multiplicity, disorder, contradictions in the world, seen from various points of view . . .

The world and becoming meant movement-transformation, an incessant inclusion of new elements.

Commenting on Husserl's concept of time, Maurice Merleau-Ponty uses the example of the river; the train, too, is a significant image.[15] Merleau-Ponty speaks of man 'anchored' to his body: in order to go out into the world, we need reference-points, strong anchoring points, welcoming stations along the territory traversed.

If one travels by train from Marseille to Paris, one goes through Lyon, then through Dijon; Marseille–Lyon–Dijon–Paris follow one another in order. But the four cities also exist in the same horizon, in the same 'country', at the same time: what is different is the experience of the meeting, which is a simultaneity of space and time.

Again everything depends on the point of observation, the point of view and 'retention'. Dijon is an anticipation in relation to Lyon; it is what is in front of the subject, a 'protention'; in relation to Paris, Dijon is what is behind, in a state of 'retention'. Each of the cities is co-present in the 'story' of the subject in movement. Since time is 'one', the distinction between past, present, and future is only a question of point of view. For this story to be explicit and coherent, the carriages must be well articulated with one another; there must be good rails, capable of being articulated with the landscapes and scenes of the world. 'For Husserl', Merleau-Ponty writes, 'time is not a line, but a network of intentionalities.'[16] When there is a movement from one point to another in space and time, there is always something that is 'retained' (retention or *Abschattung*), that is part of the present. The reality of the journey is also a reunion of all the impossible *Abschattungen*. If Husserl introduces the notion of retention it is to represent a historical profile of the 'itinerary'.

The schizophrenic's difficulty lies in his inability to articulate his discourse: he constantly feels that he is about to go off the rails. The schizophrenic's discourse is fragmented, disordered, disarticulated: in order to understand it, it must be grasped in its real discontinuity, one must not try to integrate it from the outside and to create the artifice of a false continuity. That is why it is so difficult to write the clinical history of a schizophrenic individual; this difficulty represents the semiological sign of the degree of the disintegration of the patient's ego.[17]

In the 'mental itinerary', in the points of view of the psychotic conception of the world, one notices an intuition that anticipates the future. I have already indicated, in an earlier work, what 'primitive' means of communication are developed in certain psychotic states in the course of situations of separation or abandonment.[18] A sort of 'telepathic capture' (I would almost say 'parapsychological') seems to develop in moments of absence on the part of the object of need, in the form of primary perception and transmission equivalent to the 'moment of illusion' between mother and infant described by Winnicott.[19] The capacity to be 'in the other' (projective identification) increases when 'one cannot live without the other' and when separation is experienced as a catastrophic situation.

If psychotic patients speak more in 'premonitory' dreams (Freud speaks of 'prospective' dreams), it is because they have a magical, defensive view of the world. To control 'the becoming' of the world and to make it present constitutes in fact a way of not assuming the 'crisis of presence' – that is to say, the absence of the object of need. That might represent Utopia, the 'nowhere' . . .

The space–time in which anticipation is situated or, rather, in which absence or illusion are made present is a 'nowhere' (*u-topia*) or a 'non-place' (*a-topia*). The categories of space and time in psychotic experience do not necessarily correspond to the dimensions of the conventional or 'scientifically' verified categories.

Sometimes one chooses a shaman or astrologer, who must assume the act of making present, the destiny of anticipation, for us.

Latent fantasy is reduced to an omnipotent projection into the other, the master of time. Thus the subject's ego abdicates his life and confides himself to the words of the Other, establishing a reassuring but risky alliance to defend himself against the all-too unpredictable vicissitudes of life.

Life implies waiting and projects: when there is no project, we are confronted with a paralysis of time present or the repetitive approach of history, we fear opening, error. Suicide, too, is a way of avoiding projects in order to avoid death, if the project means 'project up to death'.

The notion of dream as message allows us to rediscover, not only the traces of abdication, but also the signs of a possible project. Even a counter-transference dream, a dream dreamt by the analyst, may make it possible to discover a new perspective. Everything depends on the concept of time: if time is dynamic, all time present is connected to a history, and therefore to a past-present. And in so far as one assumes the present, one always projects, one projects into the 'to come'.

Notes

1 *Morte e pianto rituale*, Turin, Boringhieri, 1977.
2 Karl Jaspers, *Psychologie der Weltanschauungen*, Berlin, 1925, ch. 3.
3 Ernst Cassirer, *The Philosophy of Symbolic Forms*, New Haven, Conn., 1955.
4 Martin Heidegger, *Being and Time*, Questions IV, Paris, Gallimard, 1976.
5 J. Seglas, *Leçons cliniques sur les maladies mentales et nerveuses*, Paris, Salpêtrière, 1887–94. Jules Cotard, 'Délire d'énormité', in *Etude sur les maladies mentales et nerveuses*, Paris, 1888.
6 Eugène Minkowski, *La Schizophrénie*, Paris, 1927.
7 Friedrich Nietzsche, *Gesammelte Werke*, IX, Munich, 1923 p. 361
8 See Wilfred Bion, *Transformations*, London, 1965, p. 59: 'The chain of causation was designed with the express purpose of preventing coherence. . . . The patient's communication, in so far as it must be defined as logical, is a circular argument, supposedly based on a theory of causation, employed to destroy contact with reality, and not to further it.'
9 Heraclitus, Fragments 52.
10 In my case, the reading was rather 'post-monitory', that is to say retrospective.
11 Aristotle, quoted by Freud: 'Dreams may very well betray to a physician the first signs of some bodily change which has not been observed in waking' (*The Interpretation of Dreams*, Pelican Freud Library, Harmonds-worth, vol. 4, p. 59).
12 James Strachey, 'The nature of the therapeutic action of psychoanalysis', *International Journal of Psycho-Analysis*, 1934.
13 The patient might have dreamt the same situation, or been under the delusion that he had experienced it, rather than in a train, in a bus or restaurant, where there might have been a client with a South American accent opposite him. . . . The fact that the patient had recourse to the same symbol of the train rather than to another has special significance.
14 Descartes, *Oeuvres*, Paris, Charpentier, 1844.
15 Merleau-Ponty takes up in a critical way the Heraclitian metaphor of the passing of time: 'If time is like a river, it flows from the past towards the present and future. The present is the consequence of the past and the future the consequence of the present.' But, Merleau-Ponty goes on, 'time is not a real process and actual succession that I do no more than record. It springs from my relationship with things. In things themselves, the future and the past are in a sort of eternal pre-existence and survival.' *Phénoménologie de la perception*, Paris, 1945, p. 171.

16 *Phénoménologie de la perception*, Paris, 1945, p. 477.

17 The clinical histories of schizophrenic patients ought to convey the 'truth' about discontinuity in a comprehensible way, rather than over-structured formal anamnesis, which in no way expresses psychotic experience.

18 Salomon Resnik, *Personne et psychose*, Paris, 1973.

19 D. W. Winnicott, *Through Paediatrics to Psycho-Analysis*, London, 1975.

7

The archaeology of the dream

'But there is also a madness which is a divine gift, and the
source of the chiefest blessings granted to men. For
prophecy is a madness, and the prophetess at Delphi and
the priestesses at Dodona when out of their senses have
conferred great benefits on Hellas, both in public and
private life, but when in their senses few or none. And I
might also tell you how the Sibyl and other inspired
persons have given to many an one many an intimation of
the future which has saved them from falling. But it would
be tedious to speak of what everyone knows. There will be
more reason in appealing to the ancient inventors of
names, who would never have connected prophecy, which
foretells the future and is the noblest of arts, with madness,
or called them both by the same name, if they had deemed
madness to be a disgrace or dishonour; – they must have
thought that there was an inspired madness which was a
noble thing; for the two words, $\mu\alpha\nu\tau\iota\kappa\grave{\eta}$ [mantiké] and
$\mu\alpha\nu\iota\kappa\grave{\eta}$ [maniké], are really the same, and the letter is only
a modern and tasteless insertion.'

(Plato, *Phaedrus*)[1]

Freud privileged the interpretation of dreams and, through interpretation, he sought the profound meanings of symbols.

The notion of symbolic representation is already present in the
writings of Freud's pre-analytic period, when he speaks of language
disturbances, for example in his book on aphasia,[2] or his studies on
hysteria,[3] where hysterical conversion is described as 'a symbolic
dramatization' at the level of the body, an expression of a certain
repressed content.

Paul Ricoeur, in his book *De l'interprétation*, analyses the relationship between symbol and interpretation, and stresses the dialectical relation: the presence of a symbol is a request for interpretation within a specific meaningful context.[4]

Otto Rank and Freud both privileged the link between dream thought (the dream is a way of thinking), myth, and delusion.[5]

In cultural history one notes a certain link between *mythos* and *logos*. Mythical discourse, or 'cultural dream', and dream discourse, or 'personal dream', are expressed by means of a metaphorical logos, specific symbolic mediations. The work of the oneiromancer was presented as a cryptological, philological exploration of the dream message, as a search for the particular meaning of symbolic language, in order to attempt an appropriate reading and hermeneutic 'decoding'.

Being a hidden or 'masked' language is a characteristic of dream language. The interpretation of dreams is therefore a reading of the mask, a 'physiognomonia' of the dream discourse, of the 'soul' of the dream which, like the 'person' (in its general Latin sense of *persona*), is not expressed directly.

According to Freud the drive is expressed through the imaginative process (*Phantasieren*), which is above all transformation. What we are witnessing is a representation of the drive speaking the 'language of the organism' under the appearances of unconscious masks', which constitute the discourse in a material way. The body animated by the imaginative process exists through its expressive corporization, which is bound up with the gestual and verbal aspects of the corporal mask. As an expression of the animated body, the drive is materialized and appears before the interlocutor.

Freud uses a sort of 'stratified' view: what is hidden by the mask, what is therefore to be found behind the manifest dream discourse, seems to constitute another content, the latent content.[6]

'Working on the dream' means studying in what way this production was produced, from drive to dream representation, through the mediation of conscious and unconscious 'fantasies'. This explains how Freud, well before Bion, could speak of 'dream thoughts'.[7]

On the other hand, in psychosis the frontier of the dream is eliminated. Everyday life, waking life, the non-dream is invaded and inhabited by dream elements: this is the alienation of 'the space of life'. It is a spatial phenomenological element: dream thought 'in' the dream and dream thought 'outside' the dream. The work of the reader, the interlocutor who reads and interprets the dream, is above all a work of translation: the translator must know the language that he translates as well as the language into which he translates.

On the first page of Chapter 6 of *The Interpretation of Dreams*, 'The dream-work', Freud writes:

> 'The dream-thoughts and the dream-content are presented to us like two versions of the same subject-matter in two different languages. Or, more properly, the dream-content seems like a transcript of the dream-thoughts into another mode of expression, whose characters and syntactic laws it is our business to discover by comparing the original and the translation.'[8]

It is as if Freud's words awaken the life that had slumbered and 'coagulated' in the definition of the dream as 'hallucinatory fulfilment of an unconscious wish'. Freud, then, is in a position to tolerate a certain ambivalence with regard to the definition in general, which corresponds to his qualities as a scientific observer.

We can now understand better the reason for the theory of desire in Freud: when he says that in passing from a language (that of the 'unconscious') to its translation (the 'conscious'), stress should be put on the drive; instead of saying, 'the unconscious speaks when one dreams', he says, 'the drive speaks'. What could the drive speak about if not need and desire? The drive is not concerned with the relation, but only with its 'impulsive desire'. That is the ontological and ideological trajectory of the drive in the Freudian metapsychology.

We must also draw a distinction in semiological nature between the drive (the living element of the unconscious) and the unconscious itself (a complex pre-linguistic world, the a priori of consciousness, a heteromorphic whole). It is therefore by allowing the drive, rather than the unconscious to speak that we obtain the fulfilment of desire. Indeed, if Freud had written, 'the unconscious speaks', we would still be at the stage of interpretation of the oneiromancers of antiquity; it would be like listening to Artemidorus of Daldis. In Freud the voice of the drive is constituted as a prophetic, charismatic message, its language recalling that of Groddeck: the id speaks in a certain way, the id appears as the essential subject of the unconscious, sometimes as an almost mystical, religious entity; the id assumes the 'features of godhead'.[9] (In classical Greece, the gods spoke through the masks of the person.)[10]

The unconscious is not an abstract, a-corporal entity: it settles into the face, which is matter. The unconscious has its own way of entering the presence of the mask-body. The unconscious is a mask-body, a masked, present, buried reality, rooted in the 'bio-logical' subject, in cultural, onto- and phylogenetic diachrony. The subject speaks in accordance with its essential *arches*, by means of a series of transformation phenomena (as in dream-work), which are responsible for the meaningful intentionalities of the dream discourse in time.

The classical concept of desire gives voice to the drive, which does not concern the subject as a whole, the mask of the 'person'. The unconscious is a presence personified by the mask and it expresses its own desires, which are more than the drive: the unconscious is not only a 'psychical area', an 'abstract entity' *sine corpore*, it is not a mere instinctive drive, but also everything that expresses a globalizing discourse, which is *shown* as body-face.

In the dream, representation may be, in an overall sense, a *Vorstellung*, in the sense of dramatization and theatricality a *Darstellung*, and *qua* mediation, intermediary, a *Repräsentanz*.

To represent is a way of 'making present' in another space and in another time.

From a phenomenological point of view, the place of the dream representation is found on another stage, just as the unconscious has its *andere Schauplatz*, its 'other stage' (Fechner). But the imprint of repressed or insistent desire is always present in an enigmatic way; absence has its sign and its place – the locus of lack. Not always tolerable absence, Heidegger points out, must often be understood as 'ab-s-ence', which means 'to be deployed at a distance'. But presence or absence also depend on the judgement of the super-ego, on the censorship (system of values in a dream sociology).

The censorship, exerted by the super-ego, is present within the dream and is responsible for the distortion and mechanisms that must make the message obscure, mask it, in order to avoid the judgement of the censor (Freud): the super-ego decides what will be the actor or the censored message, which must not appear on the stage in an 'obvious' way, as representing a certain desire (*Repräsentanz*).

The direct expression of desire is too risky and anxiety-inducing for Freud and, therefore, unacceptable. The unconscious appears to belong to a private 'mythology', animated above all by the drive, which may be either the life-drive or the death-drive. Immediacy is a risk, whereas mediation reassures. The child is very close to consciousness, he is much more 'immediate' than the adult (his preconscious is not yet very developed), that is why his dream language – according to Freud – is also more direct, more immediate to him. With time, it will alter, become more and more complicated and indirect, and also less expressive.[11]

Freud describes the phenomenon of substitution (*Ersatz*) of the past by the present, of the original childhood scene by more recent, present, and complex elements. From an evolutionary point of view, life consists of a long chain of transformations, modifications, and substitutions, the bases of the symbolic, oneiric, and linguistic process.

Another mode of dream thought is what Freud calls the 'condensation' (*Verdichtung*) of experiences, which are manifested sometimes as a new 'sign', a neologism, made up of a set of condensed meanings in a single sign: a symbolic multiplicity that must be broken down by analysis, then recomposed like a puzzle, until all its amalgamated meanings are rediscovered.

On the subject of 'displacement', or *Verschiebung*, Freud writes that 'the dream is centred differently'. Silberer observes that displacement 'pushes the unreal forward and brushes the real aside'; it is thus that the dream appears 'displaced' in relation to its latent thoughts. Displacement acts in such a way that images, places (space), moments (time), and their meanings 'shift' from one place and one time to other space-times. So an image is displaced or projected *within* another image, moves from one disguise to another, in order to try to deceive the censorship and elude it. A reading of dreams allows us to check these facts. 'Dream-work' provides us with mediations (*Repräsentanz*), which hide and sometimes betray their meaning. But to speak of dream-work in terms of 'mechanisms' seems to me to be reductive of the complex reality of a discourse – the dream discourse – which is essentially 'irreducible'. So I prefer to speak of *artisans of the dream*, characters that represent the responsible function of the 'dreaming ego' (E. Fink). Organizing and classifying experience is necessary, but often reductive of the phenomenon: the dream discourse, as a rich, complex, *fundamental* language, develops within a space-time whose co-ordinates elude the notions of Euclidian geometry and of many post-Euclidian concepts. It was I. Matte Blanco who first stressed the multidimensionality of the dream 'field'. Displacement consists, then, of an opening movement to places, times, and unpredictable, unexpected forms. Condensation, on the other hand, is an attempt to integrate and interpenetrate different spatio-temporal categories. It concerns two poles of the same complex matrix in which many other phenomena, some 'visible', others still invisible to hermeneutic research, co-habit. What is read corresponds to the dream reality that is given as 'façade', a mask that has assumed shape and become fixed at the very moment of waking, by a sort of de-tention and re-tention proper to a 'kaleidoscopic' process. The dream image constitutes a signifier that assumes a different form within a certain present, deep semantic universe.

The reader of the dream may be in a sense the dreamer in person, as addressee of an auto-allo-message, which does not concern only the analyst (people who are not in analysis also dream!), although the interlocutor to whom the dream is addressed is always present in a latent way: the audience that observes, listens to, and judges what takes place on the dream stage is always personified: either by the dreaming subject (in his multiple roles), or by the 'other': the oneiromancer, the psychoanalyst . . .

The addressee, the dreamer, is also projected into the analyst: the prototype of self-consciousness, the observing ego in Freud, already implies a possibility of imagining oneself as an 'other'.

Looking at oneself, seeing oneself in perspective is not necessarily a symptom of 'de-personalization', but rather a concrete way of making contact with an 'inner landscape', which may be projected on to a three-dimensional screen, represented by the other. The dream stage, the 'inner theatre', is flattened, becomes two-dimensional as the projection moves away (absence is deployed as distancing . . .). The more anxiety-inducing the dream is, the more the need is felt to flatten it, to distance it. Sometimes the interpreter of the dream must personify the observing ego of the patient, who will be able to adopt an 'outer-inner' point of view, by means of the analyst's mediation, and thus discover the space and time – the moment – that will enable him to read 'what the dream is saying'.

The dream is always the expression of something that is related to the dreamer, to his personality, or to his life; the dreamer is 'egotistical', says Freud. All the characters and all the thoughts in the dream belong to a composite autocentric message.

The dreamer – *qua* 'ego-centre' – corresponds partly to the psychotic ego that surrounds itself with its 'oneiroid' world, a creature that he has put into the world and totally subjected to his omnipotent, dogmatic control: this is what Ball calls the 'autophilic configuration' of surrounding space.

In the *Summa contra Gentiles*, St Thomas Aquinas draws up a list of the limits to God's omnipotence. First he cites everything that confirms His omnipotence, then everything that limits it: some of these limits seem to correspond to the characteristics of the egocentric dreamer. This is a bit like the case of the psychotic who cannot emerge from his delusion: others do not exist as 'other'. 'God is omnipotent, but He cannot make another God', says St Thomas. God omnipotent is limited in His very omnipotence: He cannot create his own double.

The dreamer, like the psychotic, rejects all power except his own: the 'other' might wake up and be transformed into a daytime creature dependent on the real, and he would become 'omnipotent'. In his *Memoirs of a Neuropath* (1903), Judge Schreber writes:

'I have no doubt that God, in His relation to me, is ruled by egoism. . . . *God is a living Being* and would Himself have to be ruled by egoistic motives, if other living beings who could endanger Him or in some way be detrimental to His interests. . . . These egoistic actions have been practised against me for years with the utmost cruelty and disregard as only a beast deals with its prey. But success could not be permanent because God brought Himself into conflict with the Order of the World, that is to say into conflict with His own Being and His own powers. Consequently, as I firmly believe, this irregular state of affairs will be finally liquidated at my death at the latest.'[12]

Man may create different images of God according to his 'religious ideology' and his cultural premises, but God cannot allow Himself to create another God: in the last resort, only man holds that power. Man's power and the power of the ideal ego consist, therefore, in that they can create and re-create the ideal image of the superior ego: the ego ideal. Meister Eckhart writes: 'I have need of God, but God has no need of me to exist.'[13]

In *The Essence of Christianity* (1841), Ludwig Feuerbach examines the problem in depth: 'What for religion is the foundation, God, is an inferred truth: man is the fundamental state; man created the idea of God.' The idea of man is related to the supreme, ideal essence. Any human, interpersonal relationship is based on this point of view, on a religious model, on the need to create a healthy, 'intact' space: the subjective need to recreate objectively a deified image. The relationship with the idealized outside is also the expression of an inner relationship, between an internalized I and Thou (ego ideal) according to a relationship of dialectical reciprocity. 'The consciousness of God', Feuerbach goes on, 'is man's self consciousness, knowledge of God is man's knowledge of himself: on the basis of his God you know man and, conversely, on the basis of man his God.'

It is therefore man that is the more powerful; man is the real essence of the idea of God and of any mystical, religious system. The idea of God is bound up with the process of idealization, with the mystical act of ascension. Verticality offers two alternatives: ascent or descent. Idealization is related to ascent, whereas the search into the unconscious is an archaeology of being, the metaphysical basis of Freudian thought concerning the 'descent'.

In the dream of my Milanese patient, levitation represents an ascent beyond time and space, a search for the ideal image of self.

Descent implies, on the other hand, the collapse of the idealized image, the fall, the narcissistic deflation of the ideal image of the ego.

The ideal ego is projected into the ego ideal, the privileged space that contains the desire of the ideal ego in gestation. The narcissistic ideal wants to rediscover itself in the perfection of the supreme being that it has created – God.

To become aware that the ego ideal coincides in no way with the image of God involves fall, depression into space, a catastrophic descent like death.

There is a very different form of 'descent', an 'exploratory' form: the descent into the very depths of the *arche*, in order to discover what is buried in the unconscious, in the inner darkness that inhabits the 'body-cave'.

The Milanese patient specifically recounted in analysis a dream that illustrates this 'descent' in the sense of a movement of exploration, of 'archaeological' discovery of her being.

The patient was interested in archaeology; she had been to Rome and seen, in the Vatican Museum, the 'Gradiva' that inspired Jensen's novel.

'In my dream', she said, 'I found myself on a site with some other people. We were carrying out excavations and had uncovered a piece of sculpture that resembled the Gradiva, then another, similar one: so there were two Gradivas. I immediately recognized myself in the first: I was lying, immobile, petrified, a statue; the other statue reminded me of the particular beauty of my sister, who died long ago.'

She added that she had been very attached to that young, dead sister when she was herself only a girl.

The patient had cathected and idealized this goddess-sister. With her sister's death, there also disappeared her Gradiva, the ideal part of herself, the 'other' Gradiva of the dream, which was to be transformed into a statue in order to be buried beside her young sister.

'Analysis', my patient went on, 'has helped me to dig inside myself and bring out into the light of day that aspect of myself that was buried with the body of my sister who, for me, was as beautiful and perfect as a goddess. It's as if a part of me had been separated from myself and that I had remained "dead" for a long time.'

Analysis tries to bring into the light of day what is buried. One may speak of an 'archaeology of the dream' as a certain form of 'discovery', which tries both to 'bring into the light of day' and to 'shed light' ('to discover' means 'to remove the covering').

In my patient's dream, there was a subterranean light that illuminated the statues and enabled us to recognize the features of the two sister–Gradivas. The patient spoke of a 'warm' light, which reminded her of a painting by Memling representing the nativity. The central, luminous, warm light gradually invades the space of shadow, and gives life and reality to the whole.

I interpreted to my patient that a part of herself, bound up with the non-elaboration of mourning, had 'died' and been buried with her sister's body. Usually, when a love-object dies, there is always part of ourself that dies with it and remains emotionally and 'corporally' anchored to the lost object. The process of mourning has the function of 'recovering' not only the lost object, but also that part of the suffering subject that followed the lost object and whose absence is felt. This patient's dream recounts, in a sense, the story of her own death, the story of the loss of her ideal ego, which is reflected in the idealized 'double' (ego ideal) personified by her sister. Both are turned to stone. An infinite time in which life and death do not exist: the paralysis of time immobilizes life and death, and sends back the reflection of the eternal fantasy.

The patient recounts how her body was always cold, devoid of warmth, which she often felt as 'dead'. Through the analytic process, she succeeded in digging within herself and rediscovering movement, life, warmth: the warm light of Memling's picture, which accepts life, and gives light to its buried aspects.

Analysis recovered a living part of the subject that had been buried alive in a body-grave (*soma-sema*). The light also means that the patient rediscovered a luminous, warm aspect of herself, different from that cold, rational intelligence that had been habitually hers.

Part of her experience had been buried with the love-object, her specular ego buried in the shadow of a dead, cold time. Her sister represented an aspect of her ego that was heavily invested with narcissism.

The archaeology of the dream means precisely to recover a buried reality, which is sometimes difficult to rediscover and recognize. The analysis of narcissism is indeed painful and is not always tolerated. The dream work represents a fundamental element of analysis, which consists in deciphering, interpreting, recovering the 'other language', and confronting the dis-illusion experienced when we realize that we are not as we would like to be. The image of the

101

Gradiva is, therefore, a condensation of several meanings of a part of the self that the patient over-valued and which correspond to her 'brilliant, but cold' intelligence.

Generally speaking, the individual finds it difficult to understand his own dreams and needs to entrust them to a mediator – an oneiromancer or analyst – to interpret them. The patient's narcissistic ego does not readily agree to become 'an object of exploration', for he is anxious to remain the 'subject'. Analytic exploration may also be felt as a 'violation' of the frontiers of the space of personal life: that is why analysis must be extremely rigorous and prudent.

The super-ego so arranges matters that some things that are forbidden or dangerous may be seen, despite the censor. The action of 'looking' poses the problem of light and the gaze. The analyst throws light on what we normally cannot or 'must not' see.

Sometimes the dream appears practically free of content: this was the case with one of my patients, who always recounted to me two dreams – which I interpreted as a double request on his part: he wanted to make first one 'analytic breast' speak, 'empty itself', then the other; the account of the dream was merely the necessary mediation to take both breasts.

The dream appears as a transaction, an indirect way of expressing oneself; but, when the symbolic process is reified, the significant content is 'coagulated' and all that is left is the mechanical, manipulatory aspect of the signifier. Beyond what is apparent and known in the dream, what matters during the interpretation is not only the hidden meaning of the content, but also the intentionality and the sense of the dream vehicle: that is to say, the account of the dream, the content of the discursive form, the signified of the signifier (and therefore the way the account *acts*, its gesturality, its shape).

The account of the dream is part of the *transference*; the patient–analyst relationship is based on a sense of empathy, dialogue, the co-expressiveness of the signifiers that 'travel intentionally' through intersubjective space. Intersubjective space opens up a perspective; it is a way of looking 'through', as Albert Dürer would say: the 'through' is essential . . . For if for reasons of an ethical nature everything cannot be said 'directly', the analyst must respect the distances and mediations necessary to the good development of the analysis.

Two elements can exist only thanks to a third, structuring element: 'the space in between' (Martin Buber).[14] The space of both stresses the function of the third space, the mediating space, which is a precursor of the paternal super-ego.

In the patient–analyst relationship interpersonal space may be filled by silence or by words, which makes the 'silence' that gives its meaning to the dialogue 'insignificant'. In a dialectical relationship there is sometimes a significant silence that is hidden, filled with words; sometimes silence is adopted in order to efface and indicate the significant word.

Silence represents the profound, universal nature of what is private, that which hides and at the same time denotes the metaphysical anxiety that seizes us when we are confronted with the unknown.

The unconscious is not a silence, but it is veiled in the 'silence of reason'. One thinks and speaks in order to mask the primordial silence: the language of the unconscious in the delusion of the psychotic, his words detached one from another, swim silently (or noisily), without moorings, without a future.

Throughout the spaces that allow the dream to speak, silence moors and pronounces a discourse that is more or less coherent, more or less articulated: silence is not there to fragment discourse.

Notes

1 *The Dialogues of Plato*, trans. B. Jowett, vol. I, Oxford, 1892, pp. 449–50.
2 Sigmund Freud, *On Aphasia*, London and New York, 1953.
3 Sigmund Freud, *Studies on Hysteria*, Standard Edition, XX.
4 Paul Ricoeur, *De l'interprétation, essai sur Freud*, Paris, 1965.
5 Otto Rank, 'Traum und Dichtung' and 'Traum und Mythus', in Freud, *The Interpretation of Dreams*, Standard Edition, IV, pp. 103, 369, 477, 508n.
6 On the basis of Merleau-Ponty's critique of Heraclitian time (a past that impels the present), one might also say on the subject of the spatiality of the mask that apparent 'stratification' is merely the artifice of everything that exists in space at the same time.
7 Wilfred Bion, 'The Psychoanalytic Study of Thinking', *International Journal of Psycho-Analysis*, XLIII, 1962.
8 *The Interpretation of Dreams*, p. 381.
9 G. Groddeck, *Le Livre du Ça*, Paris, 1977.
10 Angel Garma (*La Psychanalyse des rêves*, P.U.F.) rightly observes that the traumatic situation in the genesis of dreams comes before the gratification of unconscious wishes: 'When one has undergone a profound psychological shock, the ensuing dreams are a monotonous representation of painful sensations experienced at the time of the shock. . . . Dreams

often reproduce traumatic infantile experiences.' In a sense the traumatic situation intervenes in all dreams and is one of the fundamental factors of their genesis.

11 The preconscious may not be a mere mediation. It might also be a 'necessary' separation between conscious and unconscious: the sons of night must not mingle with the sons of day. Night may cover light and efface it, or a too powerful light may blind 'souls' that live in darkness, like those condemned to live in Plato's cave.

12 Daniel Paul Schreber, *Memoirs of my Nervous Illness*, trans. Ida Macalpine and Richard A. Hunter, London, 1955, pp. 251–52. Cf. Sigmund Freud, 'Psycho-Analytic Notes on an Autobiographical Account of a Case of Paranoia (Dementia paranoides)', Standard Edition, XII.

13 Reiner Schurmann, *Maître Eckhart ou la joie errante*, Paris, 1972.

14 Martin Buber, *Between Man and Man*, London, 1966.

8

The dream of Irma's injection: Irma and Freud[1]

So far we have dealt with the relationship between the dream, life, and psychosis; we have discussed the part played by the dream in one's view of the world, in the dream view of reality, and we have also stressed the difference that exists between ideology, delusion, waking, sleep, and dream.

I think it would now be useful to go back to the source, to Freud and his *The Interpretation of Dreams*, and to examine, in the light of our hypotheses, the *fundamental* work represented by 'the dream of Irma's injection': I use and stress the word 'fundamental' for this dream was the first to which Freud devoted a deep, detailed semiological analysis and through his study of this dream he undertook an analysis of his own problems.

It must be remembered that early on in these experiments, Freud was on friendly terms with most of his patients: those who asked to undergo analysis with him were often quite close to him.[2] One such patient was Irma, a friend of his wife and her family.[3] As was the usual practice at that time, she was under analysis with Freud for a very short period.

Freud met Otto, a doctor friend who had recommended Irma to him, and asked him how his patient was going after the treatment had been completed. Otto replied:

'She's better, but not fully recovered.'

Freud was very irritated by this answer: Freud wanted the efficacy of his treatment to be recognized and, for him, Otto's words were a great narcissistic wound. But, aware of this narcissistic attitude, Freud admitted that this observation was very useful to him.

Irma was a friend of his wife's, and the success of the treatment enhanced his prestige with her. Irma, then, was a social symbol, the object-projection of his therapeutic ability.

Freud's ideas began to interest and occupy an important place in the cultural life of Vienna: the drawing-room in which the dream took place was vast, the theatre of the dream constituted in itself a 'dream metaphor' of the importance that Freud's thought was assuming.

'*Dream of July 23rd–24th, 1895.* A large hall – numerous guests, whom we were receiving. – Among them was Irma. I at once took her on one side, as though to answer her letter and to reproach her for not having accepted my "solution" yet. I said to her: "If you still get pains, it's really only your fault." She replied: "If you only knew what pains I've got now in my throat and stomach and abdomen – it's choking me." – I was alarmed and looked at her. She looked pale and puffy. I thought to myself that after all I must be missing some organic trouble. I took her to the window and looked down her throat, and she showed signs of recalcitrance, like women with artificial dentures. I thought to myself that there was really no need for her to do that. – She then opened her mouth properly and on the right I found a big white patch; at another place I saw extensive whitish grey scabs upon some remarkably curly structures which were evidently modelled on the turbinal bones of the nose. – I at once called in Dr M., and he repeated the examination and confirmed it. . . . Dr M. looked quite different from usual; he was very pale, he walked with a limp, and his chin was clean-shaven. . . . My friend Otto was now standing beside her as well, and my friend Leopold was percussing her through her bodice and saying: "She has a dull area low down on the left." He also indicated that a portion of the skin on the left shoulder was infiltrated. (I noticed this, just as he did, in spite of her dress.) . . . M. said: "There is no doubt it's an infection, but no matter; dysentery will supervene and the toxin will be eliminated."[4] . . . We were directly aware, too, of the origin of the infection. Not long before, when she was feeling unwell, my friend Otto had given her an injection of a preparation of propyl, propyls . . . propionic acid . . . trimethylamin (and I saw before me the formula for this printed in heavy type). . . . Injections of that sort ought not to be made so thoughtlessly. . . . And probably the syringe had not been clean.

This dream has one advantage over many others. It was immediately clear what events of the previous day provided its starting-point. My preamble makes that plain. The news which

Otto had given me of Irma's condition and the case history which I had been engaged in writing till far into the night continued to occupy my mental activity even after I was asleep. Nevertheless, no one who had only read the preamble and the content of the dream itself could have the slightest notion of what the dream meant. I myself had no notion. I was astonished at the symptoms of which Irma complained to me in the dream, since they were not the same for which I had treated her. I smiled at the senseless idea of an injection of propionic acid and at Dr M.'s consoling reflections. Towards its end the dream seemed to me to be more obscure and compressed than it was at the beginning. In order to discover the meaning of all this it was necessary to undertake a detailed analysis.'

(SE pp. 107–08)

It seems to me to be important that Freud is proposing a semiological technique that consists not only in interpreting the dream as a whole, but in following the linguistic sequence of the message with the greatest rigour – in other words, the associations of ideas.

'*Analysis. The hall – numerous guests*, whom we were receiving. We were spending that summer at Bellevue, a house standing by itself on one of the hills adjoining the Kahlenberg. The house had formerly been designed as a place of entertainment and its reception-rooms were in consequence unusually lofty and hall-like. It was at Bellevue that I had the dream, a few days before my wife's birthday. On the previous day my wife had told me that she expected that a number of friends, including Irma, would be coming out to visit us on her birthday. My dream was thus anticipating this occasion: it was my wife's birthday and a number of guests, including Irma, were being received by us in the large hall at Bellevue.

I reproached Irma for not having accepted my solution; I said: "If you still get pains, it's your own fault." I might have said this to her in waking life, and I may actually have done so. It was my view at that time (though I have since recognized it as a wrong one) that my task was fulfilled when I had informed a patient of the hidden meaning of his symptoms: I considered that I was not responsible for whether he accepted the solution or not – though this was what success depended on. I owe it to this mistake, which I have now fortunately corrected, that my life was made easier at a time when, in spite of all my inevitable ignorance, I was expected to produce therapeutic successes. – I noticed, however, that the words which I spoke to Irma in the dream showed that I was especially anxious not to be responsible for the pains which she still had. If they were her fault they could not be mine. Could it be that the purpose of the dream lay in this direction?'

(SE pp. 108–09)

Two points emerge from this account, which are fundamental to this stage in the development of the analysis: on the one hand, Freud's honesty and, on the other, his narcissistic intolerance of uncertainty, his wish to ignore why his interpretations, his 'solutions' were neither absolute nor effective. Freud was already well aware, therefore, of the problem of narcissism and of the analysis of the analyst's narcissism; the theme of narcissism as relational experience also appeared. And even if, in theory, Freud speaks of primary narcissism from the genetic point of view, in analytical practice, the actual experience is always 'secondary': time – the historical sequence of the analytical discourse – corresponds in the transference to a spatial experience. Time exists, therefore, as an intersubjective (patient–analyst) rhythm that is built up between both subjects: diachrony is synchrony. The dualism between diachrony and synchrony is inconceivable: each implies the other; there is no more than a difference of register.

The analysis of the dream is also a relational experience: the time of the dream is manifested as the rhythm of the narrator's discourse, and the dialogue between patient and analyst is revealed as an 'a-historical' dramatization of history. The accurate moment in time at which the thinking being expresses himself takes on the configuration as a locus of thought, the space of the being of thought, the moment when history relapses and becomes an 'a-historical space': a time 'in parentheses'.

Through the mediation of Irma's dream, Freud brings out the theoretico-practical aspects as well as the spatio-temporal aspects, which form a striking contrast with those of his formulations on the 'dream experience' that are bound up with his theory of the unconscious, in which one finds no notion of either space or time.

Freud could not imagine the importance of the transference, caught up as he was in his researches into analytic discourse, in the notion of causality.[5] And for Freud, who lived in the midst of a 'Victorian' society, the notion of cause was synonymous with guilt;[6] to find a cause was to find the person or thing responsible, the 'guilty' person or thing that lay at the origin of the symptom (thus ethics is based on and is infused with aetiology). This was the foundation of anatomo-clinical medicine. His concern, like that of the phrenological tradition, was in fact to locate the 'guilty' organ or the ill-functioning responsible for the disease.

In the history of psychiatry, phrenology based its queries on anatomo–pathological research (the guilty element must be found concretely), with the aim of identifying the part of the body 'responsible' for the mental illness. The anatomical body was for a time the locus in which 'somatic' psychiatry concentrated its research and became a 'corpse psychiatry' (*soma* in Homer means 'dead body', tomb-body, a sense that has been preserved in the English 'corpse').

The locus of mental illness has always been located in the brain. Aetio–pathological hypotheses correspond to a basic fantasy: that of discovering, controlling, and removing the pathogenic cause, the cause of the madness. The idea of the 'contamination' of mental disease appeared reactively in classical antiquity with the profound respect for divine possession (the sacred notion of mental disease that demands its own – sacred – space, far from everything), and again in the Middle Ages, in the form of 'epidemics': collective hysterias, which were real psychotic states of exaltation.[7]

To the concept of the psycho-toxins as elements responsible for schizophrenia was added, in the psycho–biological domain, the strictly organicist one (bacteria, microbes, metabolic disturbances, and so on) of certain authors who also spoke of a possible location of the 'cause' in the intestine (colibacillary psychosis). Tubercular, haepatic, endocrinic, post–influenza, and toxic psychoses formed different ways of situating, 'making transparent', and giving a name to the unknown 'cause'. Even psychoanalytic theory, sometimes used in a mechanical way, can become a 'materialist' exploration: a way of discovering in topography a historical locus that lies at the origin of neurotic and psychotic conflict. This way of posing the problem, based on the traumatic theory (which Freud later criticized), puts the patient in the situation of being helped to discover or to get rid of the cause of his illness. Freud also looked into Irma's throat in an attempt to locate the supposed cause of the illness, just as, in his theories on wish-fulfilment in dreams, he looks for the initial and ultimate cause of the drive in the state of conflict.[8]

The throat, through the mouth, is a space between inside and outside, a gateway, an entrance leading to a deep space: that of the origins of verbal and mental thought, that of the 'body of the unconscious', the place where the explorer-oneiromancer tries to reach dream space-time.

Melanie Klein made the individual responsible for his own fantasies. She tried to help him assume the 'guilt' of his desires and its implications in the relational framework. In the analysis of the transference, the individual is confronted with his own intentions, which are all the more narcissistic and egoistic the more neurotic he is himself.

The actors on the dream stage constitute different versions or various parts of the dreamer's world that are organized dramatically around an ideology that is that of the dream's author.

The narrative of the dream requires an interlocutor, the analyst, just as a pupil needs a master.

For Freud, Fliess represents the friend, the father, the privileged interlocutor, who receives his verbal and epistolary messages, and answers them. Fliess represents the 'other', Freud's alter-ego and super-ego. The area they share is that of the language of the organism – a theme that Groddeck was to take up later. Neuro-endocrinology tended to crystallize Freud's thought in an organicist discourse, based on physio-pathology. Freud's prospective imagination put its trust in neuro-hormonal research as the true determination of the psycho-neurotic process in the 'physiological body'.

Let us return to Irma's dream, in which we find all Freud's ideological contradictions and his difficulties in reconciling official medical thought and his new ideas on the psyche.

'*I took her to the window to look down her throat. She showed some recalcitrance, like women with false teeth. I thought to myself that really there was no need for her to do that.* I had never had any occasion to examine Irma's oral cavity. What happened in the dream reminded me of an examination that I had carried out some time before of a governess: at a first glance she had seemed a picture of youthful beauty, but when it came to opening her mouth she had taken measures to conceal her plates. This led to recollections of other medical examinations and of little secrets revealed in the course of them – to the satisfaction of neither party. "*There was really no need for her to do that*" was no doubt intended in the first place as a compliment to Irma; but I suspected that it had another meaning besides. . . . The way in which Irma stood by the window suddenly reminded me of another experience. Irma had an intimate woman friend of whom I had a very high opinion. When I visited this lady one evening I had found her by a window in a situation reproduced in the dream and her physician, the same Dr M., had pronounced that she had a diphtheritic membrane. The figure of Dr M. and the membrane reappears later in the dream. It now appeared to me that for the last few months I had had every reason to suppose that this other lady was also a hysteric. Indeed, Irma herself had betrayed the fact to me. What did I know of her condition? One thing precisely: that, like my Irma of the dream, she suffered from hysterical choking. So in the dream I had replaced my patient by her friend. . . . Irma seemed to me foolish because she had not accepted my solution. Her friend would have been wiser, that is to say, she would have yielded sooner. She would then have *opened her mouth properly*, and have told me more than Irma.'

(SE pp. 108–11)

In a footnote Freud speaks of the feeling that he had had that the interpretation of this part of the dream had not been carried far enough to make it possible to make it follow the whole of its concealed meaning.

To his moral concern as to what was true and what was false was added the difference between the 'imaginary' illness (hysteria and hypochondria) and the 'real' or somatic illness. The light of analysis, comparable to that which floods in from the window of the dream, made it possible to discover and to distinguish the true from the false. With Irma's analysis, Freud is confronted by his system of narcissistic values, in relation to which he feels himself to be a critic: 'The patient who allows herself to be explored and penetrated by my light, by wisdom, and who is docile to my researches, is an intelligent woman.' The phallico–narcissistic aspect of Freud penetrates without argument, while the non–narcissistic aspect is confronted with the true man who exists inside him, who feels his own weakness.

The Irma dream poses the problem of the psychoanalyst's drama in relation to his own body, to his own sexuality, to his own mental and physical health.[9] This problem was already present in Freud's studies on hysteria and on the symbolic representation concerning the body (conversion symptom). In this dream we find once again the problem of mental and bodily symbolism, as well as the problem of identity and otherness.

On the evening of his meeting with Otto, Freud felt the need to write a letter relating the facts to another more competent physician whom he calls Dr M. He thus felt that he wanted to discharge himself of responsibility for the therapeutic situation. In 1895 Freud still believed partly that if one communicated the causes of the symptom to the patient, the symptom should disappear 'magically'.

The Irma dream was the first that Freud studied in detail, but he did not publish it, for it was too personal. It should also be added that the attitude of Victorian society to the sexual theory implied for Freud a difficult confrontation with himself and with his moral principles concerning sexuality. Furthermore, publications, articles, and books are ways of making the private public. Like any other dream, the Irma dream represents the private, personal world of the dreamer, Freud, in this instance, who was exposing himself publicly. This brings us back to the theatrical problematic of the dream and to the relation between the structure of the dream message, the meaning, and the relationship with the audience: the witness-audience.

'*What I saw in her throat: a white patch*[10] *and turbinal bones with scabs on them.* The white patch reminded me of diphtheritis and so of Irma's friend, but also of a serious illness of my eldest daughter's. . . . The scabs on the turbinal bones recalled a worry about my own state of health. I was making frequent use of cocaine at that time to reduce some troublesome nasal swellings, and I had heard a few days earlier that one of my women patients who had followed my example had developed an extensive necrosis of the nasal mucous membrane. I had been the first to recommend the use of cocaine, in 1885, and this recommendation had brought serious reproaches down on me. The misuse of that drug had hastened the death of a dear friend of mine.

I at once called in Dr M., and he repeated the examination. This simply corresponded to the position occupied by M. in our circle. But the "*at once*" was sufficiently striking to require a special explanation. It reminded me of a tragic event in my practice. I had on one occasion produced a severe toxic state in a woman patient by repeatedly prescribing what was at that time regarded as a harmless remedy (sulphonal), and had hurriedly turned for assistance and support to my experienced senior colleague. There was a subsidiary detail which confirmed the idea that I had this incident in mind. My patient – who succumbed to the poison – had the same name as my eldest daughter. It had never occurred to me before, but it struck me now almost like an act of retribution on the part of destiny. It was as though the replacement of one person by another was to be continued in another sense: this Mathilde for that Mathilde, an eye for an eye and a tooth for a tooth. It seemed as if I had been collecting all the occasions which I could bring up against myself as evidence of lack of medical conscientiousness.'

(SE pp. 111–12)

For Freud the problem with death and the comments on cocaine may also represent the harmfulness of psychoanalytic methodology when badly used.[11] Cocaine, in excessive doses, caused the death of his friend, a death for which Freud felt guilty.

Destruction is bound up with the analyst's destructive narcissism, which in turn is bound up with the dogmatism of analytical knowledge.[12] This is potentially an ally of the patient's destructive narcissism.

A psychoanalysis in which the analyst's narcissism is never discussed (and is therefore unbound from the counter-transference) may link up with the patient's destructive narcissism and lead to a bad dependence, like a drug. Thus Freud is very critical of himself: at the same time as he is idolizing cocaine, he is struggling against it. But, like any other ideology or scientific, political, and religious position, psychoanalysis may become a *drug*; this depends on the *qualitas* or *quantitas* of the subject's narcissistic cathexion. One of the phenomenological conditions of any relationship is accepting the diversity of the other: a diversity in externality that leaves respite in the intersubjective space. Allowing oneself to be penetrated, to penetrate, to amalgamate prevents communication and stifles the breathing space necessary to the logos.[13] Being 'oneself' requires solitude, whereas the infantile ego, which is naturally agoraphobic, tries to seek space in others, or in an ideology that gives it security and identity, thus sacrificing at the same time its identity and its own personal space.

The fusional, symbiotic tendency in analytic practice is always linked with unconscious models in both patient and analyst. This is why it is difficult for the analyst to have as patients, relations or friends that belong to his familiar space, to his everyday environment.

If the analyst cannot avoid such a situation, he must necessarily strive to preserve a continuous alienation of the transference and counter-transference, in order to prevent the analysis from becoming stifling or even stifled in turn.

Freud is aware that, in the dream under discussion, pathological narcissism (on the part of both patient and analyst) constitute a danger that, without adequate supervision, becomes harmful and 'necrosal'.[14]

Using psychoanalytic knowledge as an explanatory justification for one's own actions or one's own behaviour involves a danger and indicates an inadequate understanding of its methodology: one cannot explain and 'analyse' everything.

The context and foundations of any experience form an axiological web; the systems of values of a particular area must be coherent with the availability and flexibility of the subjects involved in the research. Psychoanalysis is both research and therapy and the researchers themselves are part of the space explored.

'*When she was feeling unwell, my friend Otto had given her an injection.*
Otto had in fact told me that during his short stay with Irma's
family he had been called in to a neighbouring hotel to give an
injection to someone who had suddenly felt unwell. These injections reminded me once more of my unfortunate friend who had
poisoned himself with cocaine. I had advised him to use the drug
internally only, while morphia was being withdrawn; but he had
at once given himself cocaine *injections. A preparation of propyl . . .
propyls . . . propionic acid.*'

(SE p. 115)

This image is associated with the story of some pineapple juice that
Otto had given Freud's family the day before; the smell of that juice
was reminiscent in an associative way of that of *ananas*, pineapple
brandy.

'The smell of fusel oil (amyl . . .) evidently stirred up in my mind
a recollection of the whole series – propy, methyl, and so on – and
this accounted for the propyl preparation in the dream. It is true
that I carried out a substitution in the process: I dreamt of propyl
after having smelt amyl. But substitutions of this kind are perhaps
legitimate in organic chemistry.'

(SE p. 116)

Trimethylamin played an important role as a product of the
decomposition of 'sexual substances' and was associated with Fliess's
researches.

'Thus this substance led me to sexuality, the factor to which I
attributed the greatest importance in the origin of the nervous
disorders which it was my aim to cure. My patient Irma was a
young widow; if I wanted to find an excuse for the failure of my
treatment in her case, what I could best appeal to would no doubt
be this fact of her widowhood, which her friends would be so glad
to see changed. . . .
    Injections of that sort ought not to be made so thoughtlessly.'

(SE pp. 116–17)

Here the criticism of thoughtlessness is turned directly against his
friend Otto. Grinstein, in his studies on the Irma dream,[15] speaks of
the importance of Otto, Dr M., and Leopold. Otto and Leopold
were both assistant physicians at the Brücke Institute, where Freud
had worked. Otto was always enterprising, even bold, very quick to
understand things, while Leopold's attitude was more prudent and
modest, though also more serious and therefore safer. In the dream,

114

according to Freud, there is an opposition between Otto and Leopold, to the advantage of the latter. Freud seems to esteem Leopold more for his prudence. Grinstein stresses Freud's identification with Leopold, with the prudent person; and Irma speaks of the 'imprudent' injection.

> 'Here I was evidently collecting instances of my conscientiousness, but also of the reverse.
> *And probably the syringe had not been clean.* This was yet another accusation against Otto.'
>
> (SE pp. 117–18)

The problem facing Freud was how to distinguish between his personal life and his public life, the private drawing-room at Bellevue and the ballroom, in other words, between the social space of the family and the professional space.

Freud guessed that a dogmatic, possessive, invading position could infiltrate into the other's mind and body: up to a point he associates Irma with one of his friends, who had probably had a tubercular infiltration; but it might also have been that what was wrong with her was not tubercular, but merely 'imitating' the disease (pathoplastia). Freud also associated it with his own pain in the shoulder, a pain apparently due to rheumatism, and he goes on: 'Psychical treatment cannot be held responsible for the continuation of diphtheric pains.' In the dream, in order to shrug off all responsibility, Freud invents a situation in which Irma is suffering from a serious disease that is gradually infiltrating into her body. The dirty syringe and the infiltration refer to 'unclean' aspects of the counter-transference; they also refer to a transgressive, phallic, penetrating attitude on the part of the analyst. This aspect of penetration, of destructive possession of the object, corresponds to a form of projection that we have already cited and which has been described by Melanie Klein – pathological projective identification.

Lacan paid a great deal of attention to this aspect of the Irma dream in his seminar for 1954–55.[16] He speaks of the urethral eroticism in Freud's life, which was bound up with the childhood memory of urinating in his parents' bedroom, a memory that Erikson also regards as of particular importance.[17] These comments by Lacan and Erikson correspond to the theme developed by Melanie Klein on certain archaic, universal fantasies on the part of the child who may have urinary attacks against his mother's belly. These urinary attacks reveal an aggressive, destructive reaction to the encounter with the maternal space. It is a question of a very great ambivalent attachment (self-hate): a relational intensity inversely proportional to the ability

115

to tolerate frustration. The exaggerated attachment to the mother's belly and breast is accompanied furthermore by an intense, pregenital eroticization.

The symptoms of Freud's dream and its associative implications link together and merge the history of the 'transference', the relationship between the analyst and the patient, and the personal history of each of them. The double resistance would thus seem to be based on this historical duality. Analytic understanding makes it possible to overcome such a duality and its corresponding resistances.

Freud's preoccupations with Irma and with the therapeutic results are the expression of his *preoccupation* with the destiny of his drives and unconscious fantasies.

Freud's study of this dream is also very important from the point of view of linguistic research. The interpretation of the dream is a reading of the figurative and non-figurative aspects that appear on the dream stage.

When Lacan takes up the discourse on the imaginary, he suggests that the figurative character of the dream is part of dream's perceptual-visual experience. According to Lacan, Freud needed to introduce the hypothesis of regression in order to advance his discourse on the quantitative aspect of the drive, which was already present in his 'project', leaving to one side the qualitative character of the dream imaginary.

The qualitative aspect of the Irma dream is related to the intentionality of the drives of the analyst who wants 'to cure' in a penetrating, invading, and absolute way, following the metaphoric model of the laws on cancerigenic infiltrations.

Fliess's theory on the relationship between the nose and sexuality is expressed here through the danger of 'sticking one's nose too much' into the patient's private life. Furthermore, the analysand often tends to want to stick his nose into the analyst's private life: the development of the analytic 'setting' will depend, therefore, on an analysis appropriate to this double transgression. The Irma dream is *fundamental* because it theoretically foreshadows various technical aspects of psychoanalytic theory that were later to be developed in a more formal way.

Frieda Fromm-Reichmann, in her work on analytic psychotherapy, maintains that, in order to analyse psychotics, who so often tend to act and to confuse analytic thought with the action of the drives, the analyst must have sufficient affective and sexual gratifications not to seek to obtain them in a perverse way with the patient.[18]

One of the protections of the narcissism of both patient and analyst consists in cathecting the analytic material and 'disguising' it erotically, eroticizing the transference and the counter-transference in order to compensate for the affective and cognitive powerlessness of narcissism, which does not tolerate a failure in understanding and an inability to help: its 'omnipotence'.

Such a configuration of transference and counter-transference bears down on pathological narcissism and the inability to tolerate ignorance (not understanding the material).[19] Dogmatic analytic exploration, which does not doubt, tends to reify, idealize, and eroticize the logos, turning it into a fetishistic act.

This is absolutely not the case with Freud, for whom personal ethics and the sociological implications of the theory of the super-ego guarantee an appropriate destination of the transference and the quality of the encounter.

The Irma dream is material for a creative, self-critical counter-transference, an example of Freud's ability to tolerate doubt and ambiguity, and to question his own thoughts and feelings. His behaviour arouses admiration, but not adoration: psychoanalytic mediation must be distinguished from shamanic practice.

In Freud self-criticism is a confrontation with his ideal ego and with its counterpart, the ego ideal – a confrontation that is sometimes excessive and incompatible with his usual modesty. The counter-transference is an internal dialogue, a critical confrontation involving the whole person.

The dream of Irma's injection is for Freud an essential stage in the development of the theory of the drives and that of the psychical apparatus. The structuring of the manifest text of the dream suggests the presence of a certain ego that thinks 'with its eyes shut', and which reflects on the fundamental aspects of life, present, past, and future (the 'projective and protensive' aspect of the dream message). In applying the interpretative method, Freud discovers that the dream is full of meanings and that his language is structured according to the rules and laws of the unconscious.

Freud never ceased to declare the importance of his researches into the interpretation of dreams. In a letter to Fliess, of 12 June, 1900 (Letter 137), he speaks of the house at Bellevue that was the setting of the Irma dream and writes that it would be right for a marble tablet to be placed one day on the house inscribed with the words:

'In this house, on July 24, 1895 the secret of dreams was revealed to Dr Sigmund Freud.'

Notes

1 What happens during the counter-transference when the patient is not present? This is the question that Freud asks in the case of Irma's injection. 'What is the destiny of the transference?' he wonders. What is the destiny of the object internalized by the patient and the analyst? The analyst is in a position to understand his own dream only in so far as the material provided by his patient succeeds in arousing his own personal history. In the counter-transference the patient may become the analyst's therapist: it is his turn to question his analyst's way of thinking, feeling, and 'acting'.

All these problems are already present in *The Interpretation of Dreams*, but Freud was not to develop the notions of transference and counter-transference until ten years later, in 1910.

The dream of Irma's injection is also a 'premonitory' dream: an anticipation of Freud's illness, the memory of a future inscribed in the body and present in a 'manifest' way, but which had not yet been made 'public'.

2 Freud's position, especially at the beginning of his psychoanalytic practice, is complex: his self-analysis and the analysis of his counter-transference were the necessary tools to preserve the analytic setting (and also to understand its alienation). Jacques Lacan rightly points out the importance of the notion of 'interference of subjects' in relation to the analysis of the dream of Irma's injection (*Ecrits*, Paris, 1966, p. 16).

3 One of the richest and most complete documentations on Freud and the dream of Irma's injection has been collected and developed by Didier Anzieu, in his *Autoanalyse de Freud* (Paris, 1957, 1975, p. 187). 'A dream about Irma and Freud', he writes, 'constitutes . . . a programme-dream for all the subsequent discoveries that were to constitute psychoanalysis. It declares the identity of body and dream and of dream and body.'

4 I believe that I can read into Freud's words: 'We shall use the catharsis of the body, dysentery, and everything will go well.'

5 To demand a cure of Irma is a mistake that Freud admits as an expression of his research into the transference. On the other hand, influenced by the medical thought of the time, he seeks confirmation for his theories on cause (aetiology) and the meaning of the symptom.

6 Aetiology, from the Greek $\alpha\iota\tau\iota o\lambda o\gamma\iota\alpha$, is made up of $\alpha\iota\tau\iota\alpha$ (cause) and $\lambda o\gamma o\varsigma$ (speech, discourse). Aetiology is a rhetoric on the origin of things, a theme that in Greek thought is often confused with myths of origin. A phenomenological study of aetiology is a study of the *arche* that comes to meet us, that is to say, an archaeology of the present.

7 Mental illness is identified with the plague. Speaking of the plague at

Marseille in *Le Théâtre et son double*, Antonin Artaud says: 'The rats were not responsible, they merely awakened the plague that was already in the city.'

8 He is also looking, 'without knowing it', for an anticipated memory of his own future. 'Freud's cancer' is already speaking in the present, or in any case his worries and 'tissular' fantasies are being summoned in his transference with Irma, a transference that he was later to call 'counter-transference'.

9 The dream of Irma's injection reveals the drama of the psychoanalyst Sigmund Freud in relation to his own body. Freud had started smoking at the age of 24 and, from that time, was concerned with the effect of nicotine on various parts of his body (even though his father, a great smoker, died at the age of 81). These are the preoccupations that appear in the letters from Fliess, who, after reassuring him about his father's death, began to advise him against continuing to smoke. Thus the prohibition to smoke and 'closing his eyes', or one eye at least, are superimposed. In a letter of 17 November, 1893, Freud writes to Fliess: 'I am not obeying your prohibitions about smoking; do you really think there is any point in living a long, wretched life?' Fliess considered that all Freud's pains, even the cardiac disturbances, were a reflection of the problems that he had in his nose. Fliess also suffered from his nose, in a pathological way, and in the end he worked out a theory that connected the nose with sexuality. A specialist in otorhinolaryngology, he tried to find the ætio-pathogenic – and not only symbolic links – between the nose and the genital organs. To deaden the pain, Fliess used cocaine; Freud, too, was to have recourse to cocaine over a long period.

On the subject of Freud's cardiac disturbances, his physician, Max Schur, was convinced, on the basis of descriptions that Freud himself gave of his 'cardiac miseries', that Freud suffered from *angina pectoris* and had probably already had at the age of 38 a minor coronary thrombosis.

10 In the Irma dream, in what might already be called one of Freud's 'counter-transference dreams', the concern with the scabs in Irma's throat corresponds to the leucoplasia that, in 1923, was subjected to a 'preventative operation', to be followed by several other, rather traumatizing operations. Indeed it would seem that much of the pain connected with 'Freud's cancer' was merely the result of bad feeling and the contraction of tissue in the areas operated on. The histo-pathological studies on Freud's cancer are somewhat contradictory both as regards Professor Pichler's 'medical notes' and the notes of Max Schur and of other doctors. This would suggest that Freud was the victim of his own hypochondriacal concerns and that, despite his loyal, grateful attitude, he induced in his doctors similar anxieties.

Recently an Argentine cancer specialist, Dr José Schavelzon, who has made comparative studies on the histo-pathological preparations of Freud's 'cancer', has reached rather interesting conclusions (see *Sigmund Freud, un paciente con cancer*, Buenos Aires, 1983). In a letter to me, dated 17 February, 1982, he writes:

'What last July was for me merely a hypothesis has now been confirmed from a histo-pathological point of view. . . . I was lucky enough to see the histo-pathological preparations of a disease that had been evolving for several years. I can now say that Freud suffered from a leucoplasia of the right cheek extending to the mucous membrane of the mouth and of the palate (nicotinic palatitis) of which he complained as early as 1917 (see Freud's letter to Ferenczi, vol. 2 of Ernest Jones's biography of Freud). . . . Whether this lesion encouraged the production of a carcinoma or not gave rise to divided opinions, especially in Vienna in 1923. Indeed on April 23 of that year, Freud was "savagely" operated on, as he sat on a kitchen chair, with a local anaesthetic. The right part of the palate was resected, opening up the maxillary sinus, and the edge of the upper right jaw was extirpated. All this was done with a scalpel and a hammer. A serious haemorrhage followed and the operation had to be postponed. The gaping surfaces were covered neither with mucous membrane nor with skin grafts. . . . This led to very serious complications: the formation of scabs, shrinking of the mucous membrane, i.e. retraction of the scars (see his commentary on his father's death). It is also highly significant that the last book he read was Balzac's *Le Peau de chagrin*. Freud remarked that this was just the book he needed – it was about contraction and death by inanition – by which he meant the gradual contraction not of his scars, but of his whole body, towards the end of his life (see Ernest Jones, *Sigmund Freud*, London, 1957, vol. 3).

The tumoral process present in Freud was not a cancer in the usual sense and this type of tumour – florid papillomatosis or Ackermann's verrucous carcinoma – was not studied until much later, in 1949. It consists of a local lesion, which does not usually lead to either metastasis or adenopathy, but may infiltrate the neighbouring tissue. When radio therapy is imprudently administered, it may turn into a real carcinoma, but this requires a long evolution. Nevertheless this is what happened to Freud, who underwent ray treatment eleven times. The histology shows that only in 1936 did a real carcinoma appear. What did Freud die of? Several hypotheses may be advanced, but certainly not from cancer. Probably his difficulties in eating and drinking (the contraction of his body), the repeated pneumonopathies, added to the septic process with osseous radionecrosis. . . . The large white scab in the dream of Irma's injection is, therefore, his own leucoplasic lesion.'

Freud's studies on the death drive, and on the confrontation between Eros and Thanatos, seem to personify the presence of the body, that is to say, the notion of finitude as an awareness of the idea of death as forming part of life.

The theme of contracting skin is echoed in a letter of 1896 to Fliess, to whom he writes about his dying father: 'he is shrinking regularly . . . up to the fatal day'. If the unconscious is a memory, as Freud says, he would have confronted his own life, the 'history of the body', the whole time. Shortly before his death, Freud said to his physician, Max Schur: 'You promised not to desert me when my time came. Now there is nothing but torture and it no longer has any meaning . . . thank you.' On 23 September, 1939, Freud went into a coma from which he did not emerge.

11 Freud, who was the first to discover the therapeutic function of cocaine, turned it into an intermediary figure between himself and Fliess. Cocaine represents the 'great other', the drug of concretizing dogmatism of the thought of a therapeutic ideal (a God who turns out to be diabolical).

12 A concept developed by H. Rosenfeld (*Psychotic States*, London, 1965), who deals specifically with the increase in the destructiveness of the drives caused by certain drugs. See also note 19.

13 Descartes speaks of a breathing-space in relation to the capacity to think: 'I breathe, therefore I exist', he wrote to Renneri in 1638.

14 The remedy, like analysis, has to be calibrated; at high doses, both may become toxic.

Freud had discovered indirectly, and in accordance with linear causality, the destination of Irma's 'symptomatology'. This was worked out only shortly before the omnipotent project of psychoanalysis as 'absolute' remedy intended to eliminate 'symptoms surgically'.

15 A. Grinstein, *On Sigmund Freud's Dreams*, Detroit, Mich., 1968.

16 Jacques Lacan, *Séminaires*, Paris, 1978, vol. II, pp. 177 and 193.

17 Erik H. Erikson, *Identity; Youth and Crisis*, London, 1971.

18 Frieda Fromm-Reichmann, *Psychoanalysis and Psychotherapy, Selected Papers of F. Fromm-Reichmann*, Chicago, Ill., 1959; *Principles of Intensive Psychotherapy*, Chicago, Ill., 1950.

19 Herbert Rosenfeld, 'On the Psychopathology of Narcissism: A Clinical Approach', 1964, in *Psychotic States*, London, 1965, p. 169; and 'Introduction to the Discussion on "A Clinical Approach to the Psychoanalytic Theory of the Life and Death Instincts"', in *Scientific Bulletin of the British Psycho-Analytical Society and the Institute of Psycho-Analysis*, no. 55, 1972.

9

The traces of the Gradiva

'On the bridge linking dream to reality, "slightly lifting her dress with her left hand": Gradiva.'

(André Breton)[1]

Sigmund Freud's theories and methods profoundly influenced art and literary criticism. Freud's attitude to art and to the various forms of literary expression is based on a substantial, cultural research that tends to uncover and reveal the author's message through an analysis of the biographical traces and of the 'personal' signs found in the work itself.

Each sign is the expression of a certain meaning, but the meaning has been made public only through the mediation of the signifier.

Freudian thought, which was contemporary with the phenomenological approach in philosophy (Freud attended lectures by Franz Brentano at the same period as Husserl), anticipates structuralism in certain respects, by offering a 'reductive' description drawing on the 'factum' and the associative sequence, which determine the 'historicity' of discourse.

Freud's approach is fundamentally genetic, but his experience is 'factual' and phenomenological: the psychoanalytic theory is a methodological research into the phenomenon of the transference, that is to say, into encounter.

The genetic foundations, the research into the *arche*, find their starting-point in the immediacy of the exploration of the terrain on which the analytic situation takes place. In the case of a literary or artistic work, the relationship between the analyst and the work is not immediate, but mediate. The aesthetic object is 'subjectum', the presence of the artist. The empathic relationship with the work becomes co-presence, reciprocity, inter-prestation. Interpretation is always an inter-prestation, an exchange, a prospective intuition, a judgement.

Freud, who is interested in the creative process, assumes the role of spectator and witness 'in the field', in the space that is developed between him and the object of analysis.

Freud's study of Jensen's 'Gradiva' is an example that shows how a work may transcend and attain the operative space of the critic.

Freud becomes an essayist, a critic, a meticulous observer, a hermeneut concerned to understand the hidden meaning of the various characters that correspond to the various ways of existing for the author of the work. The dream is 'egotistical', all its characters relate to the dreamer: so the characters of a novel dramatize the author's living dream.

The study of Jensen's 'Gradiva' reveals Freud's continuing interest in poetry, an interest that finds expression in his own qualities as a writer.[2] The dream, with its analogies between day-time and night-time metaphors, leads Freud into a vast, productive cultural space. 'Between the fables of various mythologies, fairy tales, the inventions of certain poets, and the dream that takes place inside me', writes Albert Béguin, 'I see a profound kinship.'[3]

Literature always stimulated Freud's thought; the study of Jensen's book is a model of applied psychoanalytic exploration, as well as an essay in literary criticism.

The concept of essay, indirectly related to the Greek σοφός, poses the problem of the relationship between knowledge, consciousness, and the unconscious.[4]

The unconscious is 'made flesh' in the discourse of the consciousness: the 'root' of thought is unconscious, but also present and substantial: it is part of an 'arborizing' discourse.[5]

Freud suggests the idea of an organic (arborizing!) language of the unconscious and Otto Rank stresses its creative aspect. However, neurosis is not synonymous with creativity in itself. Only the artist is in contact with his 'roots': he is the man who creates, the man who bears fruit.

Jensen is an artist who unconsciously guesses the meaning and importance of dreams, of the imaginary, of fantasy, of day-dreaming, and delusion. At least this is what Freud thought about Jensen, even if Jensen would not have shared that opinion.

Specifically the characteristic of Jensen's story is that its unconscious discourse transcends the author's apparent, 'voluntary', conscious intentions. Generally speaking the writer cannot see himself 'whole' and, in a way, seems to need a certain amount of inner 'blindness', or to find an ideal perspective to contemplate, to express himself, without necessarily having to recognize himself in a 'factum' or in each character.

The neo-Platonists cultivated 'wisdom' and, following the Socratic tradition, exalted the ability to look inwards. For Plotinus, the sage draws from himself what he shows others; the sage is a critic, serene and objective, without being indifferent. The serenity of atharaxia is not a matter of isolation or renunciation, but of awareness and judgement.

It is with all the serenity of the sage that Freud interprets Jensen's text, reads it, thinks about it, and lives it 'objectively', from an assumed subjective point of view. Critical analysis is both a way of seeing and a way of showing.

Freud speaks of two directions in research: the first consists of deepening a reading of the dreams imagined by a novelist, the second of bringing together and comparing the works of various authors who speak of dreams. In his work he chose the first type of approach.

The short novel on the Gradiva, which Jensen also calls a 'Pompeian fantasy', centralizes the drama, the main scene, in a Pompeii that is both imaginary and real.

This ambiguity, which situates the description between dream and reality, light and dark, day and night, imagination, dream thought, and delusion, is maintained throughout this narrative. The dream forms part of life, and everyday reality is a living metaphor. Everyday space and time make up the scenes of the novel.

The stones of Pompeii bear the trace of a history, a tragedy personified and made present.

Norbert Hanold, hero of the novel, wanders through the past, the present, and the future, through dream, day-dreams, uncertainty, love, and nostalgia, elements in the work that are articulated in the form of a poetic adventure.

The image of a girl, seen for the first time in a bas-relief in a Rome museum and which Norbert baptized 'Gradiva', that is to say, 'she who moves forward', is merged with the personal story of the main character. Norbert's interest in the Gradiva, in her living physicality, expresses his aesthetic, vital ideal in a moment of paralysis in his own life.

Norbert Hanold, a professor of archaeology, is fascinated by the Gradiva's movement, her graceful foot, which, through its vertical position, breaks the statuary immobility of the bas-relief. Struck by his encounter with the work, which has become, for him, a living character, he bears its image within him, an image that he seeks everywhere to materialize, throughout space, closed or open, seen or dreamt.

In the end Norbert is persuaded that the image of the Gradiva, animated by his imagination, must be found at Pompeii, a city of which he has made a special study, and that Gradiva is walking across those flagstones revealed by the excavations . . .

He was in Germany, his native country, when an anguishing dream transported him to ancient Pompeii, the very day that Vesuvius erupted, in 79 BC. In this dream, he was near the temple of Jupiter, when suddenly he caught a glimpse in front of him of Gradiva, 'a short distance away'. She was walking calmly towards the temple of Apollo, where she sat down on one of the steps, quietly awaiting the death that would come with the eruption.

On waking, after this anguishing dream, Norbert went to the window of his room and, looking out, he seemed to recognize in the street Gradiva's outline, her supple, graceful feminine walk. He ran out into the street to look for her but, as in a 'real' dream, the figure had vanished.

Back in his room, his attention is drawn to a canary in a cage, in the window of the house opposite. He recognizes himself in that canary; his own cage is his body, which has been turned to marble. Only the presence of the Gradiva gives it warmth, life, and movement.

Following the dream, he is more and more convinced that Gradiva lived at Pompeii and was buried there in 79 BC. The image of the Gradiva obsesses him; and since he has no reason to stay, he decides to set out, 'for the South'. The 'South', unconsciously, is to become Rome . . . Naples . . . Pompeii.

In the end, in his hotel room, he does not fall asleep straight away. He listens to the rather too loud noises and voices that reach him from the room next door: the voices of a young couple, who disturb him somewhat, for they make him aware of his solitude. Next day, he leaves Rome, almost fleeing it, for Naples. His journey 'to the South' ends, of course, two days later, at Pompeii, where he stays at a hotel quite close to the site of the excavations. And there he plunges once again into his dream–novel, pursuing his adventure; his search is disturbed only by the noise of flies, which reminds him of all those pairs of lovers that he has met on his way, and he wishes he had a 'fly-swat' to get rid of those insect–couples that seem to mock him.

Pompeii does not turn out to be the quiet place he hoped for. His tormented, disturbed inwardness is distinctly spatialized and materialized around him. Several times our hero goes into the ruins of the old city, sets about interpreting the graffiti and any trace likely to inform him and guide him in his amorous search. And while he is plunged in his day-dreams, he catches a glimpse of 'his' Gradiva, the unforgettable shape of the bas-relief, leaving a house: she is wearing some light material, which no longer has the coldness of marble, but which is rather warm and yellow. Norbert then rediscovers, in a corner of his memory, an image of his dream, that of the Gradiva on the steps of the temple of Apollo. The Gradiva must have been resuscitated and is now moving towards the house where she was living on the day of the catastrophe, a house that Norbert identifies as being the one known as Meleager's house. And, indeed, in front of Meleager's house, Gradiva disappears. Norbert pauses for a moment to read an inscription engraved on a mosaic on the house, which reads: *Ave* (hail).

This 'factum' is a favourable clue. Indeed, shortly afterwards, the image of the Gradiva appears to him again, continuing to live in his apparent life at noon, the hour of ghosts.

Norbert asks her several questions, first in Greek, then in Latin. The Gradiva replies with a smile: 'If you want to talk to me, you must speak in German.'

The young archaeologist is suddenly aware that the Gradiva is a real image. He thinks he recognizes her and says, 'I knew your voice sounded like that.' And he tells her that he has already seen her and heard her in dream. Then, before she disappears again, Norbert asks the Gradiva if she will come back the following day.

Thus his dream-world is looking for a space and a time in reality, where it would be capable of materializing his desire. Next day, he sees her again among the columns, at the same place where he had met her the day before; she is still wearing the same dress and appears to him once again by chance. Hanold speaks to her, praising her graceful movement, her body, her face, all that he had discovered when he saw her for the first time on the bas-relief, in Rome.

This time, Gradiva interrupts our hero and answers simply that he would be better to keep his over-fertile imagination in check. And she adds that her real name is Zoe. 'Zoe' means 'life'. Norbert, alone once more, feels that Pompeii is enveloped in a cloud of mist and the sunbeams that pierce it seem to him like gold threads.

Next day, Norbert is once again at Meleager's house, looking for Zoe-Gradiva, whom he does in fact meet. She even calls him by his name: Norbert Hanold! This is very odd, since nobody at Pompeii knows him. At a moment in their conversation, Zoe-Gradiva speaks of a little canary, locked up in its cage, hanging in the window of his house, in Germany. A distant memory has invaded Norbert's thoughts, a memory that he is unable to situate, either in time or in space. Zoe goes on: 'In that house lives my father, Richard Bertgang, a professor of zoology.'

'Bertgang . . . ', Norbert explains, 'so you must be Fräulein Zoe Bertgang?'

Zoe Bertgang was indeed a childhood friend of Norbert's. Zoe Bertgang and the Gradiva are one and the same person.

Norbert, overcome with emotion, wakes up and emerges from his dream: the fog has lifted. Gradiva–Zoe Bertgang becomes a living reality, as brilliant as the sun. The hero's half-oneiric, half-delusional imagination recognizes the object of his love, buried in his childhood, paralysed, deprived of history, locked up in a cage, enveloped in a thick mist – the delusion of his passion . . .

The image of his childhood appears not only as an emotional expression of his world, but also as part of his life, of a time that is personified by the Gradiva.

Between delusion, dream, and reality, Norbert must now choose: wake up or go on dreaming with his eyes open. Norbert noticed the allusion made by the delusion in his confrontation with reality: 'Zoe' means 'life', 'Gradiva', 'she who moves forward', and Bertgang 'a fine step'. This philological sequence indicates a precise determination: find the road, the greeting (*Ave*), the love object.

The caged canary represents the 'autistic solution', the 'debris' from the collapse of a fragmented 'self', contained in the cage-body inside which Norbert feels reassured but, at the same time, bounded like a prisoner. To leave the cage, to throw himself once again into the world, to transmigrate, to be reborn at Pompeii, which is, like him, in ruins, is an experience dramatized in the flies, those wild, noisy flying objects, which fly through space, lost, without purpose or reason, seeking to get themselves trapped, treated, tamed, and thought (this is reminiscent of the notion of 'wild thoughts' in psychosis, developed by Bion).

The character of the Gradiva, says Freud, is transported into Norbert Hanold's past-present.[6] Knowledge of antiquity has made Norbert familiar with a distant world, cut off from everyday reality. Not recognizing Zoe also means to deny what is repressed, what he has buried in the space-time of his whole being. With the idealized love object, part of his childhood, of his fragmented history, has moved away, losing contact with his conscious being. The buried, repressed childhood implies that part of his present infantile ego is separated off from the present. His lack of vitality and joy, his inability to play (the delusion occupies the space of play), is the sign of this loss. The infantile ego is also the expression of movement,

127

fluidity, the flexibility of body-time. Norbert's attachment to the immobile world of statues is an emotional manifestation of his ludic paralysis, of his own petrification.

Zoe-Gradiva, buried in Norbert's memory and petrified in the city, represents a pathological solution to his catatonia; time must be paralysed and petrified, he must become a creature dead in life, in order to be able to avoid absolute death, or to avoid life.[7]

Norbert's world, distant and beyond reach, or close but lifeless, separated from co-existence, reminds Freud of his experience when he visited the Acropolis for the first time. In a letter he wrote to Romain Rolland on the occasion of the French writer's seventieth birthday (1936), Freud relates his experience of 'false recognition' the sense of *déjà vu*, or *déjà raconté*, of something unlived in the present, experienced at his first contact with the Acropolis.[8] Freud feels depersonalized, derealized. In his state of 'double consciousness' or split personality, he recognizes himself as he who is 'fulfilling' a dream (he had always wanted to make this journey), but cannot experience it. It is only by becoming aware of his inner split that Freud wakes up and makes contact once more with his emotions, with his desire, which had previously been reified and petrified.

De-realization is the external counterpart of de-personalization. De-personalization and de-realization (intra- and inter-personal dissociation) are transformations, deep modifications of perceptible experience. 'Lived' memory is incompatible with the objectivity, for which one blocks the evocative, or recreative ability. This phenomenon is characteristic to a certain degree of psychotic experience. The psychotic does not remember, but he recreates at another level what is memory, in the form of reminiscence.[9]

In Latin, memory is *recordor*, a composite word made up of the prefix *re-*, 'again', and *cor, cordis*, 'heart, feeling'. Affectivity speaks with the heart, while memory, cold, unexperienced, speaks with thought, a de-vitalized thought. In Latin, to remember, 'to have memory of', is to say 'with the heart' the emotional content of an evocation, the living reactivation of the past. Psychotic evocation, on the other hand, is not a memory, but a reminiscence, a historical reactivation without warmth, without vitality, *sine cordis*.

Norbert Hanold, depersonalized and derealized, tries with archaeology to resume contact with a memory that has become arrested in time. His sexuality and affectivity, all his infantile world, have remained in suspense, half-way, paralysed, as if buried 'after the flood'. The psychotic crisis is a catastrophic phenomenon (the flood) and the sub-acute and chronic forms represent the psychotic solution:[10] to cool the memory and bury the time and place of the catastrophic experience – for Norbert, Pompeii.

All that is not psychotic in Norbert tends to revive the characters of the catastrophe: re-vive, after being dead, means to re-create the buried world, to assume contact with his emotional world, to be able to remember. But in order to re-member, he must assume his own anxiety, the sign of the presence of the pain that is involved in bringing back to life. For Norbert, the lack of pleasure is also lack of pain; there is no pleasure without raising the sense of loss: to return to life, one must remember and make contact, return (*nostos*) to painful (*algia*) experiences, in a word, assume 'nostalgia'.

The relationship that Norbert sets up with his own 'objects', which he has buried, is a passionate one. Passion is not exactly love but a *raptus*, an uncritical elevation of an overwhelming emotional world that escapes violently from its 'cage'.

Love, passion, and the 'delusion of love' are different degrees of an intensely lived experience, which is manifested each time under different symbolic or proto-symbolic forms.

This is related to the problem of narcissism, for passion is fundamentally narcissistic: it does not demand, does not consider the object *qua* subject. The 'desire of the other' takes possession, but is itself possessed: by its own desire. Passion is blind, it neither sees nor demands, it seeks only to grasp its illusion, to materialize its own 'hallucinated' desire.

Dissociation is a more primitive mechanism than repression: repression already implies the presence of an ego capable of dissociating and differentiating, of pushing towards the space of the unconscious (re-pression) what involves pain and threat for the space of consciousness. The ability to differentiate is based on the possibility of 'discrimination' between the various zones of the psychical apparatus, between corporal reality and the dream-world.

Repression means a capacity to categorize, to separate pleasure from pain, or painful pleasure from what is incompatible with life.

Freud encountered considerable difficulties in defining repression in relation to psychosis. In his studies on hysteria and the anxiety neuroses (1892–95),[11] and when speaking of the factual drive and paranoia (1896),[12] he uses the word 'repression' (*Verdrängung*) to define projection: 'Bei Paranoia wird der Vorwurf auf einem Wege, den man als *Projektion* bezeichnen kann, verdrängt, indem das Abwehrsymptom des Misstrauens.'[13]

In paranoiac delusion the ego rids itself of a sense of inner persecution by projecting it outside, into the other, thanks to suppression (*Unterdrückung*) forcing the external object open and letting it be buried through the mediation of repression (*Verdrängung*).

The 'pressure' exerted on the world in the form of suppression represents in Norbert Hanold a way of keeping his catastrophic experiences at a distance in others. Pompeii becomes the place, the other, where painful, persecutory memory is laid and buried. The Gradiva personifies, therefore, in her static aspect, Norbert's childhood feminine ideal, which both hides and reveals the 'time of disaster', in which the hope of his ideal ego has lost strength and consistency.[14] Only the Gradiva's foot, forming an angle in the horizontality of the everyday, remains a living, phallic, ludic part of his being, his masculine ego.

Then there occurs the moment when Zoe, by empathy and love, understands Norbert's delusional passion and agrees to assume the role of the Gradiva, as it had been assigned to her. The caged canary, the Gradiva, Pompeii, represent in turn different aspects of the Hero's personal archaeology.

In psychoanalytic experience the Norbert–Zoe relationship represents the patient–analyst dyad; similarly the 'Pompeian adventure' sums up the many vicissitudes of the transference.

Norbert makes an 'archaeological' contract, as in an analytical experience, with what has been projected, suppressed, 'repressed outside his lived corporality' (outside into the world, that is to say, projected *into* the world of objects).

Zoe-Gradiva is also the place into which his immobilized affectivity is projected and which it inhabits. The discovery of the bas-relief already means that he is bringing to the light of day what was buried by the darkness of night and which, engraved in time, 'takes relief' in stone: what was repressed is shown in the form of appearance, of 'phenomenon'.

The study of Jensen's Gradiva enabled Freud to resume his discourse on repression, suppression, and regression. Gradiva, which means 'she who moves forward', is contrasted with a concept of regression, which means 'to go backwards'. The 'move forward' of the delusion is an escape 'in progress', towards a new space in time. Delusional thought has a tendency to assume – following the Gradiva's foot – a vertical position and to depart from the horizontality of the earth.

The horizontal line is the line of the earth; the vertical line, which rises, is the mystical dimension of the psychotic ideal. Delusion imitates the canary, it takes flight, and moves away from the earth.[15]

According to the Freudian model, regression is a journey backwards, to the past, to the fundamental point of 'normal' repression in each individual: the 'dispositional point'. According to Freud, everybody goes through a period of neurotic conflict, which is then repressed at a certain level of personal history; this is 'pro-gress'. Suppression arouses latent conflict and allows the debris of the catastrophe to rise to the surface, in the case of a psychosis. The 'locus' of repression, whether oral, anal, or genital, represents different areas and stages of the pro-gress that the conflict has chosen in order to remain buried.

The Gradiva, petrified in time, is revealed as a project, a 'movement forwards', the possibility of moving on, of 'beginning again'.

Zoe-Gradiva also plays the role of the reality principle that confronts the principle of unreality represented by the delusional proposition. Passion, like delusion, constructs too much and too quickly, at an ever faster rate. The illusional progress of the delusion is not maintained and has a tendency to collapse 'catastrophically' into dis-illusion.

Reality disinvested of delusional illusion is 'deflated' and comes up against the expansive, autocentric tendency of the delusion: the inflation and deflation of the ego.[16]

The analytic method that Freud applies to his study of Jensen's short story is very close to the method of *The Psycho-pathology of Everyday Life* (1901), since it is a semiological, linguistic approach based on Jensen's associations of ideas. The sequence of the story is in fact the author's associative articulation.

Zoe also means life, life held back, imprisoned. Zoe says: 'I long ago got used to being dead'. Zoe has always inhabited Norbert's world, seeking, in reality, keeping her distance, her 'salvation', her *ave*, her *salve*.

At a given moment, says Freud, representations are repressed because they are attached to feelings that are far too intolerable and which the ego cannot assume; that is why it tries to suppress (*Unterdrückung*) them.

Symbolic representation is a product of a substitution of some primary need, of the desire that is incompatible with the norm, with the law of the super-ego, an entity that judges and forbids the fulfilment of the sexual drive outside certain rules. The symbol is the necessary transaction, the price that the drive must pay in order to exist 'in a way'. But guilty sexuality is a source of anxiety and a cause of persecution on the part of the super-ego. Some authors, Melanie Klein for example, give much more importance to this aspect in the genesis of the symbolic process: the symbol, according to them, is the socialized expression of an intolerable, a-social anxiety.

Erotic, fetishistic attachment to the Gradiva's foot paralyses the sexual drive and the corresponding anxiety in such a way as to 'solidify' feelings that are incompatible with the 'move forward' of desire; but it also represents at the same time a modality of the drive that culminates in a 'petrified' pleasure: the marble of a bas-relief.

At the first stage, love is for Freud a transformation of the libido, a sublimated modification of the sexual drive. Fetishistic erotomania dissociated from love is a displacement, a transposition of the sexual drive and not a transformation of it. The fetish-object (*factitium*) is a concrete reality, a fact (*factum*), invested with sorcery, attachment, and adoration. The fetish, when a foot or shoe, Freud stresses (1910), represents a symbolic 'substitute' for the possessed, lost female phallus.[17]

For Norbert Hanold the Gradiva's foot is the lost phallus, the absence of a *corpus erectus* on the surface of the earth, which turns him into a 'fallen' creature.[18] The worship of the fetishistic object is a rather 'magical' way of regaining strength, the lost erotic energy. Norbert Hanold's fetishistic ego magically desires the object of need and seeks to obtain it and to include it in his delusion-world by appealing to his omnipotence.

Fetishistic passion unleashes a state of war: if one cannot appropriate the object, the object becomes an enemy-beloved: Mars-Gradiva, god of war, which means 'move forward to combat', represents a bellicose state, an amorous struggle.

The fetishistic individual ought not, Ernest Jones declares (1920), to regard his attachment as being sexual.[19] The significant essence of sexuality is corrupted, perverted (a perverse form of sexuality).

Desire in a delusional form detests reality, the everyday factum, and does not want to be aroused. Zoe senses that to arouse Norbert may be risky and painful, that his delusion is full of love and desire. The delusional dream leaves its territory of origin, the dream space, and moves forward to occupy as much space as possible, over different territories . . .

The dream abandons its own space in order to invade and 'colonize' a reality that is outside time. Dream and delusion, says Freud, spring from the same source.

The dream comes from darkness, from the opacity of night; the person who chooses to pursue his dream is deluded: megalomania is a form of delusion and delusional faith a mysticism in action.

The reading of the 'Gradiva' is fascinating on account of its atmosphere and its experiences, which pierce through the reader's mask. Behind the mask of the person, in that very mask that for the subtle observer is already a presence of what it represents, there is a hidden Norbert Hanold, a caged canary trying to get out and express itself: delusion is freedom and the psychotic contents of delusion are, in a latent way, universal. Indeed, the dream is the plastic, literary creation that makes it possible to bring these contents out into the light of day and to shape them.

Jensen is a writer with the soul of a poet; he perceives, grasps, and formulates 'artistically' the 'psychopathology of everyday life'. Passion is fulfilment in the artist and every creative expression that affects us is a small revolution, a striking trans-formation.

Notes

1 A. Breton, *La Clé des Champs*, Paris, 1967.
2 Sigmund Freud, *Delusions and Dreams in Jensen's 'Gradiva'*, Standard Edition, IX, pp. 2–95.
3 Albert Béguin, *L'Ame romantique et le rêve*, Paris, 1929.
4 'To be aware' of something is *sapēre* (to know), *sāpere* (savour), *sapor* (the sense of taste), *sapidus* (prudence) – a whole related series of metaphors of truth.
5 Raimond Lulle has recourse to the image of the tree as an expression of a 'living' whole, whose trunk represents unity in multiplicity: the branches and roots communicate between the earth and the cosmos and with everything that is deep, varied, obscure in life ('Metaphors of the Unconscious', S. Resnik, 'Inconscio', *Enciclopedia Einaudi*, Torino, 1979, VII).
6 One of the phenomena characteristic of the psychosis described by Bion is the tendency in these delusions to protect themselves at a great distance in time and space; the more anxiety-inducing the significant content of the delusional feeling is, the further it is 'transported'.
7 Nosferatu, the 'undead', is the expression, at once human and diabolical, of a being who finds no space either to live in or to die in – S. Resnik, 'Nosferatu ou l'épouvante', *Rivista Bestiario*, no. 2, Rome, 1981.
8 Sigmund Freud, 'Eine Errinnerungstörung auf der Akropolis', *Gesammelte Werke*.
9 For Plato 'reminiscence' is the mythical form of rationalism, whereas for Aristotle it is contrasted with 'memory', which is a spontaneous movement. Reminiscence implies will, intellectual effort, rather than a spontaneous 'involuntary' experience.
10 But not every delusion is psychotic: there is also the poet's creative delusion, which belongs to a metaphysical space.
  The Chilean poet Vincente Huidobro provides a 'lucid' example of this in his 'Manifiestos' (1925): 'When I write "the bird perched on the

rainbow"', he says, 'I am presenting you with a new phenomenon, something you have never seen, that you will never see.' Vincente Huidobro, 'Manifiestos', *La Revue mondiale*, Paris, 1925, p. 36.

11 Sigmund Freud, 'On the Grounds for Detaching a Particular Syndrome from Neurasthenia under the Description "Anxiety Neurosis"', Standard Edition, I, p. 315.

12 Sigmund Freud, 'Further Remarks on the Neuro-Psychoses of Defence', Standard Edition, III, p. 159.

13 'In paranoia, self–reproach is repressed in such a way that it might be described as projection.'

I have kept the quotation in German in the text in order to bring out Freud's curious formulation, which seems here to anticipate the notion of 'projective identification'. *Verdrängt* (repressed) seems indeed to describe phenomenologically the idea of 'projection into an object'. The word *Projektion* had already been used by Freud in a letter to Fliess dated 24 January, 1895.

14 For Melanie Klein excessive idealization is the corollary of an intolerable persecutory situation.

15 Among drug addicts one finds the anti–gravitational, hallucinatory aspiration: an expression of the search for a new space and a new time, 'superior' to reality, which is seen as flat and monotonous, as well as an opening to a sense of omnipotence, which lends wings to desire.

16 S. Resnik, 'A propos de la dépression narcissique', in *Regard, recueil, absence, hommage à Daumezon*, Toulouse, 1980.

17 Sigmund Freud, *Leonardo da Vinci and a Memory of his Childhood*, Standard Edition, IX, p. 252.

18 In my latest work the vertical position of the body corresponds to the internalized paternal image as a structure of the habitat-body – the 'spinal column' – that which enables us, with the 'maternal', containing function of the surface of the body, to trace the corporized image of the 'combined parents'. The theory developed by Melanie Klein is therefore integrated into the Lacanian theory of the structuring function of the body.

19 Ernest Jones, *Psychoanalysis*, London, 1920.

10

Dream, hallucination, and delusion

'To hallucinate in dreams' is for Freud a 'normal', 'physiological' experience. Certain perceptual and ideational experiences, as well as certain modes of dream representation, correspond to a psychotic structure of the world.

From a phenomenological point of view, the signifiers and signifieds are many and various within the complex web that unfolds on the dream stage. Just as what is played out in the course of a theatrical representation has a meaning within significant space, so the actors of the dream drama, the objects and atmosphere of the stage, the development of the work, form a special grammar, proper to dream discourse. The subject of the dream web is expressed through the infinite play of roles and is always articulated according to the point of view of the 'director'.[1] The manifest expression of the dream is a formal, specific way of articulating a theme and its messages that are constituted according to modes that are not those of everyday reality. What is manifest in itself is the content, the text, and the masks: the interpretation of the dream is the reading of a mask, a hermeneutics that interprets, grasps, and contains its unconscious messages.

One of the semiological characteristics of the manifest aspect of the dream in the case of the schizophrenic lies in the very special structure of the dream, in the dream's 'physiognomy', which is often experienced as a strange, sinister, sometimes badly articulated ensemble.

A dream is a complex scenic landscape, made up of several pieces: fragments of houses, bridges, figurative or abstract shapes, which are the expression of a world based on multiplicity, a world that does

135

not respect the conventional rules and is organized 'in its own way', governed by the 'unreality' principle: unreality is merely reality that is different from daytime reality.

The various 'forms of appearance' are sometimes mixed and articulated in an 'incoherent' way, without any 'anatomical' and 'physiological' harmony: the roles overlap and the characters of the dream merge into a single, irregular, asymmetrical, strange mask.

All dreams, according to Freud, have a delusional aspect. This does not mean that all dreams are psychotic. The development of an appropriate, specialized hermeneutics may lead us to differential diagnosis between norm and psychopathological discourse, and enable us to distinguish from a dream point of view neurotic language from psychotic language.

Sometimes the neurotic patient has experiences and dreams of a 'psychotic' kind. This is the expression of an anxiety that does not necessarily indicate a 'psychotic' illness. The dreaming ego (Fink's 'dreaming ego') has all the flexibility given it by its own 'weakness' and fragility, its lack of coherence.

The dissociative aspects of the 'normal' ego correspond, as models, to the classic body–psyche dualism, peculiar to our culture.

Some psychical anxieties move into the body and sometimes hypochondriacal symptoms anticipate a psychotic process. The reading of the dream text has sometimes enabled us, as in the case studied in Chapter 3, to detect certain processes related to still latent disturbances, which were nevertheless slowly finding expression.

At the beginning of the illness, the psychotic often expresses his own fantasies, using his body as an intermediary (how can we forget Schreber, with his hypochondriacal fantasies of a delusional type and his somatic hallucinations – the transformation of his body into a woman's body?).

The 'classical' psychiatrists had already described hypochondriacal phenomena appearing at the beginning of the psychotic process, as anticipations of delusional aspects that had not yet been intellectualized, but which would develop sooner or later.

Freud refers in one of his articles to the importance of the study of the pathology of the imaginary and to the possibility of deepening our understanding of delusional thought and analysing the imaginative function in dreaming. He uses Scherner's terms and speaks of 'dream imagination'.[2]

From the point of view of the archaeology of the dream, it may be said that dreaming and unconscious activity of the imaginary share a common experience: the construction of a primordial, personal language.

Dream thought and the metaphorical thought[3] of the dream are, in phenomenological terms, close to the formal aspects of delusional thought. In his book on dreams and in particular in the chapter on 'The Relation Between Dreams and Mental Diseases' (1899), Freud illustrates this type of connection: in the case of mental illness, the dream is capable of profound and specific modifications, which make it possible to 'diagnose' still latent disturbances.[4]

There were many studies that dealt with the relationship between dream and psychosis before Freud's analytic contribution. One might cite the work of Maury in 1878, Radestock in 1879, Spitta in 1882, Tissié in 1898, as well as De Sanctis in 1896 and 1898, of which Freud also speaks.[5]

As far as the premonitory aspect of the dream is concerned, Hohnbaum, as early as 1830, observed that the first sign of the delusional process may be present in an anguishing, terrifying dream, in a nightmare.

Sante De Sanctis was to develop the same idea: a dream may throw light on latent delusional material.

Some authors, like Allison, speak of 'nocturnal insanity' in the cases of patients who, apparently healthy during the day, begin to hallucinate at night.

The state preceding the act of dreaming is defined, in psychiatry and according to the work of E. B. Leroy, as a 'hypnagogical hallucination' if the dreamer is asleep and as a 'hypnopompic hallucination' if the dreamer is awake.[6]

One may, with Freud, speak of a psychopathology of the dream. Emmanuel Kant, cited by Freud, writes: 'The mental patient is a person who dreams while awake.'[7] This point of view seems to confirm my hypothesis: the problem posed by cases of psychotic disease is not that of knowing 'whether one can dream or not', but rather the fact that 'he can't wake up'.

The dream space of the psychotic, which grows and expands according to a centrifugal force, seizes on external reality; the dream-delusion becomes spatialized and transformed into a 'world system': delusion is a dream that has lost self-control, which leaves its original space to take up new positions in the space of the world.

Megalomania is manifested, therefore, as attempted expansionism on the part of the dream space, at the expense of waking space.

In 1862 Schopenhauer wrote that the dream is a brief madness and madness a long dream.

Many philosophers have studied the relationship between dream and mental illness. Cabanis and Maine de Biran devoted a great deal of time to this subject. This confirms me in my hypothesis: in order

137

to rediscover and penetrate the essential aspects of being *in statu nascendi*, research into the dream and mental illness is of crucial importance.

Man in crisis and the existential crisis of the psychotic are a form, as normal as it is pathological, of self-questioning and questioning of the external world. Fundamental ontological anxiety is present in states of crisis, but the protagonist does not manage to know and to recognize unaided the roots and implications of his own character and drama.

On the basis of such work on delusion, it may be said that the dream of the psychotic is a 'way of living', a way of facing the world and transforming its reality, by proposing a different personal view, invested with pathological narcissism.

The subject realizes his proposition from his ego-centre: pathological narcissism rests not only on a confrontation with the world of others, but also on the occupation of their space and on the assumption of a position within their ideological view, in order to control the space of others, which is invested with a threatening intentionality.

It is in this way that one can speak of 'fantasy' or a desire for 'propaganda'. It might be said that the ideology of delusion, the dream that abandons its 'natural' habitat, its 'domus', the primal scene, wages its own political and religious propaganda. This propaganda is invested with a will to convince (as in the case of delusional conviction), necessary to conquer and persuade the world to accept its 'colonizing' proposition.

In the psychoanalytic experience of the treatment of psychotics, the fact of recounting one's dreams may already be regarded as a positive, important element of communication, possessing the sense of a prognosis.

We shall now examine the case of a young schizophrenic, Karl, 18 years old, who at first sight seemed to have begun his schizophrenic process during puberty. But he himself was to make frequent reference to pre-pubertal experiences in the transformation of 'his world'.

Karl himself traced the beginning of his 'illness' to when he was 13, the year in which he went on holiday with his father and thus found himself for the first time separated from his mother, with whom he had lived in a fusional symbiotic relationship. It was from that time that he began to perceive the reality around him in a 'different' way.

'For example', he recounted, 'one evening during those holidays

138

I went to dine at a restaurant with my father and noticed a woman, who seemed about the same age as my mother, and seemed to be making strange signs to me; I also noticed the strange look in her eye. I was convinced that this woman was making fun of me.'

Since then he observed the same feeling on many occasions: in the street, for example, he constantly had the impression that people were turning round to look at him, because he looked odd and ridiculous. This feeling gradually coincided with his bodily experience: he felt that his body no longer belonged to him, no longer existed; in its place, he thought he had a steel cylinder, which enveloped him and formed a 'second skin', a hard, rigid, armoured skin, which prevented him from communicating with others, but which also served as a protection.

Such an autistic experience of withdrawal and rejection of the world was connected with the change that had occurred in the structure and intentionality of the external world. Karl gradually became the centre of a space invested with strange meanings, directed against his own person: this situation seemed to follow closely the process that Bleuler termed 'relational delusion' (*Beziehungswahn*).

From my point of view, the idea of relation corresponds already to an attempt at opening and an initial abandonment of the autistic defence, a massive projective emergence, in which the inner world of the ego and of the entire self is projected expansively into the environment.

The *Umwelt*, the environment, is inhabited by bodies and objects invested with the subject's unconscious intentionality, which is of a persecutory kind. This is why he needed to possess, control, and transform according to his own point of view: the 'point of view' is as much a way of being of the visual perspective as a latent 'visual ideology' that is materialized in others.

The unconscious process, which Karl experienced as undifferentiated from the conscious, gave him the sense that what surrounded him was absolutely real and had a close link with him. What was lacking was the awareness of this undifferentiated, defensive, massive, and omnipotent projection, with which he invested the world. This poses the problem of identity and otherness, and of the confusion between the One and the Other, being and non-being; the other is now merely a part of oneself, which one cannot distinguish or control. In fact what characterizes the strange object referred to by Bion is its very fragmented projection, invested with great power.

With analytic treatment Karl began to dream, which had not happened to him for a long time, since his view of the world was already strongly invested by an oneiroid precedent. The fact of not dreaming – and therefore of not being able to wake up – preserved his will to power through a delusional spatialization. Furthermore, an exaggerated expansion may be transformed into a 'dispersion', and therefore into a danger to his own identity. That is why Karl needed his steel cylinder: but remaining constantly enclosed triggers off a claustrophobic anxiety. He felt caught in a trap, imprisoned, and isolated, and could see no way out.

To emerge from his own limits, from his armour, was already a fact invested with delusional, oneiroid meaning, which accorded external reality no more than a well-determined meaning: that of obedience to the systematic world of delusion.

The physical sensation that Karl felt most frequently during his illness was one of cold, paralysis, petrification of his whole body – a physical experience coinciding with sensations of cold and pallor. This situation was transformed during the transference, at the time when Karl was in contact with the analyst and with his own dissociated, confused aspects. His face then took on colour and gradually expressed warmth and vitality – concrete manifestations of awakened feelings that had difficulty emerging and expressing themselves. We were confronted by a veritable 'congestion' of feelings that were revealed through the mask, which prefigured the appearance of the secret, the riddle hidden in the icy darkness.

This change that was taking place at the level of the face, with the reappearance of colour, anticipated a new way of being for Karl, a situation that he had to confront in its existential reality.

He began to doubt the 'dominant ideology' that he had constructed: the doubt that he experienced towards his own identity led him to ambiguity, to a 'crisis' in his dogmatic universe. He noticed changes: people in the street no longer looked at him as they had done before, he no longer felt criticized and persecuted, he was no longer the centre of attention, the point at which all eyes converged. He began to feel a person among others, and among others, *in* the spatiality of the world.

The new situation reached the egocentric, narcissistic image that he had created. But he now wanted to become like others; he no longer wanted to feel important and to remain imprisoned behind his iron mask, which defended him from a threatening world, but which also prevented him from having any contact with reality.

Such ambiguity towards change – an uncertainty that was expressed in acceptance or rejection of the deflation of an egocentric view – appeared in Karl's dream as a loss of power, in the form of a depressive process of loss of the most valid personal aspect – delusion is fundamentally auto-centric.

The dream that follows might be regarded as both a summary of this pathological form and as the beginning of its change (the 'turning point').

'I'm in the street', Karl recounts, 'in a car, with people I don't know. The street is called "Avenue of Apparitions". In front of us there is another, smaller car, and I know that there is another "me" in it. I'm also in that other car. The scene outside is a strange one: all along the Avenue of Apparitions I see houses made up of clouds, there is also a Greek temple, with columns, which is made up of smoke and white clouds.'

This is a true surrealist landscape, reminiscent of certain pictures by Magritte, of whom Karl is very fond.

'I feel very anxious in the car', he goes on, 'then I get afraid, because suddenly, just as I am looking at the small car in front of us, in which my double is sitting, I see the road open up and the car disappear, swallowed up. We are all afraid and stop our car. We turn around and flee in the opposite direction. Where the small car disappeared there is now water, blue water.' In his comment on the dream, Karl admitted: 'I was anxious in my dream because I knew that the temple represented my illness, the illness that wants me to believe that I am a god, a god in Olympus. I now realize that the temple I have built had become my tomb and that I could not get out of it, could not get out of that image of myself that I had created.'

Karl's split ego, which had remained, on the one hand, mature and intelligent, invested his own delusion with aspects that reflected a certain education and certain abilities; the non-delusional side, on the other hand, had been pushed aside and impoverished. When the delusion began to be 'deflated', the non-delusional aspect of his self became once again intelligent, imaginative, and cultured.

Speaking to me about his dream, Karl had also said: 'Those images are driving me mad.'

The 'material' chosen – the web of delusion in the dream – is made up of clouds and smoke, gaseous substances with which one can construct a whole world. With smoke one can make shapes, invent landscapes; if the web of delusion is more consistent and co-existing with psychotic omnipotence, one can even give a certain solidity and density to the smoke and clouds.[8] This makes it possible to shape new spaces or to alter pre-existing space. When the psychotic speaks

141

of his delusion from the point of view of space and time, as in our case, it may be that what had been felt as a delusional experience may reappear in the patient's narrative in the form of metaphors.[9]

I wish to stress once again the difference between delusion and metaphor: it is only when the delusional discourse becomes more coherent and less psychotic that it can relearn the use of metaphor and of an appropriate symbolic language.[10]

Karl also told me about the anxiety aroused in him by his fear that this world of smoke and clouds might disperse and vanish. The anxiety that he felt when faced with the possibility of using the 'materiality' of his delusion was expressed in the dream as the acquisition of an internal point of view: he became aware – and it was a painful experience – of the imminent disappearance of his intelligence and his architectonic ability to shape the world of illusion.

This is the phenomenon that I have described as 'narcissistic depression' or 'deflation of delusion'. When one abandons the image of the ideal ego associated with delusion, the sense of what remains of the 'self' is a sense of emptiness, because the ego has not yet recovered its imaginative and cognitive capacity. Faced with his pathological ideal ego, Karl experienced a moment of dis–illusion and began to devalue his delusional creativity.

The small car that was swallowed up in the dream by a 'solid' road, which then liquified, posed a problem of 'construction' for me: why had there been a 'solid' that dissolved and a liquid that was transformed into smoke, into vapour?

The material of which the dream was made up ('We are such stuff as dreams are made on . . . ', cf. Chapter 1) is, in Karl's dream, a dream language made up of smoke and clouds. It is a material that contrasts with iron, the 'metal period' (the 'iron age'!) of which Karl spoke in the first stages of his delusion. Between the solid steel armour and the dream settings modelled in smoke, clouds, and vapour, there is a semantic gradation in the 'being' of the material that makes up a language.

From solid to liquid (the road that is transformed into a stretch of blue water), to smoke, there is a whole series of gradations and modalities of texture. (For the 'tex–ture' of the living experience of body and language, see Resnik, *Personne et psychose*.)

In his article, 'The Statue in Pushkin's Poetic Mythology', Roman Jakobson speaks of the 'cement' of phonetic language and analyses three of Pushkin's poems each of which deals, not with a human being, but with a statue.[11] In each case the adjective defines the material of which the statue is made: (1) The Stone Guest, (2) The

Bronze Horseman (taken from Molière's *Don Juan* and Mozart's *Don Giovanni*), (3) The Fairy Tale of the Golden Cockerel.

Karl explains again:

> 'The small car represented in fact my mechanical aspect, the fleeing, unconscious aspect that travels along the road out of control, unaware of the dangers.'

I pointed out to him that this small car might also represent an aspect of his infantile, magical ego, which still clung to the power of illusion, to which he now no longer attached great importance, which he had ceased to idealize. The infantile ego, when at the mercy of a delusional personality, becomes a danger that merely increases anxiety and disillusion.

In dream, Karl was still trying to oppose change and seemed to prefer to follow his delusion, even if it involved a risk of death.

The delusional personality goes forward with all the certainty and blindness typical of delusional dogmatism: an expression of the deepest conviction of a petrified, monolithic ideology that fears to vanish into smoke and refuses discussion, dialogue, or any change. This fearless, risky way of moving forward brought out not only the negation of the danger, but above all faith in the personal dogma and the challenge issued to a therapy that challenged the delusional conviction.

Karl's faith in his dogma turned out to be an ideological rampart opposed to cure, which was felt as a catastrophe, as a dissolution of the ideal ego, of the temple that had been built up. A problematic of a depressive, narcissistic kind involves for the individual in crisis the need for an existential choice: he must choose between the world of delusion and that of everyday life.

The same problem was posed again in another dream recounted by Karl: there he had to make his choice, not between different materials, but between different spaces.

> In this dream, there was a train made up of an engine and several carriages. Karl was in one of the carriages, with his father and sister. All three of them got out of the carriage and climbed on to the roof. [They were the only passengers.] What they were doing was very dangerous, because the train was moving. All three hesitated: they wondered whether it might be better to get back into the carriage or to jump off the train. The countryside around was arid and lonely looking; Karl felt a feeling of emptiness as he looked at it. Suddenly the train stopped, then moved off again, but backwards, and slowly. This movement backwards dramatized an

attitude towards the present and the future. It was a form of reflection on what had to be done, an interval of time in which to decide whether it would be better to go on, get out into the world, or go back. The three characters each represent a different aspect of Karl: his sister is his feminine ego, which does not always manage to distinguish itself from the masculine ego. . . . Indeed Karl often told how, as children, his sister and he (they were almost the same age), had identical macs (their mutual impermeability) and that sometimes they mixed them up. His father represented an aspect of the super-ego that wanted to take him back to earth, conscious of the risk that such a step involved: he, too, was therefore an aspect of the analyst, *qua* judging social witness.

In the dream, the actors of the scene in the train had to get off, come to a decision: stop (jump off the train) or go back.

During the treatment of a psychotic individual, the most delicate, the most 'crucial' moment is when the patient becomes aware of his own inner space, a space that offers him infinite possibilities, but also appears as threatening and resistant to all domination. The patient wants to get out of himself and make contact with the outside world; but when the delusional, megalomaniac outlook is deflated, he sees himself at the mercy of a persecutory experience.

Melanie Klein stressed that excessive idealization is the corollary of a persecutory situation in which is born the claustrophobic anxiety bound up with one's own body,[12] the body that is represented in dreams by the railway carriage.[13] Furthermore, the external world appears as full of dangers, which means that the patient may also develop an anxiety of an agoraphobic type.[14] The dis-junction requires an existential choice: in the course of treatment there is always a crucial moment when the patient is not at his ease anywhere – either in his world, or in the outside world (claustrophobic and agoraphobic anxiety). At this moment, the relationship with the analyst as real super-ego is essential. Confronted with the paternal transference (the analyst-guide), the relationship with his mother seems to be bound up as much with the analyst's body as with the 'body' of the analytic session (the 'therapeutic space'), that is to say, with the capacity for containing and 'comprehending' the 'terrain' (the analytic field).

To cure means to pass from the terrain of illness, from pathological closedness, to another terrain, which is open and available – the world. Psychoanalysis is a journey into a 'past' that must lead the patient to face the present and the future. But for Karl to 'go out' still meant to take with him and to project his inner landscape: the desert-space of dream dramatized his inner emptiness. To pass from delusion to normality is a painful, difficult 'passage': the outer world seems to be invested with one's inner atmosphere.

There are also autistic aspects, which correspond to a negation of the inner world (negative hallucination), which are added to the projection outwards that appears as an external 'void' – hollows in the real.

In the dream the three characters – Kurt, Karl, and his internal objects – finally jumped off the train. Karl continued his account:

'Once on the ground, we moved forward for a long time without meeting anything. It was only after a long march that we finally came in sight of a house; an abandoned, run down house, full of empty bottles and "corpses" of cars: it was like some kind of "car cemetery".'

I explained to him that he had now 'emerged' from himself and was ready to assume the shape of an inanimate, transparent multiplicity – the bottles. He had preserved his inner disorder and was looking for a 'space' in which he might become a 'person', a living, animated being, a 'being-in-the-world'.

The setting represented a mechanical scene, cold, lifeless: a car cemetery. Karl emerged into the world carrying within him the debris of a chaotic inner world that he had just re-discovered. He was projecting his inner emptiness, 'compartmentalizing' it through the bottles, in order to be able to inhabit the external, unfamiliar reality – *das Unheimlich* – with something familiar – *das Heimlich*, something known, even if it were something depressing, 'his inner landscape'.

Emerging did not make him happy; outside he found once again his inner solitude and emptiness. In the early stages of the treatment, Karl often repeated that he felt himself to be metallic and empty (when his body seemed to him like a 'steel cylinder'). In that space peopled with metallic beings, junk cars, empty bottles, 'corpses', he was merely a 'transparent being', like glass to others; he was empty, without content, accumulative, disordered multiplicity, the expression of a state of inner incoherence. The negative inner hallucination sometimes tried to deny (the autistic defence) this chaotic state, but external reality brought it out, showing it in a wretched, chaotic light, disordered.

The acute psychotic crisis seems to be an experience of a catastrophic kind (K. Goldstein, Bion) and the autistic defence a way of containing this painful situation to the point of effacing it: the body thus becomes an empty, transparent reality, without opacity, deprived of darkness. Karl rediscovered in the glass the corporal experience of transparency (the private made public) and of vacuity. That is why he sometimes needed to 'change his clothes', have his own mask, which would be resistant and opaque, made of steel, in order to be able to exist 'materially' and in a 'consistent' way.

This antinomic comparison, between two different worlds and two contradictory ideologies, activated in dream, represents an attempt to confront diversity as a whole. The inner world, the external world, the oneiroid view of the world, daytime and nocturnal experience are so many varied aspects of the same reality.

What was to be done? What decision should be made? To flee, to abandon the power of delusion, to abandon the capacity that it gave to transform and reshape the world, or accept being different, no longer investing the external world with the elements and principles of a delusional ideology?

The relationship with the world implies a certain degree of investment; nevertheless, what matters most is the 'quantum' and the 'qualitas' of what is projected. And in Karl's case the environment manifested the externalization of an inner climate characterized by chaos and de-realization.

In fact Karl responded to all the problems confronting him with a depressive state, a sense of dis-illusion, the feeling that the world of illness was not a situation that one could easily abandon. Besides, his ideological fidelity was synonymous with death. Indeed delusion seemed to be integrated into his body, like a drug, to which one feels bound because it enables one to imagine and to recreate a Utopian world.

For the drug addict or for the psychotic who experiences his delusion like a drug 'to cure' means to abandon the previous solution: delusion may be a drug, a sometimes hesitant, pathological solution.

After a period of intense analytic work (five sessions a week), some aspects of Karl's view of the world began to be revealed: it was a view that differed from the norm, but which already revealed a reality challenged by analysis. The analysis proposed a change, led Karl to a choice: a 'turning-point'.

In the dream the patient's reality was made up of specific phenomenological elements, representing in a dramatic way the patient's profound dream thoughts: Karl felt devitalized, sometimes metallic, or made of glass or steel, liquid or smoke; a temple inhabited by God himself (the ego ideal), in which the very idealized part of his being (the ideal ego) had taken refuge.

These ontological interrogations into his own corporality, into the matter and texture of the body, of the mind, and of 'things in general' are frequent and typical in schizophrenic patients, at a particular moment in their lives.

From a linguistic point of view, the essential feature lies in the phenomenology of the body, whether motionless or in movement, in its substantiality and consistence. The various possibilities – being iron, wood, liquid, or smoke, pale or luminous – form a substantial and/or chromatic semantics, rich in the 'tangibility' of perceptual experience. The phenomenology of 'corporality', the patient's form and movement are integrated into the production, setting, and dramatization of the dream.

The dream space, the dream stage, is the privileged locus in which the individual's ontological and metaphysical discourse, whether or not he is psychotic, may be 'shown'.

For Karl, assuming the fact that he is no longer God, but a mere adolescent who is finding it difficult to grow up and to find a space of his own (this process, as we have seen, emerged during puberty), involves a confrontation and a narcissistic wound that he finds difficult to accept: this is the process of dis-Utopianization.

Delusions of grandeur and his attachment to an egocentric, pathological ideal deserted Karl, making him resume contact with his childhood world, which had been held back and immobilized in time. His normal childhood ego was seeking help in the desert, seeking something that was still alive, a place in which to be himself, a 'real' relationship. The idea of place corresponds to the 'domus'; it is a maternal space that may give body to his desire, vitality and warmth to his dispersed, lonely, cold reality – this was the 'house' that he was looking for. But he remained disappointed, for where utopia had dwelt he now found only a ruined house, full of corpses, objects that reactivated his internal landscape, giving neither hope, space, time, nor any 'expectations', for there was no project.

Having chosen not to tolerate his crisis of growth and the narcissistic wound of finding himself once more like 'others', Karl built up for himself a delusional world of his own, he paralysed time ('Time – $\alpha\iota\omega\nu$ – is a child'),[15] arrested his growth, and entered into a state of hibernation, a world without movement, devoid of life, but where 'death' was not absolute either. The affective blocking in the catastrophic experience of growth demanded a price that Karl had to pay in order 'not to suffer' to become a metallic being, a robot, a being devoid of vitality, an unintegrated multiplicity, a multitude of 'parts': a car cemetery (multiple personality). The intention of ridding himself of this life as a 'tin man' appeared in a dream: 'ridding oneself' means pouring into the world the elements that make up one's inner landscape. The patient must therefore assume his own world, put himself in question, make a choice.

It might be said that, in the dreams of psychotics, there is 'something' that distinguishes them from the dreams of 'normal' or neurotic people. The psychotic's dream, in analysis, is above all a 'related' dream, and when the psychotic manages to dream it is because he is already on the right path and is able to distinguish between dreaming and waking. It is a difficult path to follow alone. But if it is taken with the analyst, one can understand why the psychotic's dream may seem, in a sense, something like an inversion of roles: whereas the dream usually represents the healthy person's 'physiological delusion', the psychotic's dream appears as an essential ontological reflection, an 'almost mature' representation, a discovery, an important aid in understanding; it is as if the psychotic had a special competence in certain aspects. The delusional system is often very well worked out, according to a strict internal logic. It is sometimes an admirable organization of human logic, intelligence, and even education, adapted to the needs of the delusion; this gives it good publicity, because it should not be forgotten that, in order to colonize others, to act in such a way that they become the receptacle of massive projections, one must be able to convince them. This image of a dream that 'advertises itself' helps us to understand better the ideology of groups that live a 'propaganda psychosis', a psychosis of absolute certainties, refusal of dialogue, and rigid definitions.

Karl's dreams enabled us to state that generally the psychotic's dream, occurring during analytic treatment, is a dream bound up with a first important step on the road to consciousness, one that will challenge a whole *Weltanschauung*, which wanted to be different. The challenge posed to the illness corresponds to a crisis in the world view; this case might be defined as 'an ideology put to the challenge'.

In the 'therapeutic dream', the psychotic becomes critic and self-critic. We find here the phenomenon of self-illusion and of exaggerated idealization of one's own ideas (a phenomenon that is difficult to distinguish from the concept of delusion), which can be observed in groups and certain narcissistically 'nourished' institutions.

Glover explains, on the subject of the training analysis, that often people who seem to be perfectly healthy and normal become trainee psychoanalysts only because they obviously show no symptom.[16] The training analysis is continued on the basis of this prejudice, which is that the candidate's apparent 'health' and possible psychotic nuclei cannot be affected by analysis. The unprepared, ill-prepared, or overly narcissistic therapist will leave an egocentric *Weltanschauung* intact. The awareness of spatializing or expansionist narcissism is experienced as an expropriation of one's own projective position in the world. Projective identification becomes a pathological sign when it occupies too great a space in the world, when daytime and night-time dreams invade everyday reality.

The analyst is a 'person in situation', entirely involved in the encounter with one's 'scientific ideology' and one's ideology of life. 'To be in situation' means to assume a position, a role, an ideological mask that takes care and takes into account others' masks. The problem lies above all in the bipolarity of the transference, for the analyst, like the patient, is put into question: one may even speak of a double transference, rather than of transference and counter-transference.

The existential problematic, man's ontological position, the concept of ideology, of *Weltanschauung* are all related, as phenomena, to a psychotic rather than a neurotic experience. What one might define as a 'normal neurosis' is personified by the neurotic mask, a system of adaptation based on the negation of man's 'normal' psychotic crisis. 'Psychotic truth', or the fundamental ontological discourse, filters through the cracks in the neurotic mask and may break it and bring it to the point of crisis. It would be a mistake in the treatment of 'neurosis' or psychosis to wish to put together again, in such a situation, the fragments of the mask, in order to try to construct a 'normal', effective neurotic mask. It should not be forgotten that our culture requires the presence of important 'obsessional' elements; adaptation requires of us a sense of classification and structuration, a certain emotional blocking, the ability to experience things without going beyond certain limits, and above all the capacity to be 'mistrustful'. The normal 'ideal' person, who believes others and is never mistrustful, is often not efficient. The 'normal world' requires the appropriate neurotic mask in order to conceal – to repress – the fundamental 'truths' of being, whatever arouses anxiety. To be a 'normal' neurotic means to be able to adapt to a pre-existing conception, to possess a psychical apparatus of adaptation appropriate to the situation.

This does not mean that the psychotic is a revolutionary; his reflection and his critique of the everyday world are too invested with omnipotence.

What is important is an open discourse on neurosis and psychosis. What is involved is research into the essence of man, the man who is a 'being in permanent crisis', whose life cycle is built up on crises of growth that are each time 'identity crises'.[17]

In Karl's dream another, alien, dissociated ego began to open up a dialogue with himself and with others, a painful, problematic dialogue in which it was difficult to reach agreement. If the individual is too narcissistic, he will not tolerate being challenged, will accept no disagreement in the course of the dialogue.

We all have an explicit or implicit view of the world; the psychotic wants to know why his neurotic mask is broken and is no longer capable of 'effectively denying' inner reality or of acting in such a way that his conflicts find a solution, according to the systems of adaptation proposed by society.

I would not like what I am saying to be turned into ammunition for the 'anti-psychiatrists'. In *Personne et psychose* I have already stressed that to attempt to justify and idealize psychosis, instead of *understanding* it, is a serious risk, which leads us to transform psychosis into a privileged ideology and the psychotic into a shaman.[18] What I want to do is rather to bring out the authenticity of the psychotic who has been unable to preserve his mask and characterological armour, necessary if he is to be able to 'adapt' without experiencing a crisis each time. The problem that I want to stress is not that of the psychotic, but of man in general, with his existential, ontological problematic.

One cannot understand the problems posed by psychosis, delusion, and dream, without comparing them with the problems of daily reality, 'in the light of day'.

Notes

1 Masud R. Khan, 'La Capacité de rêver', *Nouvelle revue de psychanalyse*, 5, Gallimard, Paris.

   We must distinguish within each patient's inner psychical reality between the process of the dream and the space of the dream, where the dream discourse takes place . . . 'To dream is a capacity', which depends, on the one hand, on a certain inner psychical climate and, on the other, on the fact that certain functions of the ego succeed in using symbolic discourse, the essence of the organization and formation of the dream.

   The notion of the space of the dream arose from consultations with children carried out by Winnicott; the space of the dream is used in the same way as the child uses the transitional space provided by the piece of paper on which he makes his 'squiggles'. The inability to dream leads, according to Masud Khan, to acting out as an attempt to mask the absence of a space in the dream.

2 Standard Edition, V, p. 634.

3 Not to speak of the symbol and to exclude the proto-symbolic, various analogies and metaphors would be to give a semiologically reductive and incomplete image.

4 Sigmund Freud, 'The Relation Between Dreams and Mental Diseases', ch. 1, *The Interpretation of Dreams*, p. 160.

5 L. F. A. Maury, *Le Sommeil et les rêves*, Paris, 1878; P. Radestock, *Schlaf und Traum*, Leipzig, 1879; H. Spitta, *Die Schlaf und Traumzustände der menschlichen Seele*, 1882; P. Tissié, *Les Rêves. Physiologie et pathologie*, Paris, 1898; S. De Sanctis, *I sogni*, Turin, 1896.

6 E. B. Leroy, *Les Visions du demi-sommeil*, Paris, 1933.

7 Emmanuel Kant, *Versuch über die Krankheiten des Kopfes*, Königsberg.

8 I. Matte Blanco, *The Unconscious as Infinite Sets*, London, 1975: 'Finally we arrive at a very interesting aspect of the dream, i.e. that frequently the images appear nebulous and not well delimited. If we suppose that, owing to the separation from the external world, increased consciousness of the internal world reveals phenomena which may be expressed in the comparison with spaces of more than three dimensions, *but which must be represented in terms of three dimensions*, it is not then so surprising that many things are seen as being behind others' (p. 421).

9 In the classic interpretation of the dream – suggests Hanna Segal ('The Function of Dreams', p. 50, in *Do I Dare Disturb the Universe*, Beverly Hills, Calif., 1981) – the dream function is based on the capacity to repress, to work through certain inner problems during the dream, and to symbolize. But in analysis one observes a growing number of patients who do not carry out these various functions in an adequate way – and yet dream all the same. This confirms and stresses the importance of a study of the form and function of the dream, i.e. the architecture of the dream (an interpretation, therefore, of the signifier rather than the signified).

10 In my work on creativity (a series of lectures given at the Fondazione Cini, Venice, 1977), I stressed the difference between metaphorical thinking and the symbolic process. There are two modes of representation: the symbol is more codified and conventional (socially more 'mature'); metaphor is less conventional, more primitive, but more comprehensive and invested with a flexible, creative, ludic content. G. B. Vico declared that the child's first fantasies and thoughts are of a metaphoric nature; it is to this principle that, in our own day, Silvano Arieti has appealed in his observations on the pathological thought of schizophrenics.

11 Roman Jakobson, *Selected Writings*, The Hague, 1962.

12 Melanie Klein, *Contributions to Psycho-Analysis*, London, 1921–45; *Developments in Psycho-Analysis* (Melanie Klein and others), London, 1945–52.

13 Like a 'totality' the train represents a more or less articulated language, a set of meaning-bearing signifiers. The child likes to play with the little train because, like the schizophrenic, he needs rails to direct and control his toy-signifiers.

14 The ontological anxiety *par excellence* seems to be of an agoraphobic nature and the need to return to the womb is a flight from the world, the search for a refuge in the first habitat, and not only a 'prenatal call'.

15 Heraclitus, fragment 52.

16 E. Glover, *Psycho-analysis*, London, 1949.

17 Edmund Husserl, *Die Krisis der europäischen Wissenschaften und die transzendentale Phänomenologie*, The Hague, 1954.

18 Salomon Resnik, *Personne et psychose*, Paris, 1973.

11

The dream cryptology
of psychosis

'In dreams, there is a production of desires and judgements that are manifested in the form of images. . . . The sensibility of the sense organs produces the appearance of images or impressions that are closely linked to other impressions or impulses coming from the brain.'

(P. J. G. Cabanis)[1]

The notion of a 'living machine' defined by Cabanis is a veritable 'dream sociology' formed of images arriving from various parts of the organism, which unite with or oppose sensations coming from outside: the living linguistic expression of the dream, the 'living machine's' mode of being and manifesting *par excellence*.

The perceptual possibilities and capacities seem to increase during dreams: very subtle sensations that pass unperceived during waking and at the conscious level then surface.

The Aristotelian idea of anticipatory premonition might have been suggested by the observation of this particular acuteness of the senses which is also proper to certain stages of delusion, loaded with signs that have not yet found a formulation. The dream acts, therefore, on the 'thinking organ': Cabanis already remarked that the dream is a mode of thought. Associations of ideas formed during waking are reproduced in dreams, translated into dream sequences that the oneiromancers knew must refer to a primitive meaning. The relationship between dream and delusion – and its interpretation – was noticed long ago in the history of psychiatry. Although dreams are not a delusion, their foundation is the same.

Maine de Biran, a contemporary of Cabanis, studied the problem of dreams in relation to the function of the ego and the capacity to think.[2] The alternation of the ideative process and its 'breakdown' suggests the notion of the 'breakdown of thought'. In dreams, the will seems to be 'suspended' and the conscious ego impoverished.[3]

It has been noted that various types of delusions follow the same laws and the same principles that govern the 'dream world'.

The dream process is characterized by the disharmony and discord of the sensations, and these same factors are at the root of what Chaslin defined as 'discordant madness' and which Bleuler called a fundamental element of schizophrenic psychosis.[4]

Maine de Biran decribes certain bodily phenomena bound up with dreams, to which 'popular thought' pays great attention. For example 'popular thought' interprets nightmares as the consequence of an alimentary disorder or abuse, or of the poor functioning of some organ: what is certain is that there is an imbalance in the physiological harmony of the body.

The dream is an 'oneirically articulated' discourse, a succession of events and 'causes', a special kind of mental behaviour, a 'theatrical action', in which the sense of 'beauty' has its place: all production, every social role, belongs to a system of values and implies an ethic.

The dream space of the fear of nightmares becomes persecutory and the only way out is flight into waking. The normal space of the dream, the dream stage, becomes a place of accumulation and disorder, a degrading function of the 'dream act'.

Freud was already able to suggest that the stimuli that produced and provoked the dream may come from the reality of the day before, just as easily as from the various organs of the body during sleep. The popular belief in the influence of the physiological disturbances of the body as stimuli for nightmares has been confirmed by medical experience in the somato-psychical domain. For example it is unquestionable that many disturbances of the gastro-intestinal zone and of the related organs are due to meteorism (accumulated air that may be shaped and 'take on the form' – mask – of various diseases and disturbances, for example 'irritable colon'), as well as phenomena of pressure and compression: the gas becomes the polymorphous actor that dramatizes various fantastic roles made of the same 'material' of which certain day-dreams and dreams themselves are made.

Nightmares, then, would seem to be a way of entrusting once again to the ego the task of leaving the confusional space and the time of the dream in which one has been unable to 'digest' and elaborate oneirically a given situation. This is why the individual wakes up from the nightmare with a start and in a state of 'mental indigestion', in the grip of terror.[5]

Before continuing, it would be useful to distinguish, on a

154

phenomenological and functional basis, the 'capacity to dream' – or the 'appropriate' dream in which the dream ego exercises all its acuteness – from the 'inappropriate' dream that is the nightmare. The inadequacy is manifested as a 'short-circuit', which interrupts the dream and unleashes fear: the dream leaves the stage and the actors are no longer in control of their characters.

During sleep, the individual may perceive things that are 'non-existent' at the conscious level or that exist, but relate to the unconscious imagination: dreams in colour, fantasies, shadows of things known and unknown, monsters,[6] which may be manifested as expressions of the body in a state of spontaneous, 'animal' exaltation and therefore extremely sensitive and receptive. In dream, the capacity for 'archaic' perception is even more acute and subtle and reaches its pain threshold in the nightmare.

Waking allows the individual to take refuge in the 'real' world of waking life and to escape the space in which the body experiences this primitive exaltation and in which the impoverished ego can no longer be controlled. These archaic, violent phenomena, Maine de Biran remarks, are differentiated and separated by each volitional and judgemental function and by each movement of the intellect. He proposes to call this primitive, 'animal' phenomenon 'dream intuition'. He describes intuitive dreams – also called visions – as being the most frequent and dependent on the privileged condition of proximity between the organ of sight and the brain. In the vision-dream, hallucinatory aspects predominate, whereas the other senses – hearing, touch, smell – are less represented from a quantitative point of view. One must distinguish between the archaic dreams and less archaic ones, which are closer, Maine de Biran continues, to the waking state, to the will, and to normal intellectual capacity (hallucination is close to the phenomenon of illusion).

Maine de Biran seems, therefore, to distinguish between different stratified 'layers' in the dream structure, from the deepest to the most superficial. To this topographical view one should add a structural perspective and another that might be called 'tissular' (proper to the 'texture'). The structural perspective corresponds to the association/dissociation, order/disorder, light/dark alternatives, which define, from a qualitative point of view, the form and type of 'visibility' of what is represented and acted out on the dream stage. The tissular perspective expresses a point of view that relates strictly to the 'tissue' or 'stuff', material, web, of which the dream is made.[7]

Maine de Biran stresses that one does not dream throughout the whole duration of sleep; sleep is made up of moments when the dream becomes dramatized, alternating with pauses in which one does not dream: this is reminiscent of the rhythms and pacing of a play.[8]

Another French writer, Philippe Tissié, notes, in an article on the pathology and physiology of dreams (1870), that mental diseases are usually preceded by very anxious dreams, nightmares in other words, which function as an alarm signal of psychosis, as elements that systematically anticipate the psychotic crisis or the 'loss of reason'.[9] The fear of going to sleep may also be a precedent heralding the psychotic crisis; insomnia expresses a fear to meet in dream what anticipates the psychotic crisis. There are, therefore, psychotic aspects that may be diagnosed within the dream. Tissié distinguishes between 'odd' dreams and 'extraordinary' dreams,[10] and gives examples of persecution delusion preceded by nightmares, the persecutory content of which is the same that was later to develop the delusion.

Tissié cites examples from Baillarger concerning delusional hypochondriacal dreams, in which the elements of a hypochondriacal process are manifested first during sleep, in the form of impressions related to the imaginary body, in dreams that have a strange, persecutory meaning.

But I would now like to recount another dream dreamt by young Karl, which may illustrate the relations between waking, dream, and delusion, and help us to understand them better.

'In that crazy dream', Karl relates, 'we are both on a boat, you and I: you are both captain and my analyst, you help me a lot and are very important for me. You're my captain. Then everything changes: you mean nothing to me, you also seem to have grown very small, your body seems "crazy", there are two heads, one head looks very odd, which is in its place, on the neck; and another head is stuck on to the thorax. The boat is now like one of those old caravels at the time of Christopher Columbus. Everything seems to me to be odd and crazy.'

I explain to him that he is thanking me in his dream for feeling better, but that later he turns me into his victim, uses me as a receptacle for his old madness; he is delivered from his 'demons' by making his analyst 'the rubbish dump' in which he will put all his 'garbage': his mad mask. The analyst loses his importance and becomes small, an inferior being, physically odd, dissociated (he has two heads): he represents two points of view, two different ways of thinking, contained in a single body.

'In fact', Karl goes on, 'I recognize in one of the heads the cold, metallic expression I have when I am ill, distant, emotionless. The other head, on the other hand, expresses kindness, it's a magical head, almost supernatural, which seems to be endowed with great power. The two heads have the hair of a 4–year-old child.'

Karl often declared, especially in the early stages of analytic treatment, that he had been ill since the age of 4. 'In depth' research helped him to remember that he had had certain disturbances even when a young child. The scenario of this dramatization is made up of 'past time lived in the present', time spatialized, 'embodied' in his 4–year-old's hair. In this dream we saw a spatio-temporal notion that is related to a very precise point in time – 'when I was 4'. It is quite normal that the time of the dream should appear as space, as a plastic rhythm: in Karl's case, it was a way of recovering his affectivity (experienced time), of overcoming his metallic condition. Confronted by that cold head, devoid of feelings, and therefore of experienced time, Karl was probably trying to recover the period that anticipated this phenomenon of depersonalization, to recover his 'lost time'.

The dissociation between metallic being and plastic, affective being forms a play of opposites, a space, too, between two periods, between the metallic age (which marks the beginning of the psychotic transformation of the inner world) and the plastic or human age (the time of its recovery): the illness is a 4–year-old child. [11]

The retemporalization and rehumanization of metallic time opens up a new perspective, an affective dimension of time: experienced time. Time is expressed in the spatialized elements of the body and the vicissitudes of rhythm in space, in the form of acceleration and slowing down.

An example given by Tissié concerning cyclothymia offers a diagnostic dream containing an acceleration in time into mania and a slowing down into melancholia. What we are dealing with, then, are the formal elements of time: the time of depression is slow, that of mania accelerated. [12]

Again I shall take one of Karl's dreams to illustrate dream rhythms and to explain the form and meaning of dreams in psychosis.

Karl dreamt that he was lying on an operating table in the street, where the traffic was dense.

'It's a quite surrealistic scene', he said. 'The surgeon is a woman, about 35, who looks like my physical training teacher [who is also a woman]. She's getting ready to operate on my brain; she says my illness is due to the absence of an enzyme in the brain.'

The setting of the operation is the street, but beyond the street is the landscape that recurs in all Karl's dreams: a lonely, primitive, ferocious, aggressive, petrified, frightening landscape.[13] But in this scene representing the omnipotent operation, which cures by a single, rapid cut of the surgeon's knife (instantaneous action – a 'cut' in the time sequence), the mental illness, the image of the deserted landscape, is left to one side, at the side of the street. Karl projects the image of his inner world away from that particular traffic (introjective and projective), that links him to the woman–surgeon: at the side of the street Karl 'spatializes' his inner world, petrified in the form of solitude, slow time, and reified depressions.

The young woman surgeon in the dream represents Karl's scientific hypothesis, which proposes as the cause of his illness the lack of an enzyme in the brain. The surgeon has to open up his brain to look for the precise spot, the 'locus' that produces the enzyme. The result of the operation is immediate: the lack disappears.

Karl gives the surgeon the features of his physical training teacher because he admired this woman and because he is himself very interested in physical training and in the somato–psychical aspect of his illness.

Throughout the treatment, Karl proposed various aetio–pathogenic hypotheses, which he had learnt out of books or heard on television programmes, and was constantly opposing his own theories to the 'official' psychoanalytic ones: a challenge and open struggle for the power, the omnipotence of knowledge.

'I heard of a new theory that says that schizophrenia is due to the absence of an enzyme in the brain or to some such disturbance in the brain.'

The enzyme, the essential mediation in the organic metabolism, is an important presence, which facilitates the digestion and adequate assimilation of the indigestible aspects of the 'psyche'. The enzyme, or yeast, confirms its role as a catalyst, 'fermenting' the inner situation (*en* = in, *zume* = yeast).

In fact Karl is using the enzyme theory as a challenge thrown down to psychoanalytic theory. The representation of his physical training teacher, that is to say, of his own physical hypothesis, used in opposition to psychoanalytic theory and ideology, which he regards as too 'abstract', has made itself felt in the narcissistic imagination, which is sufficient unto itself.

In fact it is Karl who operates upon himself; he is at the same time the patient and the surgeon, both signifiers of the transformation of the dream within a narcissistic, autocentric situation of self-cure.[14]

The woman who lends her face to the surgeon and to the physical training teacher appears in another of Karl' dreams; this time she represents a pregnant woman and it is Karl's turn to play the doctor who delivers the baby. The child that is born is very puny and sickly; he seems 'underdeveloped' and has a black skin; it is a baby lacking any vitality.

'One might almost say that it was "stillborn"', Karl adds, 'a little savage that seems to need help and is afraid. I look into his eyes and see an appeal for help for his loneliness, his desert reality.'

In the dream of the boat, Karl felt relieved to be embarking, after pouring into the captain, his analyst, his odd, psychotic aspect. Thus in the birth dream, in which the analyst is personified by the pregnant woman, Karl seems to accept in the end the analytic situation and project into my 'belly' his still sick, wild, primitive, inferior, 'black' infantile ego – an obscure unknown – and becomes himself the 'captain' of the analytic situation. And this is achieved through the process of cure in action, being expressed through a 'fantastic narrative' of transformation and birth, Karl's moment of self-management.

The analyst is present as 'other', in the image of the pregnant woman; it is not, therefore, merely a moment of self-management, but also one of outside management. The analyst is used by Karl as a receptacle of his psychotic aspect, although this is an 'inferior' role in relation to the characters of the captain and doctor.

The non-psychotic side of the dream lies in the failure of the delivery, the failure of psychotic omnipotence; Karl brings into the world an 'underdeveloped', sick, infantile ego, one that needs help, that is to say, treatment; what is important is that he recognizes this. The dream shows that Karl is aware of his illness and is ready to accept help.

Karl has acquired a notion of perspective; he is developing insight, is becoming aware of his inwardness. To see oneself 'in perspective' means, for Freud, to develop the idea of an observing ego that is capable of looking at itself through time and space. It is thanks to this still healthy, preserved side of himself that Karl is able to become aware of his illness and manage to tolerate it (a fact that the psychotic usually rejects).

In another dream Karl sees himself 'as carrying a mask or wearing make-up, with a very different face':

'I looked rather like a criminal – my skin was bronzed and my hair like my mother's. It was as if I could see myself in the same head and what I saw there was a criminal, with my mother's hair; it was an odd mixture. . . . It was an unhealthy, crazy dream.'

We have three characters in one: the mother, the criminal, and Karl. The result is an odd mask lacking all coherence, which he dislikes and which frightens him. Karl connects the criminal appearance to his fear of losing control of himself and doing 'crazy things'. The bronzed skin reminds him of the painting of a boat that he saw in Venice, a city to which the analyst often goes: the boat, then, is, in terms of distance, the place where the object of need and desire, the analyst, is to be found when he is not with him in Paris. The yellowy colour also has a condensed multiple meaning: it represents the odd object that Karl calls 'being crazy'. Bion, in reference to Freud's essay 'Constructions in Analysis' (1937), in which he proposes the idea of a delusion that is equivalent to a construction, in turn defines the 'odd object' as a 'delusional construction'.[15]

The 'odd object' may be fragmented and the pieces projected into the environment form a discordant, surrealistic landscape.

Delusional thought is often experienced by the patient as an intuition – the 'delusional intuition'. Certain aspects of the delusional transference are characterized during the analytical process by the presence of 'odd' objects or thoughts, which are at the service of an intuition that is both psychotic and therapeutic (therapeutic on the part not only of the analyst, but also of the patient).

The development of the transference and counter-transference, psychotic and non-psychotic, depends on the moments of 'empathic encounter' that form so many 'loci of truth', in which the mutual, experienced understanding of the therapeutic experience is concentrated.

Max Scheler speaks of fellow-feeling (*das Mitgefühl*), which would seem to be prior to love and hatred.[16] Communication, understanding, and empathy are integrated into the projective intuition that links one with the other. Intuition (*Einfühlung*) and availability to understanding belong to a cycle of empathy, or inter-availability, which has in itself therapeutic implications.[17]

Karl had a very special relationship with his mother, which was sometimes symbiotic, sometimes fusional and con-fusional. For a long time he came to his consultations with me accompanied by his mother, because he maintained that he had no body of his own, that instead of a body he wore steel armour or his mother's body.[18] Karl was *in* his mother but not *with* her; that is why he felt so alone, a 'deserted thing', which was never really with others, but always isolated, enclosed in an object.

I would now like to recount one more of Karl's dreams: this time he finds himself in a train without compartments, which has a curious undulatory movement. Then the setting changes: Karl finds himself outside the train, in a landscape representing once again the spatialized image of his inner time, his sense of desertion: it is an arid, lifeless, frightening landscape. Suddenly he finds himself on the train, a normal train, this time, with compartments; he is inside a carriage and he has to get out through a hole; for him getting out means abandoning space that belongs to him. He finally gets out of the train and starts looking for a house, a contact, some other person. He finds a house that, this time, is not dilapidated and uninhabited, like the house of the earlier dream; it is on a farm with lots of animals and food. But in this 'open' space, Karl has a sense of fear and abandonment (agoraphobic anxiety); at the same time he wants a place, a 'locus' in which he will be able to 'be' and stay:

> 'I wanted to go into the house', he said, 'but a man, a peasant, called over to me, saying that I couldn't go in, that I had no right. But he then seemed to recognize me as someone important and let me in.'

A delusional element then appeared in the dream:

> 'He let me go in because he recognized me as a "mutant".'[19]

The fantasy of cure is experienced as a new crisis, which means for the psychotic individual a new catastrophe, at the moment of impact between delusion and reality. The loss of delusion brings with it a deep depressive state ('narcissistic depression'), an experience of change during the process of cure, experienced as disaster. The patient understands that cure involves renunciation of delusion, the abandonment of a capacity to transform reality according to the model of the psychotic ideal ego. Narcissistic depression leads to the loss of a highly idealized part of oneself, invested with megalomaniac narcissism that does not tolerate the limits imposed upon it by reality.

The psychotic desire for omnipotence reappears as a modality chosen to be able to bear this 'emergence' into the world and the new possibility of encountering others.

Karl must identify himself with supermen, mutants, and resort once again to the expansionist omnipotence of megalomania, in order to be able to resume contact with his infantile ego, which is looking for a 'house', a place that might give him a personal space, food, and warmth. Karl proves that he has made enormous progress on the way to cure. The necessary condition in his search for others is

161

the existence of a community based on a magical power, a community that he meets in a transitional landscape, half-way between the reality principle of the world and the unreality principle of delusion. The mutants embody the magical transformation of a mental landscape (psychotic world) into another (non-psychotic world). Mutation is a mode of transformation that uses a psychotic semantics in order to get closer to a 'real' language that is able to understand the needs of the infantile ego, which, by accepting diversity, has also assumed solitude and the inadequacies that are proper to it. The mutant represents the idea of change, the discovery of a new world, the transition from one mode of existence to another. The matrix of this change still follows egocentric, mechanistic models, which are struggling against the non-narcissistic, human, syntonic aspects.

The bits of glass, the broken bottles, are the sign of a catastrophic experience, a destructive process, an 'atomic' explosion: to emerge from delusion may arouse a sensation of apocalyptic movement, of an explosive or implosive nature (deflagration and disintegration occurring inside his body). Psychotic narcissism combines with the death drive to demonstrate its 'life' potency.

But, confronted with the 'constructive' tendencies of the 'therapeutic' forces (or acceptance of others), destructive narcissism (Rosenfeld) attacks the 'linking' and the therapeutic product in order to prove its power and capacity to destroy, its demoniac prestige. [20] The attacks made on linking (Bion), the reaction of the death drive in the service of pathological narcissism, are a negative reaction of admiration. [21] Pathological narcissism attacks the object of admiration that challenges its power, its ideal, and arouses its envy: *there is no envy without admiration.*

Melanie Klein analyses the offensive launch by envy against the creative process: the destructive tendencies (which are at the service of the death drive) react against the life drive of the other – represented by the source–object (the therapeutic breast, in analytic experience) and against his own life drive, in alliance with the 'other' in the reparative, constructive process. [22]

Karl's last dream reveals a positive disposition: openness to light, a determination to leave the ideologizing state of delusion and closedness – a parasite in itself or in an object – that is typical of the phenomenon of projective identification ('occupation' of the object).

It is interesting to observe the associations – made by Karl – between the swaying movement of the train and the Russian mountains of Luna Park or the rocking of a cradle. To emerge into the world means, therefore, to abandon the cradle, the cradle that, in the eyes of the psychotic infantile ego, is merely a mechanical multiplicity, made up of more or less linked pieces – the carriages of the train.

To abandon the cradle means to pass from the psychotic, infantile 'zone' to the non-psychotic (neurotic) 'zone'. We are confronted here by a child who wants to grow up and separate himself from his symbiotic mother, to wean himself off his parasitic, infantile attachment.

The little train in Luna Park represents one side of the schizophrenic structure of the world. Like Luna Park, the circus also expresses a seriality or fragmented sequence, a multitude of different, unconnected scenes: the 'yeast', the link, is embodied by the clown, whose job it is to connect one number to another, to give a ludic meaning to existence, as did the fool or minstrel in medieval tradition.

To leave the cradle in order to live in the world is an expression of the risk that the infantile ego must assume in order to assert himself in life with others.

The psychotic's dreams dramatize sharply and profoundly – for the reader and analyst-oneiromancer – the experience of delusion.

In the psychotic dream we meet once again above all phenomena of fragmentation, badly articulated and sometimes highly coloured kaleidoscopic representations, which indeed represent the circus and the carnival.

The material of the dream, the 'stuff' – the texture – of dreams, is both 'intangible' and concrete, like the clouds in Karl's dream: an extremely pliable material, at the service of the omnipotence of the psychotic ego that imposes its will even in dreams.

I would like to stress the use that Karl makes, in his dream, of hair, as a 'time piece'.[23] In the adult, hair is what goes on growing, even after death: a 'space' that grows and changes colour. Karl attacks time, or rather the passage of time, experienced as loss of power and weaning off delusion. To move away from delusion means to lose the madness-mother to which he is very attached. The analyst acts as the personification of the paternal function: the law of the father that separates the child from the mother and structures the precocious Oedipal triangle. Communication can exist only in so far as there is separation.

Freud's theory of dreams is bound up with the loss of his father, with his difficulty in accepting absence and assuming mourning. The reparatory aspect of mourning is based, according to Freud, on reparation, the capacity to re-create: one must know how to give life to new, creative ideas. In order to 'create', Freud must identify with certain maternal pro-creative aspects and thus reconstitute the original triangle.

Freud sees in a dream the hairdresser who told him not to look at a painful reality – the card that bore the words 'close your eyes'; the analytic stage often contains allusions to the hairdresser, which are bound up with the relationship of proximity between thought and hair. Indeed the psychotic tends to abolish the difference and to identify hair and thought, by means of a symbolic or rather proto-symbolic equation. The mental patient has a very intense relationship with his own hair and plays a great deal in front of the mirror with a comb: thus he has the impression of curing himself, of arranging his disordered thoughts.

In order not to see, one must close one's eyes; one can close only one and 'not quite see', smoothing out a painful reality, but one can also, Bion remarks, indeed one must close one's eyes, in order to see or in order to experience certain things that cannot be seen or experienced unless one's eyes are closed.

In the *Bhagavadgita* and the *Upanishads*, the two eyes are compared with the two 'luminaries', the sun and the moon. According to this tradition, the right eye represents the sun, the future; the left eye, the moon and the past. The unitary, synthetic perception of this duality forms a 'third eye', Shiva's frontal eye. If both physical eyes correspond to the sun and the moon, the 'third eye' is an organ of inner vision, the symbol of clear-sightedness, the solar light that illuminates the darkness of the unconscious.[24]

The single eye, devoid of lids, is the symbol (again in Eastern tradition) of divine knowledge. The single, frontal eye or divine vision – also represented by the sun – illuminates and warms the world of darkness.

Confronted by the positivist knowledge of the world, psycho-analysis represents the rediscovery of inner man, the re-establishment of a broken contact. The Freudian observing ego personifies the visual ability necessary to look inwards. Freud shuts his eyes, shuts one eye, reacts in a human way to the pain of his father's loss. He is thus aware of his unconscious guilt in relation to the Oedipus complex and makes 'reparation' for the loss by discovering and elaborating an analytical, dynamic cryptology of the dream world. He shuts his eyes in order to look in the direction of the darkness inhabited by dreams, and will thus open his eyes to the scientific world and indicate the inner path that will lead to self-knowledge, the highway being the interpretation of dreams.

Notes

1 P. J. G. Cabanis, 'Rapport du physique et du moral', 1829, *Oeuvres complètes*, Paris, 1924, vol. 3, p. 153.

2 M. F. F. Maine de Biran, 'Mémoire sur la décomposition de la pensée', Paris, 1824.

3 Freud was later to develop some of these intuitions: indeed one observes an impoverishment of the ego from waking to dreaming, but functions associated with the unconscious ego make up for this.

4 Philippe Chaslin, *Eléments de sémiologie et clinique mentale*, Paris, 1898, p. 829.

5 The author points out that the English word 'nightmare' refers to a mare that flees the space of dream terror and gallops towards the space of waking [translator].

6 'Monster' derives from the Latin verb *monēre*, which means to warn, to judge, to deliver a divine admonition. The word also means a 'marvel': originally, therefore, the word had a positive meaning.

7 In Karl's dream the predominant dream material is smoke, the visible equivalent of the gas contained in the body (meteorism).

8 As one can see, the idea of phases of sleep and periods of dream (the 'REM phase') is already to be found in Maine de Biran.

9 Philippe Tissié, *Les Rêves. Physiologie et pathologie*, Paris, 1898.

10 'Bizarre' means strange, distorted, unexpected; 'extra-ordinary' means 'beyond the ordinary', like the space required to speak of delusion.

11 In 'duration' there is a space, Bergson says, where various moments are arranged simultaneously: the space covered is a movement of time in space. The real time of duration is manifested to the consciousness as representation, a symbolizing image. The inner life is made up of a variety of qualities, a continuity of experiences that occupies space. Various objects and parts of objects are juxtaposed like dramatized concepts. The inner world lives a 'continuity of flow': sometimes multiple states and rhythms that normally tend to be organized. This flow is structured from a historical point of view in order to constitute memory.

12 Binswanger (Ludwig Binswanger, *Being in the World*, London, 1963) made a detailed study of the problem of rhythm in relation to mania and depression. Exaltation (*Verstiegenheit*) is a projection upwards (ex-alto) and the exalted modality of being is contrasted with the being of fall and depression. In exaltation time accelerates, 'flies', becomes like the wind . . . The higher the flight, the longer will be the fall, and the more widely spaced the two rhythms: mania is a 'pressure upwards', depression a

'pressure downwards' (to feel 'flat', to have a 'low morale'). Eccentricity is a strange way of reconstituting pathologically the dysrhythmy of the person in crisis. In schizophrenic eccentricity, different rhythms may co-exist. In the discourse on rhythm, repetition is 'closed' and monotonous (stereotyped) or open and more personal (mannered): both may come together or alternate.

13 The image of the operation, of 'surgical' time, instantaneous and cutting, the image of the street (the rhythm of the traffic), and the image of the desert (a vast, motionless time) represent varied aspects and different rhythms of Karl's dream time.

14 According to the principle of fracture and fragmentation of the object (which may be the subject himself), the schizophrenic always follows an approach of a 'surgical' type. Bion also speaks of the 'cutting' attack that the schizophrenic may make on his own psychical apparatus.

15 Wilfred Bion, *Second Thoughts*, New York, 1967.

16 Max Scheler, *The Nature of Sympathy*, trans. Peter Heath, London, 1954.

17 Therapy, from the Greek θεραπεια. Therapeutic from θείρός (care) and εύτικος, that which is inclined to serve, to treat, to take care of. In classical Greece the 'therapeuts' were those who took care of the god. Various philosophical sects called themselves 'therapeutic': the Pythagorians, the Essene contemplatives, the Hermetics, the 'oneiromancers'. Nevertheless it would seem that originally this attribute was bound up with Moses's disciples.

18 The psychotic's difficulty consists in inhabiting his own body, in recognizing himself as 'anchored'. Hence his tendency to project himself inside other bodies: psychosis is a 'metempsychosis'.

19 The 'mutant' is a character of science fiction. The mutants are the only creatures to have survived an atomic disaster, precisely because of their capacity to mutate.

20 Herbert Rosenfeld, 'On the Psychopathology of Narcissism: a Clinical Approach', 1964, in *Psychotic States*, no. 65, London, 1965.

21 Wilfred Bion, 'Attacks on Linking', ch. 8, in *Second Thoughts*, New York, 1967.

22 Melanie Klein, *Envy and Gratitude*, London, 1957.

23 Karl tells how when he was small he had developed a phobia for watches, being unable to tolerate anything that 'worked', and was driven to smash the glass in order to break it up, to devitalize it. Nor could he bear electric wires, or anything that 'communicated' energy and had learnt to undo wires with formidable skill and speed: 'Electric wires are the body's nerves', said Karl. 'I don't like them because they make different zones communicate with one another and create conflicts.'

24 Plato and St Clement of Alexandria speak of the 'soul's eye'; Plotinus, St Augustine, and St Paul of the 'heart's eye'.

12

Dream and poetry

'The dream is a second life. I have not been able to pierce it without shaking the ivory or horn doors that separate us from the invisible world.'

(Gérard de Nerval, *Aurélia*)

The dream is a mediation, a knowledge of the inner man that is present in all cultures, in which it often acquires the form of language and mythical thought.

Religious rituals represent the dramatized, 'cultural' reflection of a mythical history. The exploration of the dream world is a way of penetrating the mystery of Night, the dark 'belly' that 'brings things to light'. Sleep flees Zeus' anger, says Homer, and takes refuge in the bosom of Night. In Hesiod, Night is the daughter of Chaos and the sister and wife of Erebus, and she gives birth to Day.

In psychoanalytic thought unconscious language reveals what is distant in the phylogenetic history, present and hidden in the darkness that the light of consciousness often fails to reach.

We call 'repressed' whatever, in conscious thought, has been rejected and buried in darkness. The unconscious, that complex entity conceived as a–corporal, 'makes one body' with the conscious-ness, of which indeed it is the foundation. The unconscious never expresses itself alone: it needs the mediation of the body, of gesture, of speech, and of all the 'spontaneous' rituals of everyday life.

From the beginning of the psychoanalytic movement, certain analysts, such as Geza Roheim, Otto Rank, and Theodor Reik, have tried to develop an anthropological, philosophical *spirit of research* around mythical thought and dream thought.

The dream is like a journey into the history of the individual and of the culture; its significant content constitutes a narrative, a more or

167

less coherent and more or less strange message, which the unaided reader often fails to understand. The dream is a present narrative, formulated in terms that, on the one hand, precede the history of the subject (pre-history), and, on the other, are the expression of a present-day language (history) connected with the daytime memory of the day before.

For Freud, to sleep means to relive the childhood of our own origins. For Otto Rank, there are even, in dreams, mnesic traces of pre-natal life.[1]

Each culture has its own myths, its own rituals, its own 'dreams'. Traditionally one entered the world of dreams with the help of a mediator, a shaman, priest, or oneiromancer. Dreams and day-dreams – the oneiroid aspect of life – have always belonged to the 'everyday' life of poets and mystics.

Dilthey remarks:

> 'the Ancients had already observed the kinship between the imagination of the poet and dreams, hallucinations, and visions. . . . Democritus said that one could not conceive of a great poet who was not possessed of a certain divine delusion. Plato declared that it was impossible for the production of the ordinary artistic intelligence ever to equal those of divine madness. . . . Horace called poetic enthusiasm an "amabilis insania". . . . Schiller speaks of the "temporary delusion" to be met with in all original creators. . . . From the great Pinel, France has not only been for a very long time the centre of science, but also that of psychiatric fantasies that may very well be compared with the fantasies of our "philosophers of nature".'[2]

Dilthey speaks of the existence of creative experience, of poetic *Erlebnis* ('*Erlebnis* is an immediate reality'), an intuitive apprehension of an aesthetic experience. *Erlebnis* is a dynamic unity, a realization of time – *Zeiterfühlung* – in the space of existence. 'In our psycho-physical nature', Dilthey goes on, 'we find the relations of an inside and an outside and we transport it everywhere with us.' Transport means transformation in space and time, a metaphorical realization of an original experience.

'What is reality?' asks René Char. 'Without the dislocating energy of poetry, what is it?'[3] Metaphor is transposition, transference of one signification to another signification, a message that goes 'beyond' (*meta*) the space of a nature that carries (*pherein*) an analogical vision that stands out from the original experience. Poetic 'distortion' completes and enriches the original meaning.

The French romantic poets, the Intimist school, the Parnassians, and the Symbolists[4] who preceded the Surrealist movement – Théophile Gautier, Lamartine, Houssaye, Victor Hugo, Gérard de Nerval, Baudelaire, Verlaine, Rimbaud – perceived and realized, through their own characters and their poetic works, the close relationship between dream, day-dream, and reality.

The imaginative, creative capacity is in itself a poetic experience, while the metaphorical, symbolic sense of existence is itself a poetic fact.

The capacity to dream 'with one's eyes open' and the metaphorical dimension of reality personify and integrate the 'dream dimension' of everyday life. Creative fantasy participates in the encounter with nature and with the world of the other. What characterizes the encounter is the *intentionality* of the message, that is to say, the desire to discover and to discover oneself, to find the meaning of existence, to experience the sense of being profoundly struck by something that one has just created, or simply discovered, something that already existed, but which we had never noticed before, or which we had never come across. To say 'I'm surprised, struck, . . . I never saw, felt, noticed that before . . . ' is to make evident the self-evident, to unveil the presence of a world that existed before, but which has only just been revealed to our senses. One may link this phenomenon with a kind of unconscious perceptual selectivity that has a personal as well as a cultural character.

In 'ordinary' culture, 'not seeing' is a projection of habit and corresponds to a cultural negation of what does not conform to a 'routine' or which is supposed 'not to be seen'. Whatever may attract our attention, the aesthetic impact, a new feeling, everything generally speaking that may 'affirm' or 'repress' our usual world, sets our inner experience in motion and arouses anxiety.

Following on from the works of Jentsch,[5] Freud, in his article 'Das Unheimliche' ('The "Uncanny"') of 1919, poses the problem of the supernatural and of everything that departs from the ordinary and natural, which is a source not only of fear, but also of much artistic creation. The word *Heimlich* means 'familiar', as opposed to *Unheimlich*, the 'unfamiliar'. *Das Heimliche* is the space and time of terror.[6]

The marvellous, the sublime, and terror are all elements in 'fantastic art': just as one speaks of a pictorial iconography, one might also speak of a 'dream iconology', a fantastic art of the dream.

Poets, mystics, and creators – including Freud and Einstein – have often drawn their inspiration from metaphors that occurred in their dreams.

The aesthetic sense in Kant is not entirely comprised in the limiting category of the 'beautiful'. German idealism deepened the sense of the sublime and poetic adventure as the attraction and temptation of the occult, of mystery, of the sinister. Thus Rilke, quoted by Heidegger, notes that the beautiful is often the beginning of the terrible.[7]

Man has always been attracted by the unknown, the *Unheimlich*. In classical antiquity the poet and philosopher were those who, when confronted with the unexpected, with mystery, with obscurity, allowed themselves to embark on a spiritual adventure – even if the adventure spells 'danger'. 'Your destiny is to love danger', writes V. Huidobro, 'the danger that is in you and outside you, and to kiss the lips of the abyss, relying on the help of the forces of darkness to bring to ultimate success all your undertakings and your dreams covered with the dew of dawn.'[8]

Poiesis also means 'adventure': poetry is a wandering towards the 'ad-venture', it is an unexpected and unpredictable experience like dreams.[9] The street of the poets is a street of 'true' dreams. Huidobro goes on:

> 'The street of dreams has no trees, nor a woman crucified in a flower, nor a boat passing the pages of the sea. The street of dreams has a huge navel from which the neck of a bottle emerges. Inside the bottle there is a dead bishop. The bishop changes colour whenever the bottle moves.'
>
> (pp. 8 and 9)

The transparency of these poetico–oneiric images discovers a faith that no longer exists, but which is not quite dead: like a kaleidoscope, the movement of metaphors illuminates and gives life and colour to a dead image:

> 'How many things are dead in us. How many dead do we bear within us. What is the point of clinging to our dead? . . . They stop us seeing the idea coming to birth. We are afraid of the new light, the light that is emerging. . . . Iseult, bury all our dead. Think, remember, forget. . . . Take care not to die before your death. . . . Cut off the head of the monster that roars at the gates of the dream. And then let nobody forbid anything . . . then you will understand the signs of night . . . the inventions of silence. The gaze of the dream. The threshold of the abyss. . . . Where, tell me, does that staircase lead that is emerging from your eyes and disappearing into the air?'
>
> (p. 13, v. 8)

The man who questions himself decides to penetrate the secret

170

meanders of the inner world. The 'inner' man confronts himself with the inwardness of the world. The experience of the open is invested with enigmatic intentionality, with an inner 'truth' that is unveiled as metaphor. The inner man confronts himself with the intimacy of nature: the alchemists concern themselves with the 'spirit of metals', just as the astrologers were concerned with the 'spirit of the universe'.

Every poetic revolution is the expression of man's private transformation and therefore of his world. The mythical imagination tends to transform the dark space, in which the riddle dwells, into a figurative, religious, 'numinous' space, in which mythical, theatrical representation is realized *in statu nascendi*.

All experiences that are out of the ordinary, whatever is extraordinary, amazes or frightens us. Hence the need to name, to represent, to symbolize. At the root of every discovery, every creation, there is the need to find a lost or destroyed object. 'For every construction is made out of débris', says Monelle.[10] The loss of the loved object is always the re-presentation of a drama that has already been presented. Analytical work tries to bring to light a sense of absence, helps us to become familiar with darkness, absence, mourning, with everything that comes to us from our secret, hidden dimension, the unconscious.[11] The experience of discovery is a way of unmasking the unknown, of illuminating darkness: an experience that is expressed through the sense of amazement.

The marvellous and the sinister are two aspects of the same complex, contradictory reality: it is only through the presence of the one that one perceives the other. One could hardly discover the origin and cause of our amazement without confronting the unknown, death.

Every discovery is invested with risk and danger. The act of penetrating the unknown has a trans-gressive sense; from the Oedipal point of view, this means facing up to a third party, the one who judges and punishes the transgression, the super-ego. If to penetrate means 'to explore', 'to recreate', the third party, the super-ego, may take up the task and support the search. Thus the hero invokes his god before transgressing the space of adventure.

The alienated artist is driven to creation by the desire to transform the real world, to adapt it to his 'delusional intuition', and to impose his own unreality principle. Thus Gérard de Nerval saw his psychotic crisis as a 'poetic delusion', a moment of extreme lucidity:

'And I don't know why I am using this term, illness, for as far as I myself am concerned I never felt better.'[12]

171

Albert Béguin, who calls Nerval the 'permanent dreamer', speaks of the poet's illness as a 'mode of life . . . that revealed lucidity'.[13]

The duality between the marvellous and the sinister, as the ground of all experience, lies at the heart of the poetic work of Isidore Ducasse, the so-called 'Comte de Lautréamont'.[14]

Enrique Pichon-Rivière pursues and deepens the research begun by Léon Bloy who, in 1887, in his short story 'Le Désespéré' 'reveals' Lautréamont, calling him the 'desperate, devouring, mad poet'.[15] Against such an attack were raised the voices of Jaloux, Breton, Artaud, Soupault, and many others. Pichon-Rivière warns us that 'any research into the life of the Comte de Lautréamont is difficult and risky'.[16] The poet himself has certainly warned his readers:

> 'Timid soul, before penetrating further into such unexplored moorland, direct your heels backwards and not forwards. Heed well what I say: direct your heels backwards and not forwards, like the eyes of a son respectfully turning his eyes away from the august contemplation of his mother's face.'
>
> (*Les Chants de Maldoror*, First Song)[17]

The poet of Maldoror, observes Antonin Artaud, could only have been understood and accepted a hundred years later, 'when the imperious explosions of the poet's ardent heart would have had time to calm'.

It was by means of a morbid poetic game, which posed the relations between life, death, dream, and creation, that Lautréamont created dream metaphors, on the frontier between the marvellous and the sinister: 'There is an umbrella and a sewing machine on a dissection table.' This encounter of paradoxical objects brings together the odd, the moving, and the lugubrious.

The 'true' poet resolves paradoxes, describes, and gives a harmonious meaning to the riddle, assuages contradictions, while respecting the soliloquy of each force of nature and of mind, ever at grips with the reconcilable and the irreconcilable.

The poet tries to doubt and to accept uncertainty in order to be able to penetrate the 'forest of symbols' that is still not yet born. 'Doubt', writes Lautréamont, 'is a homage paid to hope' (*Poésies*, p. 380).

Through uncertainty, open to the marvellous and the sinister, 'creative' doubt 'discovers' new landscapes: 'Descriptions are one meadow, three rhinoceroses, half a catafalque. They may be memory, prophecy') *Poésies*, p. 383).

The space of poetic description is a space of opening to nature: a 'meadow', a plain[18] in which three rhinoceroses, the past, memory, half a catafalque, the present (half life and half death), and the future, prophecy, intersect.[19]

Lautréamont's poetic discourse is the expression of the 'revolutionary' encounter of different tendencies trying to become integrated through a titanic struggle. For André Breton, Isidore Ducasse embodied the future resolution of two apparently contradictory states – dream and reality – into a sort of 'surreality'. What is admirable in the 'fantastic' aspect of surreality, says Breton, is that at a given moment there is no longer any fantastic, only the real.

In Lautréamont, the loss of his mother when he was scarcely 2 years old and the consequent idealization of the absent object are manifested at the crisis of puberty as an attempt to reconcile deep resentment and great love for the 'unreal', the 'other reality': an opening to another register, to another world, the other world – Lautréamont – l'autremonde.[20]

In the melancholic crisis, in the descent into nothingness, into hell, hope consists of being able to rise and find another world, an ideal world re-integrated into nature:

'There, in a copse surrounded with flowers, sleeps the hermaphrodite, in a deep slumber, on the grass, moistened with his tears. The moon has freed its disc from the mass of clouds and is stroking that sweet, youthful face with its pale beams. His features express the most virile energy as well as the grace of a celestial virgin. Nothing seems natural in him, not even the muscles of his body, which work their way through the harmonious contours of feminine forms. He has one arm flexed, the hand resting on his forehead, the hand of the other is held against his breast, as if to hold back the beatings of a heart that refuses all confidences, weighed down by the heavy burden of an eternal secret. Tired of life, and ashamed to walk among creatures who are not like him, despair has overtaken his soul, and he goes off, alone, like the beggar of the valley.'

(Second Song)

In Pausanias' version, Narcissus represents the riddle of the divine hermaphrodite: the beautiful youth who looks at himself in the mirror of the water and completes his own image by going to join his feminine double (his dead twin sister).

In the youth Lautréamont, the feminine double is con-fused with the maternal image, which moves away from the earth and becomes the moon.[21] The moon-mother strokes the youth who, in a moment of nostalgia, tries to recover the object of desire, to reconcile in

173

himself man and woman, to integrate and embody his hermaphrodite identity.[22]

Isidore Ducasse carries inside him an eternally secret burden . . . fatigue and despair, shame at the need to rejoin his primordial image, which he loves in an ambivalent way, work their way through his soul and occupy the space of hope. He tries to react, to recover his courage, and to re-create a new image of the world, another world:

> 'I replace melancholy with courage, doubt with certainty, despair with hope, evil with good, complaints with duty, scepticism with faith, sophisms with a cold calm, and pride with modesty.'
>
> (*Poésies*, I)

To write, to de-scribe, is a way of re-calling, a form of being of the memory that resurfaces.

Lautréamont leaves us his poet's memory, the living trace of a 'true', eternal discourse. As for the poets of his youth, poetry has for him a meaning that is both 'practical' and metaphysical: 'Poetry must have as its aim practical truth', he writes (*Poésies*).

Among the Symbolist and 'oneiric' poets, Gérard de Nerval is a unique example. His work is the fruit of an imagination that moves from illusion to hallucination, to irony, a lucid, tragic, poetic game involving life and death.

'I believe that the human imagination', writes Nerval, 'has invented nothing that is not in this world or in others.'[23] Nerval moves back and forth between waking and dream, between pathological delusion and poetic delusion. He moves towards another reality: 'The dream is a second life' (*Aurélia*).[24] To dream means to venture into an unknown place:

> 'I have not been able to pierce without shuddering those ivory or horn gates that separate us from the invisible world. The first moments of sleep are an image of death; a nebulous numbness seizes our thinking and we cannot determine the precise moment when the I continues the work of existence in another form. It is a subterranean wave that gradually clears and in which the pale, gravely motionless figures that inhabit the world of the shades stand out against darkness and night.[25] Then the picture takes shape, a new clarity illuminates these strange apparitions, setting them in motion; the world of the spirits opens up to us.'
>
> (*Aurélia*)

Nerval plays with the shadow, with his double, with the fantasies, oneiric and real, of his hallucinated and hallucinating world. He plays with his own fear in order to rediscover the poetic metaphor in 'creative delusion'. The poet re-veals and un-veils, makes visible the veiled face, the negative.[26] The sinister is the negative of the marvellous and vice versa: each reveals the other.

One cannot conceive of light without shade, Nerval would say. The veil thrown by shade suggests a light that itself comes from shade.

In the *Odyssey* Homer draws a distinction between prophetic or 'true' dreams, which come from the horn gate, and false dreams, which pass through the ivory gate.[27]

In *Le Surréalisme et le rêve*, Sarane Alexandrian also says: 'Commentators have explained that horn (transparent) represented air and ivory (opaque) earth'.[28] We have come back once again to the dialectic between the transparent and the opaque, light and shade, the marvellous and the sinister – what cannot be named and makes us afraid, *das Unheimliche*.

Aurélia is an inner exploration, a journey in time, an act of faith in the unknown. Freud (1927) speaks of a natural faith that is based precisely on faith in the unknown: the 'mysterium tremendum' bound up with the idea of stupor in face of the invisible immensity.

The melancholy feeling in Nerval corresponds to awareness of a lack, a break, an arrest in his personal history, which he tries to reconstitute and reconcile creatively.

The desire of the love object is expressed as nostalgia, a love and need of the distant star (*sidus*).[29] Distance, which is synonymous with separation, brings pain (*algia*), the sign of desire.

Return (*nostos*) is also a way of recalling desire; *re-cordare* means 'backwards' and 'again', with 'heart', with 'feeling', that is to say, to reconstruct the time of absence, the sense of loss: *nostalgia is a remembrance*. Nerval recalls, re-members, and de-members what pain does not manage to re-member. In Nerval, nostalgia arouses desire, in the sense of a painful verticality that tends to link earth to heaven, darkness with light, the metaphors of night with the metaphors of day – the cord.

Gérard de Nerval was born in Paris in 1808, the son of Marguerite Antoinette Laurent and Etienne Labrunie, first a soldier of the revolution, then a doctor. His mother accompanied her husband on his travels through Austria, Germany, then Russia, while Gérard was entrusted to the care of a maternal uncle, a freethinker, whose library, well-stocked with philosophical and occultist works, was to nourish Gérard's young and already fervent imagination during his childhood years, which he spent in the countryside of the Valois (today the Oise). His mother wrote short letters to him from time to time; one day, the letters stopped coming. . . . His mother died in

Russia when only 25 years old: for Gérard she was an unknown.[30] Later, he was to learn that she resembled the figure of 'Modesty' in an engraving of that name attributed to both Prudhon and Fragonard.

In that world of mourning and solitude, young Gérard found nourishment for his mind and some certainty only with his uncle. Indeed after his return, his father was to remain a distant, cold, inaccessible figure.

Half-dream, half-reality, *Aurélia* is the reactivation of his struggle between life and death. Gérard was inspired by Apuleius, Swedenborg, Dante, and lived his visionary world as a kind of 'Vita Nuova' – a new life, at which, at each moment, images of the past rise up.

Aurélia brings back to life, one after the other, the women whom Gérard has loved and which 'fate' has taken from him, or carried far from him.

'One evening, around midnight, I was crossing the district where my lodgings were situated, when, looking up by chance, I noticed the number of a house lit by a street-lamp. The number was the same as my age. Immediately, as I looked down again, I saw before me a pale-looking woman, with hollow eyes, who seemed to me to have Aurélia's features. I said to myself, "This is a sign of her death or mine!" But, why I know not, I stayed with the second supposition and I was suddenly struck by the idea that this was to take place the following day at the same hour.

That night, I had a dream that confirmed me in this thought. I was wandering through a vast building made up of several rooms, some of which were devoted to study, others to conversation or philosophical discussions. I stopped with interest in one of the first, where I thought I could recognize my old schoolmasters and fellow-pupils. The lessons proceeded on Greek and Latin authors, with that monotonous buzz that seems like a prayer to the goddess Mnemosyne. I moved on into another room where philosophical lectures were taking place. I took part in them for a time, then left to look for my room, which was in a sort of hostelry, with huge staircases, full of busy travellers.

I lost my way several times in the long corridors and, crossing one of the central galleries, I was struck by a strange spectacle. A creature of extraordinary height – whether it was a man or a woman I don't know – was flitting about painfully above the space and seemed to be caught up in thick cloud. For lack of breath and strength, it finally fell in the middle of the dark courtyard, catching and rubbing its wings along the roofs and balusters. I was able to observe it for a moment. It was coloured vermilion and its wings shone with innumerable shifting reflections. It was wearing a long robe, with antique draperies, and looked like Albrecht Dürer's Angel of Melancholy.'

The street, his age (the magic of numbers!), the corpse-like image, Aurélia's face with its 'deep-set' eyes, the reflection of death (and, therefore, his mother), who carries within her and anticipates death, form an articulated sequence made up of various registers of the real. The every-day 'reality' of the district and the illusory, hallucinated image of Aurélia merge with his own death mask, his own 'living history'.[31]

The idea of time appears in the dream as a sequence in space, the spatialization of experienced time: 'I was wandering through a vast building. . . . I thought I could recognize my old schoolmasters and fellow-pupils.' Gérard 'traverses time' in dream, he rediscovers the Greek and Latin authors of his youth in the monotonous atmosphere of a sad memory (Mnemosyne speaks with Monotony). Gérard loses his way in the labyrinth of the dream – 'the long corridors' – and suddenly sees, flying in space, Dürer's Angel of *Melancholy* – a disturbing vision that suddenly awakens him with a start from the dream. The Angel of Melancholy is the condensation of the absent image of his mother, of Aurélia, of an anticipated project of death (he was to die, suffocated, hanged . . .).

The world of falling, of downwards pressure, rises up, takes flight, carrying with it all its multicoloured memories, then falls into the darkness.

Mnemosyne's *humor melancholicus* exerted a profound fascination over Gérard's mind, imbued as it was with the occultist philosophy. According to Frances Yates, Dürer was inspired by Agrippa's work, *De occulta philosophia* rather than by Marsilio Ficino.[32]

The *humor melancholicus* is usually attributed to Saturn: when it catches fire, he becomes fury and mania, upwards pressure.

In his *De occulta philosophia* Agrippa, referring to the Cabbala, speaks of a 'supracelestial', magical, protective world, inhabited by hierarchies of angels and by the mysteries of religion. The Angel of Melancholy, with his wings, represents, for Frances Yates, the combination between magic and Cabbala, loaded with Saturnian allusions and protected by the Angel of Saturn. Dürer's *Melancholy* does not represent simply an inactive, depressive state, a weight hanging over the soul, but also a trans-visionary state, which tries to rise. The Angel of Saturn is a winged spirit that flies like time. Gérard flies off, then falls and seeks help from 'on high':

'In the evening, when the fatal hour seemed to be approaching, I was talking with two friends at the table of a discussion circle, on painting and on music, expounding my ideas on the generation of colours and the meaning of numbers. One of them, who was called Paul, wanted to accompany me to my lodgings, but I told him that I would not be going back. "Where are you going, then?" he asked. *"To the East!"* I replied. And as he accompanied me, I began to look for a star in the sky, which I thought I knew, as if it had some influence over my destiny. Having found it, I went on my way, following the street in the direction from which it was visible, walking so to speak ahead of my destiny, and wanting to see the star right up to the moment when death would strike me. However, arriving at a place where three streets met, I did not want to go further. It seemed to me that my friend was employing superhuman force to make me change my position; he seemed to grow bigger and bigger and take on the features of one of the apostles. I thought I could see the place where we grew up, and the shapes that gave it its urban appearance disappeared – on a hill, surrounded by vast, empty spaces, this scene became the struggle between two Spirits.'

Gérard is seeking a star in the sky: the Angel of Saturn. It is a star that he thinks he knows, one that traces his destination, his destiny: that is why he followed the path indicated by the star. He is looking for the visionary, poetic path where he hopes to find his real, true metaphor.

His torn, divided soul hesitates at the intersection of three directions (three streets) and decides to stop. His friend Paul begins to grow larger and larger, becoming a gigantic, imposing 'apostolic' figure: it is he who must serve him as a guide on earth.

Gérard would like to emerge out of depression and rise up; he 'fixes' his struggle between life and death in the image of that battle between two spirits on the top of a hill. In Gérard, dissociative duality takes on the form of a double aspect of his own being. Between dreaming, waking, and ecstasy, Gérard tries to find his 'true' mask. But there is not only a single mask: several masks are struggling for supremacy, for power.

In the psychotic crisis, the individual's different masks lose all contact with one another;[33] they become separated from one another and being thus loses its unity, its specific, global meaning, and is scattered in the world of struggling multiplicity.

'My friend had left me, seeing that his efforts were useless and no doubt thinking that I was in the grip of some obsession that might subside as I walked. Finding myself alone, I got up with great effort and set out once more in the direction of the star from which I never removed my eyes. As I walked I sang a mysterious hymn, which I thought I had heard in some other existence and which filled me with ineffable joy.'

Gérard is looking for the mask of divinity in the star. One evening he feels transported to the banks of the Rhine, before a sinister rock that stands out in the darkness. He finds a 'welcoming' house and enters; he thinks he can recognize the house of a maternal uncle, a Flemish painter who died a century earlier. An old servant, Marguerite, whom, it seems to him, he had known as a child, welcomes him and invites him to rest before dining. Gérard goes and lies down on a bed and notices on the wall in front of him a 'rustic clock', from which there emerges a bird, which starts to talk to him, as if it were a person.

'And the idea came to me that my ancestor's soul was in that bird. . . . The bird spoke to me about members of my family, who were alive or had died at various times, as if they were existing simultaneously.'

Young Gérard, 'disguised as an adult', is looking among his ancestors for ideal parental figures: in the time of day-dream and dream, several times may exist, co-exist.

The dream delusion is a 'shifting' material: everything around Gérard is constantly undergoing transformation. He sees himself, wandering in the streets of a popular town that is unknown to him. A long series of staircases take him far away from the noise of the city, which reach him like murmuring in that 'delicious oasis'. He looks out across green terraces and 'small gardens arranged on flat spaces': in his dream landscape, Gérard rediscovers his 'flat' feelings, the monotony of *humor melancholicus*, which he seemed to lie in wait for and to cherish:

'those charming beings who were so dear to me, though I did not know them. It was like some primitive, celestial family.'

The star, the celestial body, becomes an earthly paradise in which fear vanishes away. Gérard weeps bitterly at the idea of having to leave that world, which he loved already, and return to earth, to life. His body stiffens, refuses to move, to abandon the star: the poet's delusion.

He emerges from this paralysis, from immobilized time, only to go on dreaming. He sees himself in a room, in a house that he recognizes as that of his ancestor, except that it is bigger. There he meets

179

various women who had belonged to him in his childhood; he remembers their familiar gestures:

> 'The vibrant, melodious voice that I recognized as one that I heard in childhood. . . . I saw myself wearing a small brown jacket. . . . smart, elegant, and impregnated with sweet odours. I felt young again. . . . I found myself in a small park . . . and as the lady who was guiding me walked under those arbors, the shadow of the trellis-work seemed to vary, for my eyes, the shape of her figure and clothes. . . . The lady whom I was following, forming her narrowing waist into a movement that reflected the folds of her shifting taffeta dress, gracefully put her bare arm around the stem of a climbing rose, then she began to grow taller under a bright beam of light, so that gradually the garden took on her shape and the flower beds and trees became the rosettes and festoons of her clothes.'

As the lady became transfigured and disappeared in her own immensity, she also disappeared before Gérard's eyes.

These are again the feminine images of his childhood, which become merged and confused with the images of the recent, experienced past. His mother and Aurélia are no longer one and the same person. The happy vision ends tragically, heralding Aurélia's death.[34]

The landscape of his solitude is invaded by the ideal, fascinating maternal image, which becomes nature, the welcoming landscape, the earth that calls to him, draws him to its bosom.

The size and importance of the absent, idealized love object vanishes when the mother, mother-nature, becomes mother-earth, Ge ('there lay a woman's bust'). Everything returns to its place of origin, to the primordial night out of which everything is born.

Aurélia dies, disappears. Pain and anger are to give Aurélia new life in Gérard's dream, in the form of a clay divinity. Gérard will have to struggle against the 'madmen', who, jealous of his happiness, take pleasure in destroying its image.[35]

Gérard experiences his bivalence before the ideal feminine figure that he loves, and the other who abandons him and drives him mad, aspiring to the destruction of the loved image. The ideal world of illusion is mixed with the monstrousness and distortion of the surrounding landscape:

> 'Huge palm trees, poisonous euphorbias and acanthuses twisted around cactuses; the arid shapes of rocks rising like skeletons.'

Nature reacts to the insane attacks directed at the love object.

The inner disorder merges with the disorder of the natural environment; the inner struggle becomes a struggle in nature, the monstrous creations are transformed into men and women, or wild animals.

To the multiplicity of feelings corresponds a multiplicity of masks: masks of man and masks of nature struggling with one another.

Gérard pursues his tumultuous day-dream in the midst of scenes of bloodshed, orgy, and visionary religious experiences. ('Three of the Elohims had taken refuge on the highest crest of the mountains of Africa.').

The landscape of his dream-delusions often reflects an oriental atmosphere – 'to the East', Gérard repeats (and eastern Europe was where Gérard lost his mother).[36] After the nightmare images, Gérard 'takes flight' to another day-dream:

'Passing in front of a house, I heard a bird talking . . . it reminded me of the one in the vision recounted above and I felt a shudder of ill-omen. A few steps further on I met a friend whom I had not seen for a long time. . . . He wanted to take me to see his estate, and, during that visit, he took me out on to a raised terrace from which a vast horizon opened up. It was sundown. As we descended the steps of a rustic staircase, I stumbled and my chest fell against the corner of a piece of furniture. . . . I fell into the middle of the garden, believing myself struck dead, but wishing, before dying, to catch a last glimpse of the setting sun. . . . I felt happy to die in this way, at that hour, and in the midst of trees, climbing vines, and autumn flowers. . . . However, I only fainted. . . . Fever seized me; remembering how far I had fallen, I remembered that the view that I had admired looked out over a cemetery, the very same in which Aurélia's grave was situated. . . . This gave me the idea of a more precise fatality. . . . I remembered with bitterness the life that I had led since her death, forcing myself, not to forget her, that I never did, but, by indulging in easy affairs of the heart, to outrage her memory. . . . At first I had only confused dreams, mixed up with scenes of bloodshed.'

Gérard rises (*ascensus*) to join his star, then falls (*descensus*) from the staircase, to the pain of depression and punishment. In the bloody nights of his dreams, he sees himself in a threatening, vindictive attitude: the child who lost his mother, the man who lost the woman he loved, grows angry and hurt, and threatens the object of his love. He punishes himself in so far as he believes himself guilty of renouncing the places where Aurélia's body is buried. He reproaches himself for outraging his mother's memory. His fatalism is marked by the itinerary and destination that the internalized object wishes to rejoin. He criticizes himself and punishes himself for not having taken care of the 'place' that links him to the absent object and therefore experiences fall and catastrophe.

Need for the absent object is the basis of the work of mourning, the basis of reconciliation. Gérard feels divided: 'Man is double, I feel two men inside me', he says. And he does not love his double, who is destroying him and effacing the love object.

The staircases, which are such a dominant feature of *Aurélia*, dramatize, in their permanent ascending and descending movement, the oscillation of the world based on verticality. Verticality is the line both of quality and elevation. Horizontality is the line of quantity and surface. The idea of the staircase traces symbolically the earthly relation, two–way communication.[37] Of course, the perspective is not the same: height is the dimension of being seen from outside, depth is the same dimension, seen from inside.

The sense of lacking the love object, which is condensed in the name of Aurélia, becomes the geometric centre of his drama. 'Aurélia was no longer mine!' The loss of the object and the struggle to recover it in memory appear as a titanic, epoch–making struggle, a struggle against time: 'I exist and to conquer it I have all the time that still remains to me to live on the earth.'

To win means to struggle against destiny, against God himself: 'Let us struggle against the fatal spirit, against God himself, with the weapons of tradition and science.'

Gérard would like to reach his ungraspable desire and descend a dark staircase leading him to 'himself', to the angels and monsters that inhabit it: 'I saw craftsmen modelling in clay a huge animal with the shape of a lama, but which seemed to possess large wings.'

Gérard is trying to reconstruct, to repair, in the midst of the elements of earth and sky, the lost, destroyed object. The product is a strange, 'monstrous' object, a reflection of his contradictory, confused feelings.

Art is memory, re-construction of a story, an inner space, a diachronic, 'real' hierarchy: experienced history, experienced time. The result is merely suffering and pain. Nerval crosses the spaces and times of his interrupted history:

'I could make out a few people who were known to me, some alive, others who had died at various times. . . . I arrived in a great hall. . . . In the middle was a sofa shaped like a throne. A few passers-by were sitting on it to test its elasticity. . . . There was talk of marriage and the husband, who, they said, was to arrive to announce the time of the celebrations. . . . I imagined that the man they were waiting for was my double, who was to marry Aurélia, and I caused a scandal, which seemed to throw the people assembled there into consternation. . . . An old man said to me: "But one doesn't behave like that, you're frightening everybody". . . . One of the workmen . . . appeared, holding a long bar, the end of which consisted of a red-hot ball. I wanted to throw myself on him, but the ball, which he pointed at me, still threatened my head. . . . Then I moved back as far as the throne.'

Confronted with the Oedipal triangle, in which his father threatens him with rigidity, he seeks a refuge in the elastic plasticity of his sofa-mother, his 'queen'. 'To the East!' also means, therefore, to find oneself once again as the prince or king who will be able to marry the queen. Dr Labrunie, his father, will always adopt a distant, austere attitude towards him; he never made any attempt to encourage Gérard. In the midst of the battles against his father, against God, a woman's cry, filled with excruciating pain, drags Gérard from his delusional sleep.

Gérard is looking for a way out:

'I opened my window; all was quiet, and the cry was not repeated. I asked people outside – nobody had heard anything. Yet I am still certain that the cry was real and that the air of the living had echoed to it. . . . I had disturbed the harmony of the magical universe. . . . Perhaps I was accursed for wanting to penetrate some fearful mystery and thus offending divine law; I could only expect anger and contempt! The irritated shadows fled, emitting cries and tracing fatal circles in the air, like birds at the approach of a storm.'

The first part of *Aurélia* ends in despair and in the fatality of the ancestral sin, of archaic guilt, of infidelity and bivalence before the love-object.

Gérard confronts his inexorable fate, Judaeo-Christian morality, with the anti-fate of his poetic rebellion. But the 'sin' does not allow him to go beyond the fate of his love object. The anti-fate loses its wings and falls into the arms of a fatal destiny.

'It is now I who must die, and die without hope', says Nerval at the beginning of the second part. He is looking for his father, for God: 'Why, for the first time for so long, am I dreaming of *him*?'

The superior, elevated, idealized image of the father returns to earth, is 'deflated': 'The spirit of the God-Being, reproduced and so

183

to speak reflected on earth, became the common type of human souls'.

Gérard is looking for his father so that he may be able to serve as a mediator between him and his mother, but he doesn't find him; the father-bridge has broken and that means, for Gérard, 'failure'.

He is also seeking Aurélia: he seeks her in the coffer in which lies the last letter she wrote to him . . . He seeks her on the sheet of paper bearing the instructions as to how to find her grave. He seeks her and finds her; he now knows that he must not go to the cemetery, that he must no longer seek her outside himself, in the outer world, but that she is inside him and in the world of the dead.[38]

> 'The hotelier mentioned one of my old friends . . . who had killed himself with a pistol shot. Sleep brought me terrible dreams. . . . I was in some unknown hall, talking with someone from the outside world. . . . There was a very tall mirror behind us. Happening to glance at it, he seemed to me to recognize A.'[39]

It is too late, Gérard tells himself, and he lends his ear to the voices that reply: 'She is lost! . . . The abyss has taken its prey! She is lost for me and for all!'

Gérard does not find in himself the full name of the absent object and he is too late to remedy this, to make 'reparation': 'My fatal dream is merely the reflection of my fatal day! . . . I never knew my mother. . . . The virgin is dead.' Gérard is haunted by death, fatality, suicide; he finds peace nowhere; his world affords neither harmony nor *concord*:

> 'Having reached the Place de la Concorde, my intention was to kill myself. . . . The stars shone in the firmament. . . . They had just gone out, like the candles I had seen in the church. . . . I thought I could see a black sun[40] in the empty sky and a red globe of blood above the Tuileries. . . . I reached the Louvre. . . . Through the rapidly moving, wind-tossed clouds, I saw several moons passing with great speed. I thought the earth had left its orbit and was wandering in the firmament like a ship with a broken mast. . . . For two or three hours I contemplated this disorder and, in the end, I walked in the direction of Les Halles. The peasants were bringing their produce and I said to myself: "How surprised they will be when they see that the night continues".'

After the descent to the abyss, there comes the ascent in grandeur:

> 'That night it seemed to me that I had inside me the soul of Napoleon, who inspired me and commanded me to perform great

things. . . . I arrived at the galleries of the Palais Royal. . . . It seemed to me that everybody was looking at me. . . . I said to myself, "I have committed a crime", but, examining my memory, which I believed to be Napoleon's, I could not discover what it was. . . . I went into a shop to buy a cigar and, as I was leaving, the crowd was so dense. . . . Three of my friends pulled me free. . . . And took me to the Charité asylum. During the night, my delusion increased. . . . The idea came to me that I had become like God. . . .

Nothing is indifferent, nothing powerless in the universe. . . . O Terror! That is the eternal distinction between good and evil. . . . My room is at the end of a corridor occupied, on the one side, by madmen and, on the other, by the servants. . . . There I found what remained of my various fortunes, the confused remnants of furniture that had been dispersed or resold twenty years ago. . . . Panels of wood carving that had come from the demolition of an old house, covered with mythological pictures executed by friends who are now famous, a small picture on copper, in the style of Correggio, representing *Venus and Cupid*. . . . There I found again almost everything that I had possessed at the last. My books, strange accumulations of the science of all times, history, travel, religion, the Caballa, astrology, enough to delight the shades of Pico della Mirandola, of the sage Mencius, and of Nicholas of Cusa – the Tower[41] of Babel in two hundred volumes. I had been left all that! It was enough to make a sage mad. Let us see if there was also enough to make a madman wise.'

Between his delusion of grandeur and his poet's delusion, Nerval tries to reassemble the 'fragments' of his broken soul, to rediscover his Venus – again the image of the ideal woman, of his lost love.

In his con-fusion he tries to distinguish between good and evil, the pure and the impure, the creative and the destructive. He remembers the things that he learnt as a child and youth, the alchemical, hermetic science, everything that is most familiar to him. He remembers his chimeras, his travels to the East, the 'divine Cabbala', which binds the world together.

'One night, I was talking and singing in a sort of ecstasy. One of the domestics in the house came to my cell and took me to a room on the ground floor, where he locked me in. I continued my dream and although I was standing I believed I was shut up in a sort of oriental kiosk. . . . I then thought I was in the middle of a vast charnel-house, in which the history of the world was written, in blood. A huge woman's body was painted opposite me, but the various parts of her body had been slashed as if by a sabre. Other women of various races . . . presented . . . a bloody jumble of limbs and heads, from empresses and queens down to the humblest peasant women. It was the history of all the crimes. . . . "That", I told myself, "is what the power conferred on men has produced. They have more or less destroyed and cut up into a thousand pieces the eternal type of beauty." And, indeed, I saw, on a shadow that slipped through one of the holes in the gate, the descending generation of the races of the future.'

Gérard finds himself once more in his 'oriental kiosk' delusion. World history 'written in blood', the history 'of all crimes', of all the various tendencies that 'cut up' the body of the beloved.

Gérard's story is a story of revolution and blood: he is himself a 'son of the revolution' and bears the marks of a generational destiny. He seeks in himself the truth about his origins. Thus the sight of a doctor putting a rubber pipe into the mouth of a patient who refused to eat left a deep impression on him: he began to conceive of a 'journey' into the human body. Gérard felt friendship towards this patient, who seemed to him to be like the statuary form of a friend-sphynx. The sphynx becomes for him the confessor predestined to listen to the secrets of his soul, which speech would not be able to convey. 'He was the ear of God.'

Gérard continues on his journey from dream to dream:

'That night I had a delicious dream. . . . I was in a tower, which descended so deeply into the earth and rose so high into the sky that it seemed that my entire life would be spent going up and down. My strength was already exhausted and I was about to give up when a side door suddenly opened; a spirit appeared and said to me: "Come, brother! . . . " I don't know why, but it occurred to me that he was called Saturnine. He had the same features as the poor patient, but transfigured and intelligent-looking. We were in a landscape illuminated by the light from the stars. . . . One of the stars that I saw in the sky began to grow larger and the divinity of my dreams appeared to me, smiling, wearing an almost Indian costume, as I had once seen her long ago.'

Gérard sees again in the sphynx his fraternal-paternal double, who will listen to him and be close to him: unlike the indifferent Labrunie-father. In the sphynx he will be able to inscribe his dreams, which he calls, like Swedenborg's work, *Memorabilia*.

They are fragments of dreams, dreams of elevation: he sees himself on the Himalayas, where a small flower is born, which seems to say to him: 'Don't forget me!' It's a forget-me-not, the flower that embodies and represents memory.

The 'good Saturnine' reappears and urges him on in this 'final stage'. 'Adonis' magic horn echoed through the wood. O Death, where is thy victory . . . ?'

The inner and 'outer' struggle takes place in an indefinite space. The dreams leave the vital space of their stage in order to transform the space of the world into a theatre.

In the middle of nightmares and 'sweet dreams' moving between microcosm and macrocosm, Gérard wants to revisit the imagined landscapes of his childhood: Vienna, Russia, the frozen Baltic, the gentle, grey daylight of Norway . . .

His waking dream is a way of piercing the secret of life and death: he lives by dreaming, seeking to know the connection between the two existences, between dreaming and waking.

This is a last attempt to return to the world, to rediscover the coherence and articulation of his tormented soul. He seeks expiation, a solution (Saturnine, the other), in other words, his double. 'I am performing my expiation.'

Aurélia is probably one of the last things he wrote, finished or unfinished, like his own discourse.

Gérard de Nerval inhabits the stage of his last days, wandering through the streets of Paris, from the Concorde to the Châtelet, from the Tour Saint-Jacques to the Fontaine du Palmier, from Notre Dame to the Sainte Chapelle, all so many staging posts on his last itinerary.

On that freezing night he knocks on the doors of everybody he knows, without hope, 'the doors are locked' . . . For some time Gérard had always carried around with him a cord, which he sometimes claimed had been Mme de Maintenon's belt, at others Mme de Longueville's garter . . . Gauthier Ferrière 'describes' the fatal night, linking Nerval to Edgar Allan Poe, to the bird that repeats 'nevermore':[42]

'Then he took the cord out of his pocket. . . . Tied it to the bar of a basement window that he had previously noticed, slipped it round his neck, and, buttoning up his coat, sticking his hat firmly on his head, gently abandoned himself to death. It was exactly at the spot where the Théâtre Sarah-Bernhardt [now the Théâtre de la Ville] now stands.'

It is the final scene of a poet's delusion: Gérard, frozen and stiff, his hat stuck on his head, 'exhibits' his fatal destiny, his exhaustion, his 'nevermore'.

At the morgue were found in his pockets, Ferrière goes on, 'heavily emended rough drafts of *Aurélia, un passeport pour l'Orient*, a visiting card, a letter, two receipts from an asylum, and the two sous kept to pay for his bed.'

'The dream world of *Aurélia*', writes A. Béguin, 'is peopled with symbols of very varied provenance: images of his own life, myths and poems of every period, which had become incorporated into his substance, forming together a sort of submarine world, very close to the surface and ready to rise up at the slightest call.'[43]

'I was determined to transfix the dream and to know its secret. . . . Sleep occupies a third of our lives . . . ; but I have never experienced sleep that gave me rest. After a drowsiness lasting a few minutes, a new life begins, freed of the conditions of time and space, and no doubt like the one that awaits us after death. Who knows whether a link does not exist between these two existences and whether it is not possible for the soul to be bound to it even now. From that moment on, I set about seeking the meaning of my dreams and this anxiety spread over my waking thoughts. I believed that I understood that a link existed between the outer and the inner worlds; that inattention or mental disorder disturbed only the apparent links – and that this explained the strangeness of certain pictures, which are like those grimacing reflections of real objects that move over troubled waters.'

Notes

1 Otto Rank, *The Trauma of Birth*, London, 1929.
2 Dilthey, 'Discours' (1886) in *Le Monde de l'Esprit*, Paris, 1947.
3 René Char, *Les Martineaux*, Paris, 1962, p. 177.
4 P. Martino, *Parnasse et symbolisme*, Paris, 1928.
5 E. Jentsch, 'Zur Psychologie der Unheimlichen' (1906), *Psychiatrisch-neurologische Wochenschrift*, I.
6 'Terror' comes from the Latin verb *terrere*, meaning to make something tremble, to shake, to frighten. Popular tradition tends to connect *terrere* with *terra*, the earth.
7 Rilke, quoted by Heidegger, in *Holzwege*, Frankfurt-am-Main, 1950.
8 Vincente Huidobro, *Tremblement de ciel*, Paris, 1932.
9 'Adventure' comes from the Latin verb *advenire*, composed of 'ad' (to) and 'venire' (to come), of which the future gerundive, *venturus* means 'that which must come', 'that which must happen', 'that which comes to us'. 'Adventure' preserves the significant ambiguity of 'going to meet a time to come' (in the future) and the 'coming upon us' of unexpected and unpredictable space-times.

10 Marcel Schwob, *Le Livre de Monelle*, Paris, 1923.

11 The symbol is a model of absence: representation must 'wean' itself, absent itself from the original source, in order to preserve its own identity.

12 Nerval, *Aurélia*, Paris, 1855, p. 1.

13 Albert Béguin, *Gérard de Nerval*, Paris, 1945.

14 Lautréamont, *Oeuvres complètes*, Paris, 1979.

15 E. Pichon-Rivière, who was my teacher, gave a series of lectures on Lautréamont in 1946 in Buenos Aires. His work on the poet's life in Uruguay and France revealed a great deal about Lautréamont's essential poetic concerns. A wealth of information is also to be found in the work of the brothers Guillot-Munoz on the period spent in Montevideo, in the notes of Aldo Pellegrini to the Spanish version of Lautréamont's works, and in the prefaces by Genonceaux, Raymond de Gourmont, Edmond Jaloux, André Breton, Philippe Soupault, Julien Gracq, Roger Caillois, and Maurice Blanchot, collected in the 1979 edition of Lautréamont's *Oeuvres complètes*. With the studies of Gaston Bachelard and Paul Valéry, I have brought together a body of material that enables us to trace a more complete image of the tormented, adventurous, and profoundly creative life of this original poet. A. Pellegrini suggests the deterministic cycle of the birth of Isidore Ducas, on 4 April, 1846 during the siege of Montevideo by the troops of Rosas, and of his death, which occurred in Paris on 24 November, 1870, during the siege of Paris.

16 Enrique Pichon–Rivière, 'Lautréamont', in *Ailleurs*, 8, 1966.

17 *Les Chants de Maldoror*, which had already appeared in France between 1868 and 1869, but which had passed unnoticed, were published in 1874 by a Belgian publisher, J.-B. Rosez, under a pseudonym, because he feared his readers' reactions. The Belgian poet Ivan Gilkin read Lautréamont and sent several copies of the work to his friends, among others Léon Bloy.

18 The plain is a symbol of earthly space. In the Celtic conception of the world, the plain is a specific designation, it represents 'the other world' (Mag Meld), which means 'plain of pleasures' (Lautréamont = L'autre monde – 'the other world'?).

19 This passage was suggested to me by Carmelo Arden Quin, an abstract poet and writer, with whom I tried to 'read' the picture of these metaphors. For Arden Quin, a surrealist picture is an enigmatic and 'realistic' passage. The essence of realism is sometimes the underside of the real: 'Application to art, or to life, seems to have the effect of concentrating the attention not on the real or the imaginary, but, so to speak, on the "underside of the real"' (A. Breton, *Les Manifestes du surréalisme*, Paris, 1946).

20 André Breton writes: 'Life and death are not a solution, there is

something else' – another register, another dimension, another world
. . . (*Les Manifestes du surréalisme*, Paris, 1946).
21 In Nerval, the star (*Aurélia*, Paris, 1855, p. 362).
22 Pausanias, who is a participant in Plato's *Symposium*, criticizes Phaedrus'
speech, which refers to two types of Aphrodite, the heavenly and the
common:

> 'Love is not single; and that being so the better course would be to
> declare in advance which Love it is that we have to praise. I will try to
> put the matter right by determining first of all which Love ought to be
> our subject, before going on to praise him in such terms as he
> deserves. We all know that Aphrodite is inseparably linked with
> Love. If there were a single Aphrodite there would be a single Love,
> but as there are two Aphrodites, it follows that there must be two
> Loves as well. Now what are the two Aphrodites? . . . There can be
> no doubt of the common nature of the Love which goes with
> common Aphrodite; it is quite random in the effects which it
> produces, and it is this love which the baser sort of men feel. . . . But
> the heavenly Aphrodite to whom the other Love belongs for one
> thing has no female strain in her, but springs entirely from the male.
> . . . Hence those who are inspired by this Love are attracted towards
> the male sex, and value it as being naturally the stronger and more
> intelligent.'

Pausanias' speech is supported by Aristophanes, who speaks of 'double-
being':

> 'The hermaphrodite was a distinct sex in form as well as in name,
> with the characteristics of both male and female. . . . Each human
> being was a whole, with its back and flanks rounded to form a circle;
> it had four hands and an equal number of legs, and two identically
> similar faces upon a circular neck, with one head common to both the
> faces, which were turned in opposite directions. . . . Their strength
> and vigour made them very formidable, and their pride was over-
> weaning; they attacked the gods. . . . At last, after much painful
> thought, Zeus had an idea. "I think", he said, "that I have found a way
> by which we can allow the human race to continue to exist and also to
> put an end to their wickedness by making them weaker. I will cut
> each of them into two . . . " As he bisected each, he bade Apollo turn
> round the face and the half-neck attached to it towards the cut side, so
> that the victim, having the evidence of bisection before his eyes,
> might behave better in future. He also bade [Apollo] heal the wounds.
> . . . Man's original body having been thus cut in two, each half
> yearned for the half from which it had been severed. When they met

190

they threw their arms round one another and embraced, in their
longing to grow together again, and they perished of hunger and
general neglect of their concerns, because they would not do anything
apart.'

(Plato, *The Symposium*, trans. W. Hamilton, Penguin Classics,
Harmondsworth, 1951, pp. 45–7, 59–61)

23 *Aurélia*, Paris, 1855.
24 *Aurélia*, p. 359. Aurélia appeared for the first time in the *Revue de Paris*,
in 1855, the first part in January, the second in February. The first
publication in volume form dates from 1855, published by Gautier and
Houssaye, with the title, 'Le Rêve et la vie'. The work was regarded as
incomplete and the publishers introduced, where Nerval speaks of a
correspondence (pt 2, ch. 6), the 'Lettres à Jenny Colon'. But the
difference in style and the break that it constitutes in *Aurélia* made later
publishers stop this interpolation.
25 A. Béguin, *Gérard de Nerval*, Paris, 1945: 'A man who struggles against
fantasies and wanders in the darkness illuminates his account with an
immaterial light.'
26 Any revelation means 'to un-veil', to 're-veil'; in photography, observes
Ana Taquini-Resnik, the negative is the shadow that must be brought to
light, which must be 'de-veloped'.
27 By this distinction Homer categorizes the elements of the dream and its
intentions.
28 Sarane Alexandrian, *Le Surréalisme et le rêve*, Paris, 1974 p. 19.
29 'Desire' comes from the Latin verb '*de-siderere*', which means 'to cease to
see', 'to note and regret the absence of'. Deriving from *sidus-eris*, 'star',
desiderium originally means 'desire', therefore, but also 'regret'.
30 According to the biography by Gauthier Ferrière (*Gérard de Nerval*,
Paris, 1906), Nerval's mother died in Russia. In *Aurélia* Nerval speaks of
Germany (Silesia) (pt 2, ch. 4, p. 393).
31 Who was Aurélia? Perhaps Jenny Colon, a 'pretty blonde with blue
eyes', a 'star', one of the 'stars' of the Opéra Comique with whom
Gérard fell in love and with whom he had a relationship? Or Aurélia, the
heroine of Hoffmann's *Die Elixiere des Teufels*? The scene between this
Aurélia and Brother Médard is reminiscent of the speech of the double in
Nerval. Perhaps she was the Marchesa Aurelia Pallavicini? Jean
Senelier, in his 'Rébus italiens de G. de Nerval' (*Studi Francesi*, no. 69,
Turin, 1979), says that, during a journey between Genoa and Naples,
Gérard seems to have had a 'significant' meeting with the Marchesa
Aurelia . . . Or, again, the illusion of some nostalgic evening: a woman
met by chance, one magical evening, who reminded him of Jenny Colon
and whom he decided to call 'Aurélia'?

32 Frances A. Yates, *The Occult Philosophy in the Elizabethan Age*, London, 1979.

33 'Mask', in Greek *prosopeion*, comes from the word *prosopon*, which means 'face' and corresponds to the Etruscan *phersu*, meaning a theatrical mask, from which derives the Latin word *persona*. Altheim draws an equivalence between *phersu* and the Greek word *perseus* (and also between 'phersipnai' and 'Persephone'). *Phersu* refers to the bearer of the mask, who officiates during ceremonies. The bearer of the mask mimes and raises the underworld powers, as does Persephone, though the mask of Gorgô (J.-P. Vernant, *L'Autre de l'homme*).

34 Jenny Colon died in Paris on 5 June, 1842.

35 In another version Aurélia is more like an eastern goddess.

36 *Le Voyage en Orient* is a fragmented text, made up of several 'journeys': to Geneva, Monaco, Vienna, the Adriatic, the Cyclades, Cairo, Palestine . . . His father and mother also travelled from Vienna to Russia – to the East.

37 The staircase, the symbol of primordial contact between heaven and earth, exists in various myths and religions: the Talmud of Jerusalem speaks of two staircases, the short staircase of Tyre and the long staircase of Egypt. There is also Jacob's ladder, on which angels rise and descend. In the Old Testament there are three floors in Noah's ark and the steps leading up to Solomon's throne. Raymond Lulle speaks of *ars ascendendi* and *ars descendendi*: the artist goes up and down the staircase of being. Art is 'memory'. In the 'liber descensum et ascensum intellectus', Lulle illustrates a staircase made up of eight steps, representing the hierarchically ordered stages leading from nature to God (Frances A. Yates, *The Art of Memory*, 1966).

38 The 'in him/in the world of the dead' alternative manifests the vicissitudes of the 'place of the dream'. In order to restore the object of lack it must be exhumed, brought back to the light of day, so that it may recover its meaning and place in the subject's memory. The patient who had lost his mother told me that he had dreamt 'of the funeral the wrong way around' – the coffin in which his mother lay was brought from the cemetery to the house, which is experienced as having exhumed, resuscitated, not only the dead body, but also the living part of his being that had remained attached to the lost loved object, and buried with it. Thus Nerval does not manage to reintroject his dead mother and that part of his being that was buried with her; he sets off in search of it, first in delusion, then in death.

39 We do not know why the name of Aurélia is replaced here by her initial. Aurélia is certainly the starting-point of an 'itinerary', a 'historical' search that aspires to complete the name of the loved object.

40 As a child Gérard had heard his uncle say that God is the sun.

41 Jean Senelier ('Rébus italiens de G. de Nerval', *Studi Francesi*, no. 69, Turin, 1979) speaks of a letter from Nerval to Jules Janin dated March 1841, written in the middle of a 'crisis', in which Gérard says: 'The Cav(aliere) G. Nap. della torre Brunya e [Pallazza] "Napoleone della Torre" is a historical character of the eighteenth century, a lord of Milan, Vercelli, and Brescia. Gérard was convinced that there was a link between della Torre and Labrunie, for he knew that a tower did actually exist, which had since disappeared, built on the banks of Lake Maggiore at the time of the descent into Italy of Otto IV, who had among his knights a certain Labrunie . . . Nerval's logic retraces a very special genealogy.'

But there is also the image of Napoleon Bonaparte, with whom Gérard was often inclined to identify (*Aurélia*, p. 400). Napoleon went to Russia and came back defeated . . .

42 Gauthier Ferrière, *Gérard de Nerval*, Paris, 1951, pp. 288–97.

43 Albert Béguin, *Gérard de Nerval*, Paris, 1945, p. 76.

13

Dream, myth, and reality

'Man is the conqueror of chimeras, the novelty of
tomorrow, the regularity with which Chaos groans, the
subject of conciliation.'

(Lautréamont, *Poésies*, II)

The interpretation of dream, myth, and reality leads to the
fundamental ontological problem of being, namely man's position
before the mythical, oneiric, philosophical, and religious 'imaginary',
before 'terrestrial' and 'extra-terrestrial', ordinary and extraordinary,
natural and supernatural reality.

Any religious view of the world involves a distinction between the
sacred and the profane.

For Rudolf Otto the 'sacred' is a composite category, comprising
both rational and irrational elements.[1] The first relate to the need for
an idealized, respected entity, the second to the idea of the
'luminous', of 'that which we can produce ourselves', as Kant would
say.[2]

To speak of 'that which we can produce' introduces the theme of
the intentionality of the unconscious and what it produces in contact
with the sense-perceptible object or in the state of waiting that
precedes and conditions contact: the a priori element. One may speak
of a latent disposition or intuitive sense (*Einfühlung*), linked to the
capacity to perceive and create an ideal reality.

The category of the sacred is revealed through history as need and
system of belief. Natural magic is a ritual symbolic act whose aim is
to reveal or to recreate an event. Magic does not always mean
'believing in the spirits', and it probably precedes this belief.
According to Rudolf Otto it is a 'disturbing force' that itself derives
from a disturbing object.

Das Unheimliche, disturbing strangeness, constitutes a zone of curiosity and mystery that unveils the familiar (*das Heimliche*).

Animist theory, in the 'primitive' that dwells in each of us, is a mode of 'living' representation of an inanimate thing: a way of giving life to death. Death is disturbing and man cannot always control the anxiety that it unleashes.

In the prehistoric culture the hand that drank water discovered a way of bringing together the four 'primary' elements – earth, water, air, and fire – in order to create, as a materialized metaphor, *ceramics* (the symbolic condensation of a need)[3] to contain the irrepressible. Thus the funerary urn might represent the *recipiens* capable of containing emotionally what neither the body nor the mind can tolerate – the idea of death.

The ceramic, the receptacle that contains the water that is necessary for life, is also the place associated with the idea of death, the condition for living.

Funerary rites and the experience of mourning are as old as man and help him to work out the transition from life to non-life, death, the unknown.

Fear is a fundamental ontological and archaic feeling in the history of culture; magical and religious power is a way of reacting to and transforming a terrifying reality.

Whereas idealizing faith is realized to its highest degree in the idea of God, terror has its supreme personification in the devil and the idea of the 'demoniac'.

The 'devils' – friends of the dead in certain cultures – come from the subterranean world . . . The return of the dead arouses terror and introduces the demoniac into everyday life. The importance of the devil is evident at carnival time, when he is personified by the clown (the king's 'fool'), a minor version of the devil, and by certain theatrical 'masks'. In the theatre the devil's mask has been recognized throughout the centuries in the figure of 'Buffalmacco' (the ninth tale of the *Decameron*). The demoniac also inhabits the characters of the *commedia dell'arte*, Harlequin, Zanni (the 'zany' Merry-Andrew), and Punch. The mask of Harlequin has, apart from its demoniac origin, a shamanic character.

Between the space of terror, disturbing strangeness, and sacred space, there are various registers, among which the 'grotesque' is a ludic way of integrating the demoniac and the comic.

The ludic sense of life, which is related to the idea of festival and of representation, and therefore to the theatre, is creative expression *par excellence* (*ludus*);[4] the child that dwells inside each adult creates as he plays, by 're-creating' himself . . .

To penetrate the domain of the sacred means to move away from the profane and vice versa. In rituals involving the pure and the impure, the sacred and the profane, what one tries to avoid is contamination.

The notion of the 'mythologeme', formulated by Kerényi, corresponds to the cultural need to transform and categorize the unknown, to give a form to and to shape the ungraspable.[5]

The morphological formation of the mythological table is pictorial and tends to bring to the surface what is hidden and what arouses fear. Mythology is not a mere form of expression: it also changes with time and the systems of cultural values.

Mythology speaks, sings, dances, and represents itself as ritual and theatrical space.

The symbolic aspect of myth is related to the need to represent what is primordial and fundamental, *archè*.

The ludic foundation of mythical thought is present in every system of beliefs and is manifested, according to Kerényi, through the image of the 'divine child': the firstborn of the primitive period, in whom the idea of origin is present for the first time.

The dream, like myth and like whatever in 'reality' embodies the idea of an unfamiliar (*unheimlich*) space, is materialized as *mysterium tremendum*.

The element of *tremendum* or terror belongs to the mystical sense, in which absolute belief occupies the space of fear.

From the primitive human soul, questioning itself as to its origins, emerges, according to Rudolf Otto, the sense of the sinister, the sense of terror, which precedes the historical development of religion.

The origin of devils and gods, whatever is mythological apperception (cultural imaginary), constitutes a mode of materialization and objectification of these feelings.

The sense of terror is not a natural, ordinary fear, but a particular 'perception' of the supernatural and the sinister.

The interpretation of dreams is a way of transgressing and penetrating the world of devils and gods that dwells within us; it is also a way of confronting what is usually veiled and forbidden.

The path taken by the oneiromancer is, like that taken by the poet, a mysterious labyrinth that leads to the idea of the sacred and to respect for the unknown and for divine space. The supernatural, which is involved in the notion of the divine, must not alienate the natural world.

For Baudelaire, myth cannot 'live' and spread its 'luminosity' if it

196

does not keep close contact with the repertoire of nature, a repertoire that can be handled only by 'a winged, magical hand'.[6]

To separate man from nature, mind from body, means to 'de-nature' the *person*, to depreciate the idea of the world. André Breton writes in 'Les Vases Communicants' that one must cease arbitrarily setting dream in opposition to reality. The poet is a revolutionary, he says, who comes up against and opposes the divorce between the two realities. The poet's ambition, then, is to form an indestructible knot between the two, to create and re-create an 'imaginary of nature'.

The link between dream reality and everyday reality, 'living in the world', involves transformation, ludic activity, and symbolic communication.[7]

Metaphor is a link between the reality of the imaginary and the earthly reality of nature. Poetic reality is a metaphorical recreation of an inter-subjective discourse that reveals the dialogue between the different 'zones' of the real.

The world offers man a 'forest of symbols', says Baudelaire, or of omens, which he must discover and decipher.

Leonardo da Vinci, following Botticelli's example, in his lessons on artistic expression, advised his pupils to look hard and long at some old wall: to observe it until such time as they managed to see in it a completely sketched picture.

Encounter with things and of people with one another depends a great deal on the 'quality' of the encounter: the world of objects is full of 'possibilities', of revelations to be discovered. The mystique of encounter in surrealism – which continues the discourse of the Symbolists – involves, according to Alexandrian,[8] a philosophy of the found object.[9]

The discourse on the 'found object' and its representation is situated between man and nature, between subject and object.

Between presentation and representation unfolds the space-time of the confrontation and confusion between imaginary, real, and reality.

'A representation [*Vorstellung*]', writes Ludwig Wittgenstein, 'is not a mere image, but an image may speak for it.'[10]

Representation is a new presentation of the object, which thus becomes a plastic re-presentation. Moreover, the phenomenon of representation (*Vorstellung*) poses the problem of intersubjectivity, of the relationship between the inner and the outer world, between two stages, and between a stage and its spectator: such a distinction should not be taken as a clear, absolute separation between 'inner' and 'outer'.

Contiguity, ambiguity, and difference are articulated in a discourse that proposes for discussion the theme of encounter, identity, and the otherness of all experience.[11] There is a syncretic, undifferentiated reality, an ambiguous space and time, in which opposites confront one another and are then con-fused: light and darkness, revelation and mystery.

In Hesiod the primal chaos came to light following an established order, through Night (*Nux*). The 'director' (in the theatrical sense) – Heraclitus' *Logos* and Anaxagoras' *Nous* – is potentially present in that original mixture called Chaos. The transition from disorder to order finds its necessary mediation on the mythical stage, in the dramatization of darkness, the personification of the riddle, organizing itself in space and mythical thought and ritual.

In the mythical world, according to Ernst Cassirer, each phenomenon represents a personification, often the personification of a basic language.[12] Mythical discourse is the shadow of a proto-language reflected in thoughts. Mythology, Cassirer goes on, represents the power exercised by language over thought in every sphere of mental activity.

For Max Müller, who is cited by Cassirer, the mythical world is essentially a world of illusions. This implies a relationship between an illusory world and oneiric hallucination: the perception of the imaginary in dream is of a hallucinatory type. The power of myth, and that of the dream, consists in their capacity to metaphorize and 'reinvent' ordinary reality. Cassirer speaks of 'metaphoric thought' as a fundamental element in the origin of the construction of language . . . The 'physicality' of language and myth, he writes, must be taken in the sense of its intensity, not in that of extension.[13]

Mythical discourse is articulated like rhythm in space, time on the stage, and finds a particular expression in religious space.

According to J.-P. Vernant, religious space in Greek culture is distinguished from mythical space and organized according to a reversible hierarchy of a geometric type.[14] From a 'historic' point of view, memory and time are spatialized in order to constitute an 'image', a more or less categorical hypothesis concerning the supernatural, the unknown. The supernatural world is confronted with the natural world through the imaginary, 'natural' space in which *poiesis* finds its source.

The distinction between mythical, metaphorico-poetic, and symbolic thought opens up a space between subjectivity and objectivity, leads the subject to face the object, man to face nature, the theatre to face life, according to an exchange that is in each case a particular reality, a well-determined, imaginary structure.

Subjectivism, objectivism, materialism, idealism, pragmatism – every 'ism' that organizes the social – form points of view that are ideologically distinguished in terms of the dramatization of being-in-the-world:[15] each ideology is a distinct or differentiated scenic proposition that is defined by its articulation, its 'production'.

The idea of perspective is bound up with the discovery of distance and mediation; Dürer speaks of perspective (*perspicere*) as 'looking through'.

Perspective offers itself as language and develops as science and as con-sciousness, with the aim of representing the object, according to the differences that distance, proximity, and the various positions of the observer create. From the point of view of geometry, it is a method of projecting bodies in which all the lines of projection converge at a single point: the observer's eye.[16] The 'written' 'observer's eye' interprets the 'affective tonality' of his own look, according to its form and colour.

The works of Euclid and Vitruvius prove that the Ancients were familiar with a particular form of perspective, that known as 'linear' perspective (the frescoes of Pompei and Herculaneum). The theories on perspective, applied and developed by Paolo Uccello, Piero della Francesca, and Mantegna, reached their scientific maturity with Brunelleschi, Leonardo da Vinci, and Alberti.

The painters distinguish between 'linear' perspective (lines consti-tuting the 'profile' of the object that is presented to our eyes) and 'aerial' perspective (the degree of light reflected by the objects towards the observer).

The idea of perspective – 'scenography', for the Greeks – is fundamental in painting. In his *Treatise* Leonardo stresses its importance in being able to know the dimensions of things. The choice of distance corresponds to the observer's 'point of view', which indicates the position of the subject in relation to the object observed.

Alberti's studies during the Renaissance and Panovsky's in our own time complete the notion of perspective as symbolic form.

The notions of the observer's position and point of view, of the 'observing ego', are very useful in understanding the difference between internal and external projection. Moreover, one may speak of 'position' without introducing the idea of *situation* and of *relation*: perspective is the relational model of a 'looked at-looking' being.[17] What demonstrates its specificity and its destiny in perspectival space is the intentionality of the eye-being. The discovery of perspectival space is a reference point on which one may judge and situate the 'ob' of the object and the 'sub' of the subject. The categorization of space

199

is completed in the idea of 'rhythm': eurythmy seems to be the expression of a harmonious metric movement, 'good rhythm'. It is through rhythm that the movement from Chaos to order occurs: 'In the beginning was rhythm', says Hans von Bülow.[18] The notion of space corresponds to the discovery and experience of a 'rhythmic opening' between the subject and object in the world (the space of the world) or between the subject and internal object (the inner world).

The discourse between 'inner' and 'outer' embodies the idea of a system of exchange and 'commerce', of a 'negotiation' between inner man and the external world (the set of objects that make the world what it is). The reality of the one is conditioned by the reality of the other, which creates a more or less harmonious relation of reciprocity.

Spatial experience is a matter of point of view and rhythm, and therefore of time. The knowledge of being in the world is expressed through the modality of positions, rhythm, and the perspectival look in relation to the object observed. The discovery of the world is also a discovery of one's own world: to arrive at inter-subjectivity and intra-subjectivity, the individual must wean himself off his syncretic, fusional, and symbolic tendencies.[19]

The account of a dream already involves a differentiation, the awakening of an oneiroid view of the world towards a spatializing, creative facticity of the everyday. This corresponds to the movement between dream thought, metaphoric thought, and 'everyday' myth.

Antonin Artaud was the first to perceive the surrealist adventure as a mysticism of the everyday (1925).[20] The mythical and mystical aspect has a poetic signification in both Artaud and Breton, and becomes an unpredictable dialogue with chance. The dream is important for Breton, not for what it 'says', but for the parts that are effaced on waking. We should try to find out, says Breton, whether all the dreams of a life do not form part of an activity articulated in time, an expression of its integration in life.[21]

The role of the dream, therefore, seems to be dynamic in the truest sense, involving a contradiction that brings life and movement into existence.

Dream thought must be differentiated from mythical and metaphorical thought, just as the divine delusion of the Ancients must be distinguished from the 'normal' delusion of the poets (Vincente Huidobro) and from delusional thought. There is no reality that is absolute: there are only different ways of conceiving reality, and degrees of transformation and 'distortion' of the real. 'Each period in human thought might be defined', says Albert Béguin, 'on the basis of the relations that it establishes between the dream and life.'[22]

Baudelaire writes: 'A room that resembles a day-dream, a truly spiritual room, in which the stagnant atmosphere is slightly tinged with pink and blue. There the soul takes a lazy bath, perfumed with regret and desire. There is something crepuscular, bluish and pinkish about it; a dream of voluptuousness during an eclipse.'

The dream – Baudelaire's day-dream – has its 'room', its space, and its landscape, its dimensions and its atmosphere, its own cultural myths. The atmosphere of the world, the *Umwelt*, daytime memory, is an inter-prestation continuous with the interiority of one's being, which lives, creates, and dreams. It is its way of seeing the world, its sensory intention, the 'colour' of its gaze. Each individual, community, or society possesses its own 'mythical atmosphere', its breathing space, its habitat.

The atmospheric cosmos of experience acquires its own limits (*peras*, in Greek) and constitutes a personal space, a 'room', a landscape in itself, a window . . . The landscape is 'tinged and perfumed' by desire, frustration, and fear.

To observe a landscape is a way of thinking, a way of 'constructing a space', a place to 'live in', to think in: a temple (*temenos*, in Greek). One of the first intuitive feelings of every religion rests on the idea of the sacred, the space that cannot be transgressed. God speaks through the mask of man, but man speaks through the mask of God and says: 'I, the person, am sacred.' Man's body is a temple (templum): a 'templum' is a space cut off, demarcated by the augur, in the heavens and on earth. In terms of a living body, to delimit and to preserve boundaries means to assume one's own precinct. The verb *contemplor* links two outlooks at the same time: the inner and the outer world.

In the domain of psychoanalysis, a cultural question is posed with the situation of perpetual exchange between two worlds: the world of the patient and that of the analyst – in which each recognizes himself in the other, as a constituent part of a sense-perceptible whole, in which, between darkness and light, heat and cold, 'healthy' and 'sick', is placed the 'datum' of the containing atmosphere – is produced and produces in turn the modality of encounter. Between day and night appears the problem of the identity of the mask, of the style of the face, of the open or shut eyes. The dream atmosphere and the *style* of the dream might also be typical of each of us. Gérard de Nerval has his own poet's style to dream and practise delusion, to live and to die.

For psychotics, dreaming represents a personal cultural experience: delusions are specific myths in dreams. This book would like to throw light on certain signs characteristic of the psychotic dream: to dream or to be aware of dreaming is already, for the psychotic, the sign of a development, of progress. This reveals the capacity to distinguish between the *objectum* and the *subjectum*, between waking and dreaming, a situation that anticipates the spoken thoughts of waking.

In the chapter on Jensen's 'Gradiva', I analysed day-dream and dreaming in relation to immediate or mediate reality: the setting of the dream in the 'Gradiva', its architecture, the aerial perspectives, the light, and the atmosphere form a sort of Mannerist allegory, in which the position of the characters and their different visual points of view form the complexity of the scenes, the strength and impact on the reader-spectator.

To be aware of the degree of interiority and exteriority in relation to the dream space leads us to wonder: 'Is it I who am dreaming? Where am I? Where am I dreaming?' I have become the theatre in which inexplicable, strange scenes are taking place.

The ambiguous space between waking and dreaming is the preferred place of the poets: Heine, Hoffmann, Rimbaud, Nerval seek to unveil, and therefore to reveal, poetically, nature's metaphorical substantiality. The artist's 'inner' adventure takes place in the space that both separates and unites sleep and waking: to be outside also means to be inside, in the world. In the language used by Rilke, the open (*das Offene*) means 'that which does not impede' – does not impede, because it does not limit. Heidegger maintains that there is always an obstacle, a limit, that is repressed and brought back to life.[23] The limit impedes and creates a reflected relationship: 'The Open gives entry'.

The dream, intermediary between sleep and waking, is the expression, according to Aristotle, of the first movements of the mind and one may find traces of it in the sense organs. Since the senses are a mediation between man and nature, the traces consist in a modification or several modifications of a process, that of the uninterrupted dialogue between the subject and the perceptible object.

Classical Greek thought is not a mechanistic thought: it is always a metaphorical reflection on science, a reflection full of passion and earnestness.

The objective and subjective perspective of the dreamer depends on the imaginary: where did he believe he awoke?[24] The place of waking also corresponds to a position, a situation, an 'ideological' point of view: the animist, materialist, naturalist, universalist, or poetic presupposition of the dreamer sets up the atmosphere of waking, its conditions.

The dream representation, *qua Vorstellung*, implies an inner stage. *Darstellung* is the mental representation of something that is perceived and assimilated at another level: symbolic representation appears to be the expression of a transformation and substitution of the perceived object by the imagined object. If the object is absent, perception is also an ap-prehension, as Kant would say, and its context is an empty presence or, rather, the making present of a lack.

According to Hegel the second degree of the religion of nature, that of 'substantiality', is based on the formation of representation: the representation of nothingness is fundamental.[25] In order to be happy, says Hegel, one must try to rejoin this principle through experience and profound reflection.

This point of view, this re-conciliation between presence and absence, must not be confused with the call to the absolute void, with an ideology of 'nothingness'.

The nirvana of the Buddhists is interpreted by Hegel as an attempt at identification with the Buddha, at absolute unification, a sense of the 'fullness' of the void.

Bion, influenced no doubt by his childhood years spent in India, takes up this discourse and suggests the importance of the introjection of lack, of the 'non-breast', as 'reality testing' of the child's capacities to conceive and confront the frustration coming from the outside: the absolute absence of the object of desire.[26] If the capacity to tolerate the absence of the object of desire is enough and is adequate, the persecutory experience of the introjected 'non-breast' becomes the kernel of a new thought, the starting-point for the construction of an 'apparatus for thinking'. Bion continues Freud's discourse on the two principles of psychical functioning in relation to the construction of the apparatus of thought.

The perceptible object, the image, and the thought constitute a series of alternatives between presentation and re-presentation, position and situation. The 'representation' of the experience, the sense-perceptible representation, which has become a thought-image and mask, forms the imaginary space: an inner spectacle in which the actors help with the 'chorus' to produce 'mental thoughts' and 'verbal thoughts'. The construction of an apparatus for thinking is the consequence of the encounter between the constitutive elements of the cognitive stage. But to know, to think, and to become aware involve unconscious elements: the unconscious is a reality, a way of feeling and thinking prior to knowledge that forms part 'anatomically' and 'biologically' of the same living space, of the body inhabited by the consciousness (conscious/un-conscious).[27]

The representation of the dream, the presence and dramatic

intensity of the dream stage, contain the metaphors and symbolic forms that the presence or absence of the object have determined.

Absence means lack, separation, distance, mourning. The space of the dream is made up of daytime and night-time experiences (daytime memories and night-time memories), which precede the unconscious models of thought (the primary principle) in order to constitute the web, the texture of the dream stage.

The person who recounts a dream represents and dramatizes the audience, a multiplicity that is present and 'incorporated' into the discourse of the narrator communicating his message to the analyst-oneiromancer, the mediator between dreaming and waking.

The representation of the dream is a transformation of the experiences formulated according to the terms of dream thought. Representation involves a movement and a transposition in space and time, from the light of day to the 'darkness' of the dream stage. The account is a new transformation, in the opposite direction. As far as psychoanalysis is concerned, the account of the dream becomes a dramatization. The dramatization of the dream during the transference is a new representation, which is no longer quite like the original dream stage. The account of the dream is another dream.

The interpretation of dreams in psychoanalysis is relational and always related to the superimposition of two spaces and two times, that of the dream and that of the transference. The function of the analyst consists in deciphering prudently and responsibly the rather complicated transformations of the relationship between daytime thought and night-time thought.

To be a spectator and witness, the functioning of the analyst in the transference, involves remaining outside the dream. The witness, 'submerged', enveloped in the toils of the dream, asks several questions: What is the space of the dream? Who are its actors? Who is the director? Where is the analyst? The web of the dream may become the gladiator's net, which envelops and paralyses the other. In a paranoid transference, the account of a dream becomes a place of opening in which the person runs the risk of falling into a threatening world, a world that must be tamed and controlled, even with the dream material. In this case, one cannot interpret the dream without first elaborating the negative transference or placing the dream within a particular relational context.

In *Alice's Adventures in Wonderland* Lewis Carroll describes, on the one hand, claustrophobic anxiety (not being able to emerge from someone else's dream) and, on the other hand, the anxiety of a possible disappearance inside daytime space: if the dreamer wakes up, the stage and the actors disappear.

The analyst who is 'submerged' by the patient's dream (delusional transference) may develop a very intense concern at the level of the counter-transference: 'How can I emerge without disappearing?' he asks himself: 'How can I find my body, my role, my personal and professional identity again?'

In the history of culture, the account of a dream is reminiscent of the mythical account, the foundations of religious history and metaphorical thought.

In the myth, as in analytic experience, we witness a 'deployment of explanation', an opening of the drama that is emerging and showing itself to 'the seeing ear' and the 'listening eye', to the witness, the mediator of tradition, entrusted with the task of transmitting the message to successive generations. The myths of the birth of the gods, like the Hesiodic myth of the races, placed the meaning of chronology at the level of an attempt to organize temporal order out of the original mixture, out of chaotic space.

The temporal organization of myth reproduces the facts and events that make up the memory of our culture. Even in the dream there is an attempt to create order out of disorder. In the dream the past and the myth of each dream drama are confused with the present and with finality: past, present, and future are integrated into a single time, the scenic rhythm of dream space.

The mixture and disorder are only 'a manner of speaking' of conscious thought that is not confronted with the principles of time and space of unconscious thought.

The reading of the dream is, like that of myth, always a search for personal, trans-personal, and (according to Jung's view) universal myth. The interpretation of the dream is a new order, a transformation made public, a way of being seen, a point of view that follows the laws, the rules, and the models of space-time (multi-dimensionality of the *aspect* or unconscious *side* of the dream), apparently different from those of daytime life: two views that are integrated together and complement one another.

The space of the memory of the dream opens up to the eyes of the interpreter and acquires a meaning and signification thanks to the light of consciousness, which makes it possible to see and understand the features of the dream mask: the manifest meaning, its apparent *side*.

Conscious and unconscious, like light and darkness, are the two sides of the same mask that fashion a material, a space, a living energy in which man lives. Each element of the mask, each constitutive part of his world, has its own aspect, whether luminous or opaque; each internal object speaks and is animated according to

205

the perspective, conscious or unconscious, of the gaze. Just as there is a symmetry and an asymmetry of thought (Freud, Matte Blanco), it may also be said that there is a fundamental or archaic 'geometry', a primitive order in which the various aspects of the same thing are not entirely differentiated. This introduces a *phenomenology of the unconscious* – a theme that I would like, in due course, to develop.

It is through the analysis of the dream that a new psychoanalytic reading emerges on my horizon. The reading of the other is a way of seeing and of con–ceiving the imprints left by others' thought: to read means to trans–late, to re–write in my own way someone else's discourse, to assume my discourse and the condition of being, which is in turn read by the other person: two dreams confronting and observing one another.

Notes

1 Rudolf Otto, *Le Sacré*, Paris, 1969.
2 Winnicott speaks of 'hallucinative images', which precede the experience or go before the object of need (he is referring to the primitive mother–child relationship).
3 In Cabalistic thought the symbol is what in a sense makes the mystery visible.
4 Paolo Toschi, in *Le origini teatro italiano* (Turin, 1976), investigates the relations between cultural traditions, rituals, and theatre. The spring festivals and May celebrations are a theatrical representation of the 'arborescent' spirit, which contains all the propitiatory virtues.

   The New Year festivals have an anticipatory sense of death and rebirth, of prediction of the future; it is a way of foreseeing the way to be followed.
5 K. Kerényi, *The Gods of the Greeks*, London, 1979.
6 Charles Baudelaire, 'Correspondances', *Les Fleurs du mal*.
7 To deny oneself any transformation, to reject the conventional, may be a 'pathological' and ontological way of affirming oneself: in *Aurélia* Saturnin denies himself 'sounding the world', shuts himself up in himself, affirming himself in an 'auscultatory' autism with which Nerval finds an audience.
8 Sarane Alexandrian, *Le Surréalisme et le rêve*, Paris, 1974.
9 Lino Gabellone, *L'oggetto surrealista*, Turin, 1977. In *L'Amour fou* André Breton introduces the theme of the 'found object' in connection with the dream – the dream object at the moment of waking. The space of the world is a locus, a 'void' ready to repossess the object that belongs to it, a locus that makes visible the intuition of the dreamer's poetic gaze. The

discovery of the object, the *trouvaille*, constitutes an articulation of co-presence, a metonymy. According to Lévi-Strauss, the characteristic of critical thought is a *bricolage*: a cross-fertilization of various tendencies and suggestions, fragments of an event. 'The construction of surrealist objects', writes Lino Gabellone, 'appears as a mytho-poietic bricolage.'

10 In German, 'Eine Vorstellung ist kein Bild, ober ein Bild, ober ein Bild kann ihr entsprechen'. Ludwig Wittgenstein, *Philosophical Investigations*, fragment 301, Oxford, 1967, p. 101.
11 In *Identity and Difference* (New York, 1969) Heidegger develops the dialectic between identity and difference, between being oneself with oneself and being with the other as other. Identity poses the problem, on the one hand, of the 'truth' of the mask (*Einhung*) of what is proper to each of us and different in relation to the other (*Einheit*) and, on the other hand, of the importance of the bond (*Mit*) – being *with* the other, being with oneself, that is to say, being oneself.
12 Ernst Cassirer, *The Philosophy of Symbolic Forms*, New Haven, Conn., and London, 1964.
13 Cf. Ernst Cassirer, *Language and Myth*. New York, 1953.
14 Jean-Pierre Vernant, *Mythe et pensée chez les Grecs*, Paris, 1978, vol. 1.
15 '-ism' means 'tendency'.
16 'We use the perceptible sign of a proposition (spoken or written, etc.) as a projection of a possible situation' (*Tractatus logico-philosophicus*, London, 1957, p. 21).
17 See S. Resnik, *Personne et psychose*, Paris, 1973.
18 H. Maldiney, *Les Rythmes*, supplement no. 7 of the *Journal d'oto-rhinolaryngologie*, Lyon, 1968, p. 228.
19 In a forthcoming work on 'primordial confusion' in man's development I suggest the vicissitudes and alternatives of the passages between the 'confused object relation' and the 'distinct object relation'.
20 Antonin Artaud, 'Le Bureau des recherches surréalistes', *La Révolution surréaliste*, no. 3, 1925.
21 André Breton, *Les Manifestes du surréalisme*, Paris, 1946.
22 Albert Béguin, *L'Ame romantique et le rêve*, Paris, 1939.
23 Martin Heidegger, *Holzwege*, Frankfurt-am-Main, 1950.
24 Thus in the allegory of the cave in Plato, one may wonder: Where do the prisoners wake up? Where will they take their fantasies to? In what zone of the 'real' will they be centred or deployed? Will they wake up in reality or in another dream?
25 G. W. F. Hegel, *Lectures on the Philosophy of Religion*, London, 1895.
26 Wilfred Bion, *Second Thoughts*, New York, 1967.
27 See S. Resnik, 'Inconscio', *Enciclopedia Einaudi*, Torino, 1979, VII.

Subject Index

209

childhood 127, 147, 180
children, and dreams 26–8, 35
cocaine 112, 121n
coensthesis 18
'combined parents' 66, 134n
condensation (*Verdichtung*) 18, 71, 72, 97; examples of 75, 102
conflict 39–40
conscious-in-conscious 203
conscious and unconscious, *see* unconscious
contradiction 72, 80n
conversion symptom 111
corporality 146–7
corporization 58, 72, 94
cosmology: Greek 15–16, 167, 198; Indian 20–1, 164, 203
counter-transference 55, 118n. *See also* transference
counter-transference dream 90
crab, symbol of 62
creative: capacity in analysis 41; expression and revolution 133; imagination 84
creativity 22, 54, 151n
critical analysis 124
culture 9, 168
cure 144, 146, 161

danger 170, 171
darkness/light 35, 100–1, 130, 132, 171, 201, 205
Darsteller (actor) 13
Darstellung (theatrical representation) 11, 13, 96, 203
Dasein 39
day-dreaming 12, 18, 22, 36, 84, 181
death: and change 79; cultural views of 29; dream as experience of 21; and ending 78; fear of 16–17; and funerary rites 195; as losts of presence 81; of love-object 101; and mourning 82–3; *see also* mourning; and myth 30; and rebirth 79; and ritual 79; by suicide 90; and time 81–2
deflation 68, 75, 76, 78, 85, 131, 140, 141, 142
déjà vu 27, 128
delusion: creative 175; and dream 22, 43, 136; deflation of 141, 142; discourse of 142; etymology of 24–5n; of grandeur 74, 147, 185; ideology of 138; of infinity 832; of love 129; and metaphor 142; 'normal' 84, 86; paranoiac 129–30; and passion 131; in psychotic crisis 29; in psychotics 36, 85–6, 148; and reality 22, 140, 161; relational 139; self- 148
delusional: construction 160; intuition 160, 171; personality 143; system 148; thought 84, 130, 132; transference 205
demonology 43, 195
de-nature 197
depersonalization 128, 157
depression: and *ascensus/descensus* 181–2; narcissistic 79, 85–6, 142, 161
derealization 128, 146
descent/ascent 76, 99–100, 131, 184
desire: delusional 132; drive and 95, 96; repressed 96
'desire of the other' 75, 80n, 129
devils, *see* demonolgy
diachrony and synchrony 13, 83, 108
dike 15
discovery 171
'discordant madness' 60, 154
disease, and dreams 49–53, 60, 106–11, 119–20n
disillusion 142, 146
displacement (*Verschiebung*) 18–19, 73, 97
dissociation 49, 128, 129, 157
distancing 18–19, 20
dragon, symbol of 62–3
dream: adventure 5, 20; aesthetic experience of 2; archaeology of 100, 101; archaic 155; artisans of 97; and audience 112; capacity 150n, 155; characters 32, 36; content 17, 95, 102; of counter-transference 90; and delusion 22, 43, 136; dimensional register of 2; and disease, *see* disease, and dreams; 'distortion' 18; as experience of death 21; and film 36, 44n; and future 40–1, 49; hallucination 18, 73, 135; iconology 169; ideology 55; imagination 136; intuition 155; as journey 34; language 5, 10–11, 21, 34, 46, 94; mask 17, 54; material of 141, 142, 154, 155, 163; as message 10, 28, 31, 40, 54; messenger 40; as mode of communication 43,

Name Index

Abel, Karl 80n
Aesculapius 31
Agrippa, Enrico Cornelio (Elizabethan philosopher) 177
Alberti, Leon Battista 199
Alexander the Great 32–3
Alexandrian, Sarane 175, 197
Allison, T. 137
Anzieu, Didier 118n
Aquinas, St Thomas 98
Arden Quin, Carmelo 189n
Arieti, Silvano 151
Aristarchus 33
Aristides, Aelius 23n
Aristotle 31, 44n, 49, 70, 71, 91n, 133n, 202
Artaud, Antonin 119n, 172, 200
Artemidorus of Daldis 9, 10, 30–4, 40
Assurbanipal, King 30

Bachelard, Gaston 70
Baillarger, Jules 156
Ball, Benjamin 98
Baudelaire, Charles 196–97, 201
Béguin, Albert 123, 172, 188, 200–01
Bergson, Henri 10, 14, 82, 165
Biemel, Walter 45n
Binswanger, L. 34, 36, 165
Bion, Wilfred R. 2, 14, 21, 29, 34, 43, 67, 85, 127, 133n, 139, 145, 160, 162, 164, 202
Bleuler, E. 20, 139, 154

Bloy, Léon 172, 189n
Borges, Jorge Luis 8
Brentano, Franz 122
Breton, André 122, 173, 189n–90n, 197, 200, 206n–207n
Brissaud, E. 45n
Buber, Martin 102

Cabanis, P.J.G. 137, 153
Calderón de la Barca, Pedro, 21–2, 35, 86
Campanella 2
Cargnello, Danilo 80n
Carrington, Leonora 13, 18
Carroll, Lewis 204
Cassirer, Ernst 14, 30, 69n, 72, 81, 198, 201
Char, René 168
Chaslin, Philippe 60, 154
Chouraqui, André 77, 80n
Colon, Jenny 191n, 192n
Cornford, Francis Macdonald 18
Cotard, Jules 82

da Vinci, Leonardo 199
Daldis, Artemidorus of 9, 10, 30–4, 40
De Martino, Ernesto 81
De Sanctis, Sante 137
Delminio, Giulio Camillo 1, 55n
Descartes, René 71, 88, 121n
Dilthey, Wilhelm 168

216